Architectural Guide
Delhi

Architectural Guide
Delhi

Anupam Bansal / Malini Kochupillai

DOM
publishers

Contents

How to Use this Guide Book

1. Building name
2. Architect
3. Completion year
4. Metro station
5. Address / Accessibility
6. Geodata as QR codes
7. Project number
8. Number of map

Red Fort
Ustad Ahmad Lahori (1648)
Chandni Chowk
Netaji Subhash Marg, Old Delhi

018 A

The Red Fort was the palace for Mughal Emperor Shah Jahan's new capital, Shahjahanabad (present day Old Delhi). The layout of the Red Fort was organised to retain and integrate this site with the Salimgarh Fort. The fortress palace was an important focal point of the medieval city of Shahjahanabad. The fort lies along the Yamuna River, which fed the moats that surround most of the wall. The planning and aesthetics of the Red Fort represent the zenith of Mughal creativity, which prevailed during the reign emperor. The columns were painted in gold and there was a gold and silver railing separating the throne from the public. Diwan-i-Khas — the 'hall of private audience' — was used by the emperor for

Historical Architecture

49

Viceregal Palace/Rashtrapati Bhavan

Foreword

A. G. Krishna Menon

The prolific architectural legacy of Delhi is remarkable not only for its antiquity but also its diversity. However, few legatees acknowledge its significance or worth. Many, of course, are aware of its presence if only because the past and the present are routinely encountered in daily life. There is a link between the two that is self-consciously elided as our society aspires to shed its past in order to become modern. The link, and its contentious meaning, is perhaps most palpable in the last tranche of the city's architectural and urban history — colonial New Delhi — which is still used by its republican successors for the same imperial purpose for which it was built. Characteristically, its buildings and urban design are treated with an indifference that reflects a general absence of architectural culture in society.

There are, of course, many reasons for this indifference, but the paucity of reliable guidebooks on Delhi's architecture is perhaps one. It is difficult for laypeople to understand let alone engage with the architectural legacy of the city without a reliable guide. There are some guidebooks on ancient buildings, but none that present the total spectrum of Delhi's architecture. Therefore, few people, including architects, are aware of the complex ways in which past and present are intertwined in the contemporary architecture of the city, making it a 'living heritage'. For example, the architectural strategies which created historic buildings are still employed to create contemporary architecture. While this may generally be true of all Indian architecture, it is most evident in the architecture of Delhi: this is the 'aura' of Delhi. Even Sir Edwin Lutyens had to contend with it, as he remarked while wrestling with the design of the buildings in the new capital, more than a century after the early colonialists had begun their engagement with architecture in India: 'We cannot get rid of the body of tradition, murder it how we may'.

This book documents how contemporary architects have dealt with this challenge. The urban form of Delhi has now grown far beyond the boundaries of the earlier cities that preceded it, including the expectations of the Delhi Development Authority, which ambitiously drafted a masterplan in 1962 to guide the growth of the post-Independence city. It is now a city that is expected to have a population of 22 million by 2021, covering an area of 1,485 square kilometres, far larger than the city of 500,000 conceived by Shahjahan in 1648 or 50,000 by Lutyens in 1912–1913. Naturally, the urbanscape has been transformed. While older residents of the city bemoan the loss of visual identity with which they were familiar, it must nevertheless be acknowledged that the masterplan has brought some order to what could otherwise have become a chaotic megapolis. By making available large tracts of land for planned development it has, in no small measure, contributed to the architectural character of the city that this book documents and, thus, perpetuated the aura of the city.

Together, the city's form and architecture imbue Delhi with its unique identity. It is a complex construct, not easily comprehended by decision makers and architects who aspire to transform Delhi into a 'world-class city' like Shanghai or Singapore. Such aspirations can only be challenged through critical analysis and this book provides three reasons to question these aspirations. First, it combines a thoughtful selection of historic and contemporary architecture of Delhi in a single volume, thus challenging the common trope that views the city's historic and contemporary architecture as disparate categories. Brief scholarly essays contribute to understanding the cultural significance of the various periods of the city's architectural history, and address the needs of both the casual and more serious explorer of the architectural heritage of the city.

Connaught Place – The Commercial Hub in Delhi

Second (and perhaps unintentionally) this book challenges another trope defining the design of local architecture — the idea of 'Indian' architecture. 'Indian' architecture was a colonial construct that is gaining new saliency in a globalizing world; both laypeople and architects are complicit in perpetuating such simplistic overlays of a complex reality. There were several architectures of India in the past and, not surprisingly, there are several today; the term 'Indian' architecture does not do justice to this rich variety. This book provides compelling evidence of the uniqueness of Delhi's architecture; a similar case could perhaps be made for other Indian cities too. In fact, the book contains a small section on the contemporary architecture of Ahmadabad and Chandigarh that reinforces the point I am making. Cultivating this perspective can enrich the culture of architecture and urbanism in India.

And, finally, a third trope the book challenges is the idea that only ancient monuments are valuable architectural heritage to be conserved. The book has an exhaustive description of the renovation of the German Embassy in New Delhi built in the early 1950s. It highlights the need for documenting the architecture of the Modern Movement (Docomomo) on the one hand, and, on the other, settling the issues related to conservation versus restoration while dealing with them. Docomomo has taken root in many countries, but not India and, consequently, we are fast losing modern classics — consider, for instance, the recent demolition of the Chanakya Cinema. We need to think about how to treat the pioneering works of Habib Rahman and Acyut Kanvinde in Delhi, or those of Le Corbusier and Louis Kahn in Chandigarh and Ahmedabad before the imperatives of neo-liberal development or general neglect take such decisions out of our hands. The story of the German Embassy included in this book provides an exemplary model of the kind of research and debate — and, indeed, architectural culture — that we need to cultivate in order to conserve our brand of modernism and make it known to both ourselves and the world.

This book can, therefore, be read as a straightforward guide to the architectures of Delhi or as a critical commentary on the message the architecture conveys. Both will yield profitable returns.

Jama Masjid overlooking Old Delhi

Introduction

Delhi is an amalgamation of many cities built at different times during its more than 1,000 year history. The New Delhi of today is at least the eighth city to inhabit this dusty flat plain on the banks of the Yamuna River. The oldest known incarnation of the city is Indraprastha, as immortalized in the epic Mahabharata, founded in 1450 BC by the Pandava dynasty. Successive rulers from Persia and Eurasia left their marks, both constructive and destructive, ending in 1911 when King George V of Britain proclaimed that the Imperial Capital of India would be shifted from Calcutta to this spot, to be named New Delhi. The city can be compared with other historical cities like Rome and Athens in its vast history and the sheer number of empires that have ruled it over the centuries, as also in the beautiful monuments sprinkled across the urban landscape. Present-day Delhi consists of a vast amalgamation of all the remains of the former cities, villages that dotted the Delhi region, the Colonial Capital city and the post-colonial development that spreads to almost 60 kilometres, including the suburbs, around the centre of the city. The contemporary city has engulfed all the eras, periods, empires and cities, thus erasing all boundaries between what were once disparate and disjointed villages, citadels and countryside.

The vast, and endlessly interesting history of the culture and architecture of Delhi has been covered in a wide variety of literature, including travelogues, historical, socio-cultural and architectural accounts by authors of various backgrounds. However, relatively less has been written or documented of the contemporary developments in the architecture of the city post-independence. This book, while reserving judgment and critique for its readers, attempts to chronologically present some significant architectural projects that constitute one of the largest and most populous metropolises in the world. While the book focuses mostly on the post-independence architecture of the city, any architectural documentation of Delhi would be incomplete without an introduction of historical and colonial architectural developments, and towards this end, the guide covers the most important buildings from these periods.

While the city has grown at an unprecedented rate since the opening up of the Indian economy in the early nineties, a large number of the most interesting projects were developed in the years immediately following independence, a period of high ideological and social consciousness lead by the then Prime Minister Jawaharlal Nehru. Under the leadership of Nehru, a great believer in modernity and a proponent of socialist developmental policies, a great number of public buildings were commissioned for the burgeoning administrative, cultural and educational fabric of the city. The majority of the buildings of this period were heavily influenced by the modernist movement being embraced across Europe and North America as practised by Le Corbusier, Kahn and Gropius, among others. In the decades following independence, the city saw many diverse developments in the architectural styles of both private and public buildings. The austere and minimalist aesthetics of the 1950s and 1960s gave way to a more post-modernist mish-mash of Indian vernacular aesthetics and the remnants of the modernist movement. A few innovative Indian architects, some trained in the west, made great strides in developing a modern Indian aesthetic rooted in our rich built heritage, while embracing modern materials and building technologies. Along the way, the city has also seen a period of Classical Revivalism, a continuation of the principles laid down by Edwin Lutyens and Baker, particularly in buildings designed by Government departments and their architects. The opening up of the economy in the early nineties proved to be both a boon and a major disaster for the architectural profession in the city. The boon came in the form of the sudden growth of the opportunities available to architects, both for those with established practices, and in encouraging the growth of a whole new breed of young forward-thinking architects. However, the sudden increase in demand, and the corresponding dearth of architects with the ability to undertake the large-scale projects that were on offer, led to an explosion of builder-led projects with no architectural ideology or aesthetic grounding, projecting only a misplaced sense of a 'global' image consisting primarily of glass and alucobond facades. This trend continues to date, with a few exceptions that have actively tried to develop an architectural vocabulary that reflects the aspirations of a fast-growing economy with more innovative and site-specific principles of design. The last decade in Delhi has been marked by two events that have contributed to a very fast change in the shape of the city. The first was the Commonwealth Games concluded in 2010 and the second was the building of the Delhi Metro. The Metro has been the largest catalyst of development in the city since independence, and will continue to effect a lot of much-needed change in the next 2–3 decades.

This book is also an attempt to draw the attention of the interested reader towards the city's vast heritage of modernist buildings built in the era immediately following independence. As mentioned earlier, Nehru's socialist and modernist views greatly influenced the urban landscape of Delhi. While Nehru's most talked-about contribution to the modernist movement was his commissioning Le Corbusier for the design and masterplan of Chandigarh, he was also instrumental in the design of some of Delhi's most interesting public buildings, including the Lalit Kala Academy (1961) designed by Habib Rahman, who was heavily influenced by the Bauhaus and

Modernist movement. Rahman, in his capacity first as a senior architect, and then as chief architect of the CPWD (Central Public Works Department), is responsible for much of the work that gives central New Delhi its unique character. This modernist ideology was followed by other architects like Kanvinde and Hasmukh Patel, among others, and contributed to the urban landscape of New Delhi. Many of these Modernist buildings still stand, although a majority of them are in varying states of disrepair and decay. While there has been an active movement to repair and maintain the many historical monuments of Delhi, a similar enthusiasm is sadly missing when it comes to the rich modernist heritage of the city. As a result some notable examples of buildings that represent the development of Delhi immediately post-independence, like the Chanakya Cinema and Sangam Theatre, have been demolished to make way for generic malls and multiplexes. Additions and modifications have been made to others without any respect for the original design and ideology of the architect. Ram Rahman, a noted photographer and writer, and architect Habib Rahman's son, has written and exhibited extensively about the poor treatment meted out to the many important modernist buildings in the city. For now these efforts have not yielded better prospects for the modernist treasures of Delhi, which continue to exist in peril, and occasionally perish.

The guide also covers the most influential buildings that resulted from the modernist ideology of post-independence India in Chandigarh and Ahmedabad. Le Corbusier was invited by Nehru to design the masterplan for a new Capital of Punjab in the early 1950s where he had the opportunity to test the modern city planning principles of Congrès International d'Architecture Moderne (CIAM). Besides the masterplan, Le Corbusier also designed the most important administrative and legislative buildings of the

Delhi Skyline with Jama Masjid and Red Fort in background

new capital of the Punjab, working with untrained labour in a resource-scarce environment to realize some of the most important buildings in the history of modernist India. Around the same time, architects like Achyut Kanvinde and Balkrishna Doshi among others, after having studied and trained abroad, were heavily influenced by the Bauhaus and designed a large number of institutional, industrial and residential projects in Ahmedabad. Louis Kahn's Indian Institute of Management went on to influence a lot of architects who worked with him. Le Corbusier's influence is also obvious in the many modernist concrete structures of BV Doshi and other architects practising in Ahmedabad.

While we set out with the intention of including a wide selection of the many types of private residences that are spread across the city, privacy and issues of access have resulted in the selection being less extensive. A few noted examples of architects' residences, like Kanvinde's and Ashish Ganju's houses have been included. Delhi is also home to some of the most luxurious bungalows and farmhouses in the country, however these have been excluded from the guide for a complete lack of possibility for visual or physical access to them.

While every effort has been made to cover a wide variety of projects in the National Capital Region, not all listed buildings may be accessible to the

interested traveller. Security being a major concern in the city, most office towers, government buildings and industrial complexes do not allow easy access,
and are especially wary of photography,
although in some cases prior permission can be acquired from management.
Private residences, similarly, may need
prior permission from the owners for access. Because of these security and privacy concerns, we have had to rely on
the architects to source a majority of
the photographs for the projects listed
in the guide. As a result, a large number of photographs, especially of public projects built in the 1950s through
the 1980s, show the buildings immediately after they were constructed,

therefore appearing in their original glory.
Many of these buildings have deteriorat-
ed over time, and in some cases may be
unrecognizable as shown in the photographs.
Finally it is important to point out that
this book is in no way a comprehensive or
exhaustive listing of the historical and
contemporary architectural landscape of
Delhi. Many more projects, prestigious or
otherwise, truly deserved to be included
but had to be left out for lack of archival
material or poor state of the buildings,
and in many instances, for lack of the
ability to photograph or document them.
Perhaps future editions, encouraged by
an interested audience, will overcome
these omissions.

The Architectural Idiom of the Delhi Sultanate

Abha Narain Lambah

Delhi's recorded imperial Sultanate architecture spans over 4 centuries from the reign of the first slave king Qutbuddin Aibak to the last Lodi ruler defeated by the invading Mughals in 1526 and subsequently with the short spurt of activity in the reign of Sher Shah Suri. This imperial city thus witnessed the architectural contributions of six ruling dynasties of Turkish, Afghan and Arab stock. The architectural legacy of the Islamic Sultanate in Delhi is thus a multi-coloured mosaic that owes its patronage to thirty-five sultans, contributing to the creation of a distinctly Sultanate style of Indo-Islamic architecture that progressed from an architecture of demolition and recycling to later monumental constructions over a vast array of building forms encompassing the religious, secular and sepulchral.

Whether in the construction of Quwwat al Islam in Delhi over hurriedly assembled columns quarried from 27 desecrated Hindu and Jaina temples or early mosques built over temple sites in the provinces, the act of building the Friday mosque was as much a religious requirement as a political statement and a way of building faster with readily available material underscored by the economy and expediency of reuse. The creation of Islamic architectural forms announcing a clean break from the deeply rooted Hindu and Jaina architectural traditions of temple building was a means of reinforcing the identity of these new settlers.

Sultan Garhi

The initial architectural development of the Sultanates reflected its socio-political scenario and was essentially a military camp. Mercenary forces of Turks, Afghans, Central Asians, Persians, Arabs and Abyssinians driven with political ambition, religious fervour or pure greed for the riches of Hindustan, lived in a military encampment. Domestic architecture was confined to temporary camps and permanent construction was limited to defensive fortifications and mosques, of quickly assembled pillaged material plastered at most with lime mortar, a material hitherto unknown to Indian masons. The earliest 'royal' tomb of Sultan Garhi (1231–1232) reflects this defensive psychology of new conquerors in a hostile country. Its sarcophagus is placed in an underground chamber within a fortified enclosure. Later tombs of Balban and Iltutmish, though attempting a more urbane setting, struggled with establishing a truly arcuate construction model. The challenge was to translate arcuate forms into the traditional trabeate construction system of the Hindu artisans, a struggle amply demonstrated in the initial experiments with false arches in the screens of the Quwwat al Islam, as well as the failed dome of Iltutmish's tomb.

It took the Delhi Sultanate nearly a century to create the true arch to give structural authenticity to Islamic forms with the eventual construction of the true arch in Balban's tomb. Though Iltutmish's square tomb attempted a dome, it was not until the Alai Darwaza in 1305, that the dome was successfully constructed. Ala al Din Khalji constructed a gateway, not a sepulchral monument and yet it remains a key link in the development of tomb typology, successfully combining engineering prowess with a sophisticated architectural aesthetic. The double-height fenestration scheme, rosebud voussoir detailing and polychrome inlay stonework became a prototype for later Sultanate structures. In spite of the bold confidence of Alai Darwaza's arch,

Qutub Minar, 1865

True Arch in Allaudin'd Madrasa

the diffidence of local Hindu craftsmen in using the arch is amply demonstrated by the lintel placed under arched openings in Tughluq buildings well into the 14th century.

As the nascent Delhi sultanate looked westwards towards Central Asia and the Arab world for inspiration, the development of an Indo-Islamic architectural genre was greatly aided with both the abundance of good quality construction material of stone as well as the highly skilled local building craftsmen. This eventually resulted in the creation of a formidable body of Indo-Islamic architecture that laid the foundation for the magnificence of later Mughal buildings through the synthesis of architectural idioms of the east and the west and stands today among the finest moments of Islamic architectural history.

Until the dawn of the 14th century, Delhi continued to be regarded as a mere eastern outpost of Dar el Islam as the Delhi Sultans vied to be recognised by the Abbasid Caliph's court. It was only Ala al Din Khaljis' fierce resistance to the Mongol armies of Chingiz Khan that established Delhi as a great Islamic court, attracting fleeing tribesmen and courtiers from other Islamic kingdoms caught in the wake of the Mongol invasions. It was finally in the reign of Muhammed Tughluq in 1343 that the Caliph of Cairo sent an emissary to recognise him as Sultan. The architecture of the Sultanates came

of age during the Tughluqs, the most prolific of Sultanate builders. Ghiyath al Din Tughluq, Muhammed and his nephew Firuz Shah were all born to Hindu women, establishing the first recorded Sultanate dynasty of at least partly indigenous stock. Their architecture spelt a true Indianisation of the Sultanate architecture, with the greatest amount of experimentation, innovation and construction occurring in nearly eight decades of their reign, especially in the founding of urban enclaves such as Tughluqabad, Firuzabad, Jahanpanah, and Hauz Khas within Delhi as well as urban centres such as Jaunpur, Hissar, and Daulatabad outside the imperial capital.

The architecture of Multan is a recurring leitmotif through Tughluq built form, an indelible memory from the deputation of Ghiyath al Din Tughluq as governor of Multan. His tomb near Tughluqabad is the archetype of Tughluq proportion and later Tughluq buildings over the decades continued to follow this architectural idiom of battered walls, defensive buttresses and robust rubble masonry walls with minimal ornamentation.

Ghiyath al Din's successor, Muhammed bin Tughluq was quixotic, but a gifted scholar and perhaps the most secular of all Sultanate rulers. His militaristic conquest won him the largest territory in Hindustan until the time of Aurangzeb and this strategic interest in retaining the Deccan initiated the shift of capital

Alai Darwaza is a key link in the development of tomb, though it was not built as
a sepuchral monument.

Ghiyath al Din Tughluq's tomb is the
Archetype of Tughluq proportions

to Daulatabad, earning him immense un-
popularity, combined with the Ulema's
displeasure at his participation in Hindu
festivals. Firuz Shah, his successor, chose
to steer clear of such political statements and while delegating much of the
political decisions to his prime minister,
focussed on building construction, making him the most prolific builder of the
Islamic Sultanate and the first to have
recorded restoring monuments built by
the earlier Sultanate rulers. Firuz wrote
in his memoirs, 'by the guidance of God,
I was led to repair and rebuild the edifices and structures of former kings and
ancient nobles, which had fallen into decay, from lapse of time, giving the restoration of these buildings the priority
over my (own) building works'.
From the early Sultanate mosque with
an enclosed courtyard and *maqsura*, the
mosque plan evolved with the Begumpur
mosque in Jahanpanah. The Khirki
Masjid, a cruciform axial plan with four
courtyards, was unique, never to be

repeated. The Jami Masjid in Hauz Khas,
set within a larger complex of *madrasa*,
garden and Firuz Shah Tughluq's tomb
was another innovation in mosque planning, as was the imperial Jami Masjid in
Firuzabad, influencing the planning of
cellular rooms for travellers in the Atala
at Jaunpur. However, the invasion by
Timur and his sack of Delhi in 1398 dealt
the final blow to Tughluq rule. From the
zenith with the largest provinces under
Delhi's rule in the time of Muhammed bin
Tughluq, the capital's sway diminished
as provincial governors declared their
independence. Bengal had already broken free against Muhammed bin Tughluq
and much of the Deccan was lost in
the time of Firuz Shah with the formation of the Vijayanagar empire. With the
Tughluq empire reeling under Timur's attack, Malwa, Jaunpur and Gujarat proclaimed their sovereignty. The following decades saw the weakening of
Delhi's imperial control as the architectural contributions of Sayyids and Lodis

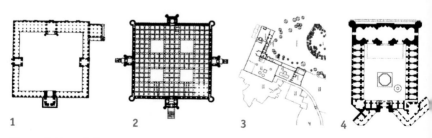

The evolution of the mosque plan
1. enclosed courtyard and *maqsura* — Begumpur Mosque in Jahapanah;
2. a cruciform axial plan with four courtyards — Khirki Masjid;
3. a larger complex of *madrasa*, garden and tombs — Jami Masjid in Hauz Khas;
4. cellular rooms for travellers — Khairul Manazil

The architectural contributions of Sayyids and Lodis, largely sepulchral monuments, Bara Gumbad mosque

The last of the sultanate expressions, Sher Shah Suri's Qila-i-Konha mosque

was largely limited to sepulchral monuments in Delhi. With the Mughal invasion in 1526, imperial Sultanate architecture came to a halt, with the short reign of Sher Shah Suri making a brief but valiant attempt to revive it.

Though not in chronological continuity and yet undeniably linked to this architectural tradition of Delhi's sultanate legacy, is the architecture of Sher Shah Suri, a short but frenetic epilogue to the architecture of the Islamic Sultanate after the establishment of the Chagtai-Mughal dynasty. Sher Shah Suri's edifices such as the Qila-i-Konha mosque illustrate a natural progression of the Sultanate genre well into the 16th century, an almost seamless extension of the Sultanate vocabulary with the minor hiccup of the early Mughal buildings of Babur and Humayun.

What was the degree of influence of imperial Delhi on the development of the architectural vocabulary of Sultanate period architecture in the sub-continent? The end of the Tughluq regime coincides with some of the finest strides in provincial architecture. Gujarat, Jaunpur, Malwa, Deccan and Bengal went on to fashion new innovations in architecture. While Jaunpur, in relative proximity to Delhi, maintained an umbilical connection with Tughluq architecture for the 100-odd years of its existence, other provincial architecture such as that of later Deccan sultanates of the Ahmad Shahi, Qutb Shahi and Adil Shahi dynasties developed bold departures from the Delhi aesthetic, forging a strong regional identity of their own. Bengal and

Gujarat continued to retain and develop their own architectural and aesthetic identities, challenging the concept of Delhi as fountainhead.

References

- Whereas Merklinger refers to five dynasties and 34 sultans of the Sultanate, I would like to stretch this definition over a chronological time line, challenging a pre-Mughal definition of the Sultanate, to include the Suri dynasty. See Elizabeth Schotten Merklinger, *Sultanate Architecture of Pre-Mughal India,* Munshiram Manoharlal Publishers, New Delhi, 2005
- This recycling of building material is not limited to the sultanate alone, as well into the late Mughal period, recorded examples of recycled building material include the scavenging of the marble cladding over the Akbarid tomb of Khan-i-Khana for the construction of Safdarjung's tomb in Delhi.
- Muhammed bin Tughluq was the first sultan to receive formal investiture from the Abbasid Caliphs after Iltutmish. See Anthony Welch and Howard Crane, *The Tughluqs: Master Builders of the Delhi Sultanates, Muqarnas Vol. 1: An Annual on Islamic Art & Architecture,* Yale University Press, 1983
- Anthony Welch and Howard Crane, op. cit.
- Anthony Welch quoting Futuhat-i Firuz Shah, ed. and trans. S. A. Rashid and M. A. Makhdoomi, Aligarh, n. d.

Aerial view from the Jama Masjid, completed in 1656 AD, over Old Delhi

Delhi under the Mughals

Meena Bhargava

The picture that the mind conjures up with the word is a city that has been the capital of India, of the dominant political formation in north India, for almost a millennium. In the literature of the past as much as of the present, Delhi has held a conspicuous space in India's history. In fact, the making of India and Delhi has been so intricately interwoven that it is often difficult to disentangle the history of one from the other. The Sultans of Delhi who had established their rule in the thirteenth century initiated the idea of walled cities, which formed only a portion of Delhi that we know today. The legacy of a walled city was visibly evident when the Mughal Emperor Shah Jahan established the city of Shahjahanabad in the seventeenth century. In a way, Delhi represents the aura and splendour of the medieval period, with its entire landscape dotted with magnificent forts, mosques and tombs. But Delhi's medieval past also lives in the *galis, havelis, katras* and *kuchas* of Chandni Chowk. We live, unconsciously though, brushing our shoulders with the rich past, which can be glimpsed through the remnants of a bygone era. A territory that has been lived in for several millennia, Delhi is an enchanting example of the link between the ancient, medieval and modern, in other words of connections, continuities and ruptures across time. To understand the character of Delhi, it is important to look at its history, its many cities — Qila Rai Pithora, Mehrauli, Siri, Tughluqabad, Ferozabad, Shergarh, Shahjahanabad — before they all evolved into New Delhi. When we look at the physiographic features of Delhi, it surprises us that it was as late as the twelfth century AD that Delhi acquired prominence. The Aravalli ranges that cut deeply into the fertile, alluvial plains of north India terminate in the Delhi Ridge. They stretch across from Gujarat into Rajasthan and Haryana and enter Delhi from Gurgaon in the southwest. The hills run through the city in a roughly north-east direction ending in Wazirabad in north Delhi on the right bank of the River Yamuna. The Yamuna is diverted from its natural south-westerly course (parallel to the tributaries of the River Indus) to an easterly one (parallel to the River Ganga) by the position of the Ridge under which it flows. Today the height of the rocky Delhi Ridge ranges approximately between 2.5 metres and 90 metres above the flood plain in north and south Delhi respectively. This implies that during the ancient and the medieval period it must have been higher and for this reason Delhi must have looked attractive for settlement. Thus the heights for settlement, rocks for stone quarries, river for water supply, navigation and defense from the east must have been added attractions for the rulers and the merchants of Delhi.

The physiography of Delhi region, if we use the local terminology, consists of the Kohi or Pahari, the Khadar, the Bangar and the Dabar. The Kohi or Pahari are the hills which we know as different sections of the Delhi Ridge; the Khadar or the 'new alluvium' comprises the more recent deposits of the River Yamuna; to its west lies the Bangar, the higher 'old alluvium' created by the deposits of the river in its older course a long time ago; the Dabar is a low-lying flood-prone area in south-west Delhi. Apart from the River Yamuna which represents a major landmark of Delhi's physical landscape, the *jheels* (lakes) at Najafgarh, Surajkund and Batkhal are also the remnants of the River Yamuna's old course. These features of Delhi's landscape, particularly its alluvial zone and the area in the neighburhood of River Yamuna rather than the Aravalli Ridge, contributed to the expanding settlements and growing population of Delhi.

Delhi of the Mughals has largely been associated with Shahjahanabad, which was established by Shahjahan in the seventeenth century. The reason for this lies in the fact that in the sixteenth and early

Humayun built the fort which was named Din Panah, now popularly known as Purana Qila

seventeenth century, the Mughal emperors hardly ever resided in Delhi. Subsequent to his triumph in the first Battle of Panipat in AD 1526 against Ibrahim Lodi, Babur had made Agra his capital (also the capital of the Lodi Sultans); Humayun had stayed in Delhi briefly after the re-conquest of Hindustan in AD 1555; Akbar also had stayed for a short period in Delhi following the demise of his father. Generally the Mughal emperors, till Shahjahan, lived in Agra or Lahore or as in Akbar's case at Fatehpur

Sher Mandal, Purana Qila
Humayun fell down the steps of this pavilion and was mortally wounded.

Sikri or at their summer residence in Srinagar. However, Delhi continued to be an image of multiple cities within a city, built since the end of the twelfth century. Even if the Mughals did not reside at *Dar al-Mulk Delhi* (seat of the empire), it does not mean that they did not consider the old historical capital as an important political symbol. It may be observed that the early Mughal emperors during the initial years of consolidation did not stay in any of the capital cities but moved about and the capital was wherever the imperial camp moved. So, whenever the Mughal court came to Delhi the 'mobile Mughal court' stayed here. Looking at the visiting patterns of the Mughal emperors, particularly Akbar, Jahangir and Shahjahan before the latter made Delhi his permanent capital, we will try to find out what Delhi represented to these Mughal emperors.

The tradition of touring the urban areas of Delhi was introduced by Babur after his victory at Panipat in AD 1526. He also sent a delegation of religious men to Delhi to read the *khutba* in his name — an act according to the Islamic practice that confirms the ruler's sovereignty. Babur also made a pious gesture by visiting the various Sufi shrines in Delhi. Inspired by his paternal ancestor, Timur, and emulating him, Babur visited Delhi several times. We may note that Timur after the conquest of Delhi in AD 1398 had got the *khutba* read in his

Humayun's Tomb

name in the different mosques of Delhi and had also visited the many cities of Delhi established since the twelfth century. If we understand Babur's relationship with Delhi in this context, we may argue that Babur was not a mere 'sightseer' but constantly made symbolic statements by his visits to Delhi, namely, to indicate his triumph, as a symbolic gesture of appropriation of land for his dynasty and to show his association with the religious and spiritual authority of the Sufi saints.

With the accession of Humayun, there was a brief lull in the imperial visits because Humayun decided to reside in Delhi. In AD 1533 he built a new capital called Din Panah (refuge for religion), which was destroyed by Sher Shah Suri after he ousted Humayun from the throne and instead built a citadel, now known as Purana Qila. Sher Shah had given the name Sher Manzil to his *kushak* (palace) within the fortified area. This name still continues to be identified with the octagonal pavilion, built by Humayun on his return from Persia in AD 1555, inside the Purana Qila. It represents the 're-Mughalization' of the fort although ironically it was from this pavilion that Humayun fell and died in AD 1556. The second site in Delhi connected with Humayun was also acquired from the Surs. This was the citadel of Salimgarh built by Islam Shah near the River Yamuna — from here Humayun had

re-conquered Delhi; later Jahangir had used the citadel for informal outings and hunting. Yet another association of Humayun with Delhi was his visits to several Sufi shrines like that of Qutbuddin Bakhtiyar Kaki and Nizamuddin Auliya.

Humayun, however, resided in Delhi for a short period of six months and could hardly make any substantial contribution to the landscape of Delhi. Perhaps his successor and son, Akbar, considered Humayun's residence in Delhi as a symbol of the establishment of Mughal presence in Delhi and built Humayun's tomb in Delhi rather than Agra, where Akbar had shifted his capital in AD 1562. Humayun's tomb dominates the landscape of southeast Delhi. The whole conception of the tomb explains the Persian architectural elements that were to be seen subsequently in Mughal buildings.

Surrounded by a park-like enclosure, the tomb is well proportioned and is the first of the monumental garden tombs in India. During the brief tenure, AD 1560–1562, when Akbar stayed in Delhi, Mughal Delhi was represented by the area between Purana Qila, dargah of Nizamuddin Auliya and the site of the construction of Humayun's tomb. Apart from Humayun's tomb, the madrasa of Mahamanaga was constructed during this same period. It is now known as Khair al-Manazil. The Jesuit Father Monserrate, who accompanied Akbar on his campaign to Kabul in AD 1581, wrote

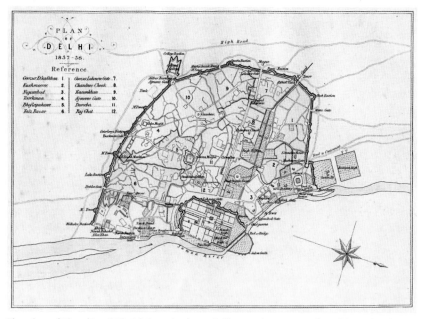

The plan of the city of Shahjahanabad was influenced, among other things, by the ancient Hindu texts like the *vastu shastras*

that as he passed through 'Delinum' he was impressed by this magnificent city, its broad roads planted with beautiful green trees, parks, gardens, fruits and flowers, with residences on both sides of the River Yamuna. He credited Humayun with these urban achievements. However, Abul Fazl, the contemporary chronicler of Akbar, mentions that in the 1590s most parts of Delhi were in ruins and only the cemeteries remained. But since Akbar considered Delhi as a place of *ziyarat* (pilgrimage) he visited the shrine of Nizamuddin Auliya, Humayun's tomb, Salimgarh and the hunting grounds in Palam.

Delhi served as transit for Jahangir while en route to other parts of the empire but like his predecessors he too visited Humayun's tomb, the *dargah* of Nizamuddin Auliya, Salimgarh — where he held wine parties and organized hunting expeditions to Palam. Shahjahan too visited the same four sites. This evolved into a pattern of imperial visits to Delhi. And since the Mughal emperors visited the same sites, it appears that each spot represented a particular relationship of the Mughals to Delhi's past — each location stood for a special historical connection of the Mughals with Delhi. It has been argued by historian Ebba Koch that Salimgarh represented the residential,

Humayun's tomb conveyed dynasticism, the *dargah* of Nizamuddin Auliya stood for religious and spiritual power and the hunting grounds of Palam, particularly its minar, demonstrated sovereignty. As the Mughal emperors visited these sites, they left behind their legacy in Delhi: Babur came as the 'new Timur', Humayun as the ambiguous 'residential visitor', Akbar as a pilgrim, Jahangir as a hunter and Shahjahan as an ideal king keen to revive the power and perfection of Delhi. Since no other city was visited in the way Delhi was and since the Mughal emperors emphasized the urban landscape of Delhi as a source of legitimation of their hold over the empire, it can be observed that in the urban context Delhi was the first capital of Muslim rule in India.

However, after AD 1639 the pattern of imperial visits changed when Shahjahan began the construction of Shahjahanabad on the advice of imperial astrologers and Ghairat Khan, the subedar of Delhi. Delhi was thus transformed from a historical political symbol (*Dar al-Mulk Dehli*) into the site of the new imperial residence and seat of government (*Dar al-Khilafa Shahjahanabad*). Muhammad Salih, an official historian of Shahjahan's reign, described Shahjahanabad as *markaz-i khak* (centre of the earth) and a scholar of the early eighteenth century referred to it as *markaz-i dairah Islam* (centre of the circle of Islam). The plan of Shahjahanabad was probably influenced by the ancient Hindu texts, *vastu sastras* (rules for architecture) that laid down the patterns for mechanical and fine arts. The *vastu sastras* described the layout of buildings (both religious and secular), settlements and their construction and habitation. For instance, Manasara, a *vastu sastra* (AD 400–600) advises that all settlements should have a semi-elliptical shape like a *karmuka* (tortoise) and that such a design was particularly suitable for a site in front of the river or seashore. In the *karmuka* plan, the most auspicious spot in a village or town was the juncture of the two cross-streets and ideally the temple of Lord Vishnu or Lord Shiva should be situated in such a spot. Interestingly, in Shahjahanabad the Lal Qila was situated in such a location, that is, at the meeting point of Chandni Chowk and Faiz Bazaar.

Shahjahanabad is enclosed by a huge stone wall — 27 feet high, 12 feet thick and 3.8 miles long. The wall, surmounted by 27 towers, had gates and entrances — both large and small — in several places. Joining the northern and southern parts of the city there were seven large gates that enclosed the urban parts of Delhi, that is an area where heavy mounted, vehicular and pedestrian traffic moved. These included the Kashmiri, Mori, Kabuli, Lahori, Ajmeri, Turkman and Akbarabadi gates. The wall, facing the River Yamuna, also had several large gates, namely the Raj Ghat, Qila Ghat and Nigambodh Ghat. These three *ghats* served as riverside crematoriums for the Hindus. Apart from these, there were small gates that provided pedestrian access to the city. Some of these gates were Zinat al-Masjid gate on the River Yamuna, Farrashkhanah gate and the gates of Gazi al-Din Khan and Ahmad Baksh Khan. The two most important topographical features within the area were two hillocks–Bhujalal Pahari that became the site of Jami Masjid and Jhujalal Pahari, near the north-west of the city but hardly of any significance. The two important thorough-fares in Shahjahanabad have been described in the historical sources as bazaars where the streets on both sides were lined with shops of variety. The largest and richest commercial complex extended from Lahori Gate of the Lal Qila to Fatehpuri Masjid; a canal, the Nahr-i Bihisht (canal of paradise) flowed through the centre of the bazaar and on each side of the canal, trees were planted for mulch and to provide a resting place. Urdu Bazaar (camp market) in Shahjahanabad catered to the needs of the imperial household, that is, soldiers, clerks, servants, artisans and others who lived in the neighburhood of the palace-fortress and who accompanied the emperor when he toured the countryside or resided in a camp. The Asharfi Bazaar (moneylenders' market) or Jauhari Bazaar (jewellers' market) was probably the section to deal with finances. The other major bazaar in Shahjahanabad extended from the Akbarabadi gate of the fort to the Akbarabadi gate of the city. Built by Nawab Akbarabadi Begum in AD 1650, this bazaar also had a *nahr-i bihisht* in its centre. An imposing structure in the bazaar was a mosque — black, red and creamy white — and opposite that a *sarai* and a *hammam*. In the early eighteenth century, Raushan al-Daulah, a noble of emperor Mohammad Shah, put strings of lights on both sides of the *nahr*. Originally named Akbarabadi Bazaar, its name was subsequently changed to Faiz Bazaar (bazaar of plenty). Another bazaar that can be mentioned was Khas Bazaar that connected Jami Masjid and the Lal Qila. Dancing girls, physicians, story-tellers and astrologers dominated this place and the shops here sold a variety of commodities ranging from cloth, medicine, cooked food, weapons, birds, fruits, flowers, wild animals, sugarcane etc. These markets represented the largest and richest markets but apart from these there were shops and stalls in almost all lanes and streets of Shahjahanabad.

The concept of gardens in Shahjahanabad was influenced both by the Quranic tradition which perceives paradise as a garden and the West Asian Islamic custom of royal pleasure gardens. Influenced by these patterns, the Mughals reworked and refined these designs to create gardens. An urban garden during the Mughal period was characteristically rectangular

Jama Masjid

in shape, enclosed by high walls but the major feature in these gardens was a central pool with a small open structure called *barahdari* (summer house). In Shahjahanabad, apart from these features, there were also canals, flowers, birds and fish. The cypress and fruit trees in the gardens had a special significance. The cypress symbolized death and therefore eternity, and the fruit trees especially mango, plum and almonds, represented life and hope. In other words, the cypress and the fruit trees, in a garden brought together the harmony of life and death, the ephemeral and the eternal, joy and happiness. The gardens, whether established by the Mughal emperors or the nobles were situated beyond the city walls, for instance, Shahjahan established a garden called Khizrabad on the west bank of the River Yamuna about five miles south of the Akbarabadi gate of the city; another garden that the emperor created outside the Kabuli gate of the city was Tis Hazari Bagh. In AD 1650, Raushanara Begum, daughter of Shahjahan laid out a large garden near the Lahori gate of the city known as Sabzi Mandi. Nawab Akbarabadi Begum established yet another garden known as Shalimar in the same style as the Shalimar gardens of Lahore and Kashmir in AD 1653–1654. The most artistic garden in Shahjahanabad was the one created by Jahanara Begum, the daughter of Shahjahan, in AD 1650, north of Chandni Chowk, called Sahibabad. Built in a rectangular design, the garden covers about 50 acres and comprises canals, waterfalls, fountains, pools, flowers, trees, *barahdaris* and a *nahr-i-bihisht* for elaborate water supply. The construction of gardens continued into the eighteenth century. Amongst these the significant one was Qudsiya Bagh, on the bank of the River Yamuna, north of Kashmiri gate, established in AD 1748 by Nawab Qudsiya Begum, wife of Mughal Emperor Mohammad Shah.

The Mughal emperors and their nobles also built caravan *sarais* (inns for travellers and merchants). Constructed as a mark of charity, religious duty or simply fame, *sarais* were accessible to merchants, scholars, religious men and all travellers except soldiers. Shahjahanabad had a number of *sarais*. For instance, Nawab Fathpuri Begum and Nawab Akbarabadi Begum had built *sarais* near the mosque in Chandni Chowk and Faiz Bazaar respectively. Bakhtawar Khan, a noble under Aurangzeb, had built a large *sarai* called Bakhtawar Nagar outside the city in AD 1671–1672. But the most aesthetically designed and imposing *sarai* was the one constructed by Jahanara Begum. A European traveller, Bernier, who had visited India in the seventeenth century,

access to it except the emperor, his sons and the household servants. The largest building in the area and the centre of collective activity was the Imtiaz or Mumtaz Mahal, later known as Rang Mahal. It was here that the emperor played with his children, watched music and dance performances by the dancing girls and listened to poets and storytellers. Near the Imtiaz Mahal was the *Aramgah* and *Khwabgah* of the emperor and, protruding from the eastern wall of the room, was a tower called Jharokah-i Darshan, subsequently called Mussaman Burj, from where the emperor received petitions and complaints.

The people of Shahjahanabad lived in a variety of houses. The *havelis* of royal princes and nobles of the upper strata contained gardens, watercourses and aesthetically built apartments whereas the lower ranking nobles and wealthy merchants had smaller houses built with stone, brick or clay and had roofs of straw. Hindu merchants, who were generally rich and prosperous, lived in houses that had six or seven stories. Ordinary merchants usually lived in quarters behind their shops but the soldiers, craftsmen, small traders and generally the common man lived in straw-thatched mud huts. As the population increased and the houses multiplied, they encroached upon the lanes and the empty spaces; this often resulted in fires during summers leading to the collapse of mud houses especially during monsoons.

In the cities of Mughal India, *masjids* (mosques) formed a significant part of religious architecture. Shahjahan too had commissioned two mosques in Delhi — an Idgah which was constructed outside the city of Shahjahanabad in AD 1650 and an enormous Jami Masjid, near the Lal Qila, completed in AD 1656, known as Masjid-i-Jahannuma (mosque of the world). Building a mosque was seen as a virtuous task and *waqf* (revenue-free land grant) was granted for the construction, maintenance and payment of salaries to mosque officials. To the north-west of Jami Masjid was a hospital and towards the south-west was located a *madrasa*.

The fact that Delhi was a significant economic centre is evident from its markets, trade and manufacture. Markets known

had observed that only the richest and most powerful Persian and Uzbek merchants were allowed to stay here.

The palace-fortress of Shahjahan, named Qila Mubarak but popularly called Lal Qila, constructed of red sandstone, was situated above the River Yamuna along the eastern wall of the city of Shahjahanabad. Ebba Koch is the only art historian who has been allowed to measure the entire Lal Qila. According to her, the whole plan was based on a mathematically proportioned grid that allowed Shahjahan to build a palace on the principles of bilateral symmetry. The Qila had four large gateways, two small entrances and 21 towers. The gates towards the west and south — the Lahori and Akbarabadi gates — were the main entrances. A moat 75 feet wide and 30 feet deep surrounded the fort, filled with water and stocked with fish; it provided shelter to the imperial household. Beyond the moat were a number of gardens — *buland* (high), *gulabi* (rose) and *anguri* (grapes). Near the eastern wall of the Qila was the sandy beach where the people assembled in the morning for the emperor's *darshan* and later in the day, elephant fights were organized on the beach for the entertainment of the emperor and the royal family. The southern half of the Qila comprised the harem (women's quarters) and no male had

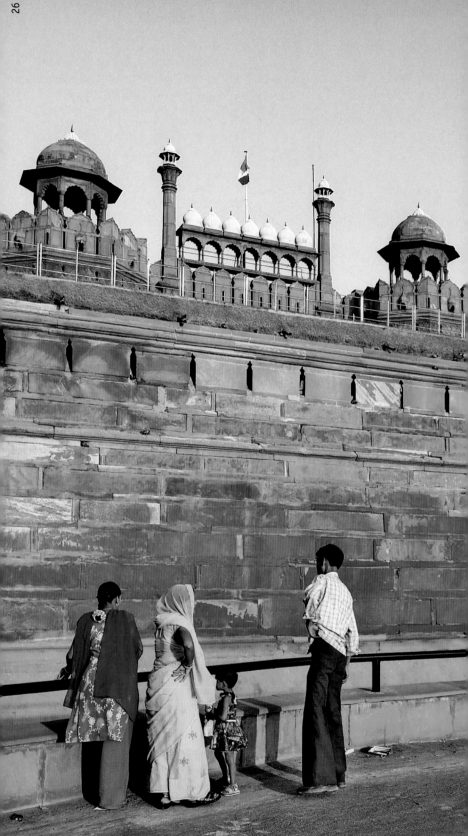

The palace-fortress of Shahjahan was named Qila Mubarak and popularly called Lal Qila. It is constructed of red sandstone and was situated above the Yamuna river along the eastern wall of the city of Shahjahanabad.

The Diwan I Khas in the Red Fort

as *nakhas* were held in several places in the morning and early hours of the evening. People from the neighbourhood visited these markets to sell their commodities, generally perishable goods and meant for daily consumption. *Dakakins* or retail outlets were a major medium of exchange — open for long hours selling not only luxurious items but also those for daily consumption — situated in the lower storey of mosques and within *mohallas*. The *dakakins* could have increased with the rise in population but the most important reason for the increase in shops was the extension of credit facilities between the wholesalers and retailers and retailers and consumers. As the population of Shahjahanabad increased, it emerged as the centre of exchange and the increasing demand for goods also led to a high cost of living. Delhi continued to be a centre of exchange in the eighteenth century despite the decline of the Mughal empire. In the early nineteenth century, family-run businesses dominated. These families had continued to live in Delhi despite the hardships following the collapse of the Mughal Empire. In fact the business transactions were now taken over by manufacturers, merchants, traders and skilled craftsmen. Shahjahanabad lives today in the Lal Qila, Jama Masjid, the mosques and temples, *kuchas, katras, mohallas* and the broken dilapidated walls but its culture and way of life retains its interest for all Dehli-wallahs.

References

· Bernier, Francois, *Travels in the Mogul Empire, AD 1656–1668,* New Delhi: Low Price Publications, 1989
· Blake, Stephen, *Shahjahanabad: the Sovereign City in Mughal India, 1639–1739,* Cambridge: Cambridge University Press, 1991
· 'Cityscape of an Imperial Capital: Shahjahanabad in 1739', in R. E. Frykenberg (ed.), *Delhi Through The Ages: Essays in Urban History, Culture and Society,* New Delhi: Oxford University Press, 1986, pp. 152–191
· Chenoy, Shama Mitra, Shahjahanabad: *A City of Delhi, 1638-1857,* New Delhi: Vedams eBooks (P) Ltd., 1998
· Frykenberg, R. E. (ed.), *Delhi Through The Ages: Essays in Urban History, Culture and Society,* New Delhi: Oxford University Press, 1986
· Gupta, Narayani, *Delhi Between Two Empires, 1803–1931: Society, Government and Urban Growth,* Second Impression, New Delhi: Oxford University Press, 1986
· Koch, Ebba, 'The Delhi of the Mughals Prior to Shahjahanabad as Reflected in the Patterns of Imperial Visits', in Ebba Koch, *Mughal Art and Imperial Ideology,* New Delhi: Oxford University Press, 2001, pp. 163–182
· Manucci, Niccolao, *Storia do Mogor,* trans. William Irvine, Vol. II, New Delhi: Low Price Publications, 1990
· Shekhar, Chandra & Shama Mitra Chenoy, trans., Muraqqa-i Dihli, *Selections from Dargah Quli Khan,* New Delhi: Deputy Publication, 1989

1200–1800:
Historical Architecture

The most iconic building of the architectural legacy of the Islamic Sultanate in Delhi: Qutab Minar and the Alai Darwaza

Qutub Minar and Mosque
Unknown (1202)
Qutab Minar
Mehrauli Archeological Park

001 I

The Qutub Minar is constructed with red and buff sandstone, and marble in the fourth and fifth storeys, and is the tallest stone minaret in India at a height of 72.5 metres (237.8 ft). The minar narrows down from the bottom up, with a diameter of 14.3 metres at the base, narrowing down to a mere 2.7 metres at the top. It is said that Qutbuddin Aibak built the first storey and Iltutmish the second, third and fourth, while Firuz Shah Tughluq repaired the fourth and constructed the fifth storey. The first storey is a polygon of 24 facets formed of alternate angular and semi-circular fluting, while in the third storey the fluting is angular again. The fourth and fifth storeys are circular. Projecting balconies, supported by stone brackets and further adorned by bands of inscriptions intertwined with foliated designs, encircle all the floors of the monument. The Minar is surrounded by several other ancient and medieval structures and ruins, collectively known as Qutub complex. Quwwat-al-Islam Mosque, to the northeast of *minar* was built by Qutbuddin Aibak in AD 1198. It is the earliest mosque built by the Delhi Sultans. The great lofty arches (without keystones) are constructed of random rubble masonry with a layer of exquisitely dressed stone on the facade. The stones can be seen to have chipped off at the edges. In the centre of the courtyard is the Iron Pillar and three sides of the courtyard have colonnaded cloisters of carved stone columns brought in from 27 Hindu and Jain temples.

Sultan Garhi ⌃ ⌄

Unknown (1231)

⊘ Chattarpur
Malakapur Village,
Near Vasant Kunj

`002` **B**

Sultan Garhi was the first Islamic Mausoleum built in 1231 AD for Prince Nasiru'd-Din Mahmud, eldest son of Iltumish, in the Malakapur village (near Vasant Kunj). The plan of the tomb structure is quite unusual with its fortress-like form and courtyard layout uncommon in the design of tombs. It is built over a raised plinth made of rubble masonry. The octagonal shape of the tomb is also unique as it has been built within the fortress like outer structure with four corner towers, over a *ghari* (cave) in front of the western Qibla wall of the mosque. It is therefore a combination of an overground tomb with towers (which is common in most of the tombs) and an underground chamber for the crypt. The exterior of the tomb structure is built in Delhi sandstone with marble adornment while the roof of the chamber is in thick lime-concrete. The marble western *qibla* (prayer wall) which has the *mihrab* boasts an exquisite Turkish and Afghan design.

The marble mihrab also has inscriptions from the Quran. The front elevation of this west wall has a marble facade, dated to Feroz Shah's rule (1351–1388). The prayer chamber in front of the *qibla* depicts a *yoni-patta* (the base slab of a Linga). The entire tomb uses a trabeate or corbel arch construction, which was common in India before the introduction of the Roman arch, seen in subsequent Islamic monuments. Old ruins of a Tugluq mosque, Jami masjid and a *khanqah* (a place of spiritual retreat) are also located on the southern side of the tomb.

Gandhak Ki Baoli ⇗

Unknown (1210–1236)

⊜ Qutab Minar
Mehrauli Archaeological Park

`003` **I**

Gandhak ki Baoli, the oldest stepwell in Delhi, owes its origin to the slave ruler Iltutmish who constructed the well to provide a continuous flow of water to the Mehrauli village. The well gets its name from the sulphur or *gandhak* in the water, which was believed to be steeped in medical properties. The well played a vital role in supplying water to the surrounding area for centuries while also offering a cool, secluded spot for relaxation and refreshment during the hot Delhi summer. Gandhak ki baoli is a large structure five tiers high, with a circular well at the southern end. Each tier is reached by way of galleries on the east and west, which give access to the well. The baoli was famous amongst the local inhabitants who used it as a sports venue for diving and swimming, but unfortunately is now completely dried up.

Balban's Tomb ❯❯   004 **I**

Unknown (1287)

Ⓔ Qutab Minar

Mehrauli Archaeological Park

The Tomb of Ghiyas ud din Balban is located in Mehrauli, in South Delhi. Erected in 1287 AD, in rubble masonry, the tomb is a building of historical importance in the development of Indo-Islamic architecture with a true arch making an appearance for the first time in India, and possibly also the first true dome as well, which, unfortunately, hasn't survived. Ghiyas ud din Balban (1200–1287) was a Turkic ruler of the Delhi Sultanate during the Mamluk dynasty (or Slave dynasty) from 1266 to 1287. The tomb of Balban was discovered in the mid-twentieth century. It is an imposing stone and masonry building, though lacking the

splendid ornamentation to be seen in the tomb of his master, Iltutmish. The tomb is surrounded by the ruins of an extensive late-medieval settlement, whose well conceived drainage system has been brought to light by recent excavations. To the east of Balban's tomb lies a ruined rectangular structure said to be the grave of Khan Shahid, Balban's son.

Nizamuddin Auliya's Baoli ❮❮   005 **A**

Unknown (1322)

Ⓔ JLN Stadium

Nizamuddin village,

North of Dargah

Built by Hazrat Nizamuddin Auliya in the years 1321–1322, Hazrat Nizamuddin Auliya's baoli is the only stepwell in Delhi to have an active underground spring that ensures a continuous supply of fresh water, and is considered holy by a lot of pilgrims. The baoli measures 37.5 metres by 16.15 metres and is enclosed by walls on the south, east and west, the descending steps being on the north. The Baoli is unique in that it contains a well that has a wooden base and is still in excellent shape even after 800 years. A secret passage linking the Baoli to the Nizamuddin Dargah was discovered by the Archeological Survey of India in collaboration with the Aga Khan Trust for Culture, and has since been restored. This passage was said to be sufi saint Hazrat Nizamuddin Auliya's personal access to the baoli. Buildings have been erected on the walls of the baoli at different times including the narrow arcaded passage on the east. The water though desilted is considered sacred and is in active use.

Tughlaqabad Fort and Ghiyasuddin Tughlaq's Tomb

006 C

Unknown (1325)

🚇 Tughlaqabad

Mehrauli Badarpur Road,
Tughlaqabad

Tughlaqabad Fort is a ruined fort built by Ghiyas-ud-din Tughlaq, the founder of the Tughlaq dynasty in 1321, the fifth historic city of Delhi. The Tughlaqabad fort served both as a defensive structure and as the imperial capital of Ghiyas-ud-din Tughlaq. There are a number of monuments within the precincts of this impressive fort. The fort's massive ramparts and bastions (as high as 15 to 30 metres, built of enormous blocks of stone with walls 10 metres thick in places) speak volumes about the might of the Sultanate. Within the fort's high walls, double-storeyed bastions and massive towers were housed magnificent palaces, grand mosques and audience halls. The city lay on the eastern outskirts of the massive fort. On the southern side of the fort is the tomb of Ghiyas-ud-din Tughlaq, which was erected by the ruler himself. The tomb is enclosed in a courtyard with fortified walls and is a fine example of Indo-Islamic architecture. The tomb is based roughly on a pentagon in plan and its entrance is guarded by massive portals. The mausoleum itself is very simple, very much the warrior's tomb, featuring the same sloping red sandstone walls which are Tughlaq hallmarks. Each wall has arched gateways decorated with beautiful latticework and white marble. The dome is entirely of white marble and is quite striking. This rather severe tomb does allow itself a few inscribed panels, arch borders, latticework screens and 'lotus-bud' edges which decorate it. Tughlaqabad stands divided into three segments. The eastern segment is entered through the Qutub-Badarpur road. It is a rectangular area enclosed within high walls and bastions and used to serve as the citadel. On the west side of the Tughlaqabad Fort is a wider area that once contained the palaces and is surrounded by walls and bastions. A huge reservoir stands on the southern side of the Fort. Bunds were put up between hills to the east to create the reservoir, which is linked with Ghiyas-ud-Din's tomb through a causeway.

Satpula

Unknown (1343)
⊘ Malviya Nagar
Khirki village,
Press Enclave Road

007 B

Believed to have been built by Muhammad Tughlaq (AD 1321–1351) this dam with sluice is unique in Delhi. It lies on the boundaries of Jahanpanah near present day Khirki village and was built to provide water for irrigation as well as be a part of the city wall and play a role in the city's defense. There are 11 elegant arched openings and a flanking tower at the eastern and western ends; four of the arched openings are subsidiary, while the seven main ones give the dam its name. On the upper level runs a wall, which is broken by recessed arches corresponding to the arched openings below. The side-walls of these arched openings are grooved for sliding gates, with which the force of the stream flowing from the south could be regulated. Both the flanking towers have deeply recessed arches facing north, inside which there is an octagonal chamber with arched recesses on each of its sides. The rear wall is pierced with arrow slits. The building is said to have been damaged by floods and a rubble wall was later erected to its south. The gates of the sluices were closed as a defensive measure against a possible attack in the dry season when no storage remained in the dam. On both banks of the weir, identical towers with octagonal shape chambers are built: as these once functioned as madrasa, the Satpula is also known as *'Madarsa'*.

Bijay Mandal; the structure that is visible today is built on a slightly raised platform

Bijay Mandal & Begumpur Mosque

Unknown (1351)

008 H

Hauz Khas

Begumpur Village, near Sarvapriya Vihar

The Bijay Mandal and Begumpur Masjid are part of Jahanpanah, the fourth city of Delhi. It was founded by Muhammad bin Tughluq in the fourteenth century. Whatever remains of the citadel lies in the Begumpur village today. Both buildings are strictly utilitarian with hardly any decoration—the hallmark of structures built under Muhammad bin Tughluq. The Bijay Mandal is a towering structure in the midst of the Begumpur village, best approached from Sarvodaya Enclave. Built in the fourteenth century, the Bijay Mandal was possibly the *Hazar Sutun* or thousand pillared palace of Muhammad bin Tughluq that was described by Ibn Battuta. The structure that is visible today is built on a slightly raised platform with a higher platform on top of it. This platform has several doors that possibly led into a hall.

The whole structure is on an octagonal plan and is built in rubble masonry. The complex on its northern side houses the shrine of a sufi saint, Sheikh Hasan Tahir, along with other graves. Designed by an Iranian architect, the Begumpur Masjid played a pivotal role in Tughluq times when it was used as a madrasa as well as a treasury. Built either by Muhammad bin Tughluq in 1351 or Firuz Shah Tughluq's prime minister Khan-i-Jahan Maqbul Tilangani, the mosque is considered an architectural masterpiece. Four walls surround the vast arcaded courtyard, with square domed chambers at the centre of each side. Three of these chambers were used as gateways. On the west side, a larger square chamber with halls on either side of it was a prayer hall. The masonry columns and arches are quite plain, the only ornamentation being the modestly carved capitals n the prayer hall. The stonework and domes were originally plastered with white *chuna* (lime). The mosque was probably in use till as late as the 17th century when Jahanpanah was occupied.

Begumpur Mosque; the mosque is considered an architectural masterpiece

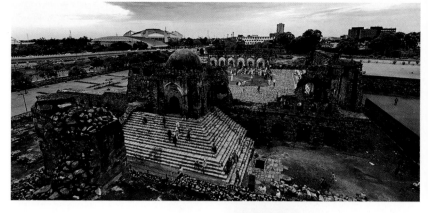

Feroz Shah Kotla ⌂

Unknown (1354)
🚇 Indraprastha
Bahardur Shah Zafar Marg
Opposite Maulana Azad Medical College

009 A

Firoz Shah Kotla was the inner citadel built by Firoz Shah Tughlaq in Firozabad, a very large city. It lies just off Bahadur Shah Zafar Marg between Old and New Delhi. The remains of a pyramidal structure topped by the Ashokan Pillar brought from Topra and a three-tiered baoli can be seen, but most of the ruins were used for the construction of later cities. Feroz Shah was a great builder and his city of Delhi was full of splendid palaces, mosques and gardens. A grand building with circular bastions mounted by *chhatris*, and exterior walls pierced with two rows of arrow slits which may have lost their battlements. The walls would originally have been completely plastered.

Khirki Mosque ⤷

Khan-i-Jahan Junan Shah (1351–1386)
🚇 Malviya Nagar
Khirki Village, Press Enclave Road

010 B

The Khirki Masjid is located in the settlement of Jahanpanah, Delhi. The north, south and east walls are pierced by windows with red sandstone grills (*khirkis*) which give the mosque its name. The mosque is a double-storeyed building, the lower of which contains numerous vaulted cells and an exterior with arched recessed openings. Sloping domed towers reinforce the four corners of the mosque. In the centre of the north, south and east sides are domed gateways projecting from the main face of the building, these are flanked by tapering minarets. The small quadrangle shaped mosque is almost entirely closed on top, making it unlike other mosques, which have large open courtyards for devotees to pray in. The roof of the Khirki Masjid is divided into 25 squares equal in size. Groups of nine small domes together alternate with flat slabs to cover the roof. Four open courtyards provide light and ventilation to the internal prayer spaces. Khirki Masjid has beautiful convoluted latticework on its windows, which were principally carved stone screens and can be said to be the precursor of later Mughal buildings marked by intricate patterns and delicate facades. The pillars and brackets of the mosque show a heavy native influence, which can be attributed to the ample use of local artisans, trained in their own schools of architecture. The external surface of the mosque is plaster; its interiors are undecorated save for traditional carved stone screens (*jaalis*) that also admit light. The rubble core construction of the mosque's walls, both exterior and interior, can be seen where the plaster has fallen off.

Firuz Shah's Tomb; the most ornate of the buildings in the complex

Hauz Khas

011 B

Unknown (1354–1388)

♻ Green Park
Hauz Khas Village

Hauz Khas Lake

The Hauz Khas Complex in South Delhi houses a water tank, an Islamic seminary, a mosque, a tomb and pavilions built around an urbanized village. It was part of Siri, the second medieval city during the 13th century Delhi Sultanate of Allauddin Khilji. The large water tank or reservoir was first built by Khilji to supply water to the inhabitants of Siri. The notable structures built by Firuz Shah on the eastern and northern side of the reservoir consisted of the main Tomb for himself, a *madrasa* (a theological college), a small mosque, and six domed pavilions in its precincts. Firuz Shah's Tomb, the most ornate of the buildings in the complex, pivots the L-shaped *madrasa* complex which overlooks the tank. The tomb, a square chamber, was built using local quartzite rubble and was originally finished with plaster. The door, pillars and lintels were made of grey quartzite while red sandstone was used for the carvings of the battlements. The *madrasa* structure flanks Firuz Shahs tomb on either side. The two arms are interconnected by small domed gateways passing through the tomb at the centre. The North-South arm has balconies overlooking the reservoir and is a two-storey building with three towers of varying sizes. Ornamental brackets cover the upper-storey balconies while the lower stories have corbelled support. The most unusual structure in the complex is the three domed pavilion located centrally in the residential part of the *madrasa* complex. It is unlike any other structure in Delhi, and may have been originally used as a meeting or discussion space.

L-shaped *Madrasa*

Square Chamber

Agrasen Ki Baoli

Unknown (14th century)

🚇 Barakhamba Road
Hailey Road, Connaught Place

012 D

Agrasen Ki *Baoli* is a 60-metre long and 15-metre wide historical step well on Hailey Road near Connaught Place in New Delhi. Although there are no known historical records to prove who built Agrasen Ki *Baoli*, it is believed that it was originally built by Raja Agrasen during the Mahabharat era and rebuilt in the 14th century by the Aggrawal community which traces its origin to Maharaja Agrasen. The *baoli* has striking features and a design layout that resembles both the Tughlaq and the Lodi dynastic styles of architecture, and may have existed even before the Tughlaq reign and rebuilt during that era. Erected during the 14th Century AD, the *Baoli* is known to be one of the most stunning step wells ever built in Delhi and it is adorned with rubble and stone dressed with inventive designs. Agrasen Ki *Baoli* presents a long staircase leading right to the bottom of the well with over 103 steps seen perpetually immersed into the waters. The steps are flanked by a very thick wall made of stone that runs along three levels and each level is seen fringed with a series of arched niches. The lowest level is submerged in water while the other two lay above the surface, creating a space for residents of the neighbourhood to sit on, providing some respite in the intense Delhi summers.

Rajon Ki Baoli
Unknown (1506)
🚇 Qutab Minar
Mehrauli Archeological Park

`013` **I**

Rajon Ki *Baoli* is a famous stepwell near Adham Khan's Tomb in Mehrauli. This magnificent three-storey stepwell is believed to have been built by Daulat Khan during the reign of Sikandar Lodi in 1516. The baoli was used by masons for some time because of which it got the name Rajon Ki *Baoli*. The *baoli* is oblong with steps leading downwards from the north. The entire structure is subterranean: as one approaches the entrance, one can only see the top-most storey. Each level of the baoli reveals itself to the visitor as one walks towards its steps. The walls of the lowest visible storey are decorated with deeply recessed arches, while the top storey is surrounded by an arcade with massive piers. On the south side is a well. The top storey had *chajjas* which have now disappeared. The *baoli*-complex also has a 12-pillar tomb and a mosque with some pretty plaster decoration on it.

Bada Gumbad flanked by the caravanserai on its right and mosque on its left

Shish Gumbad

Mohammed Shah's Tomb

Bada Gumbad Mosque

Lodi Tombs and Garden `014` G

Unknown (Between 1444–1517)
🚇 Jor Bagh 🚇 Khan Market
Lodi Road, New Delhi

Lodi Garden is a public park designed around four tombs of the Sayyad and Lodi dynasties. The gardens were land-scaped by Lady Willingdon, wife of then Governor General of India under the British Empire, and were originally called Willingdon Gardens. They were re-landscaped by Joseph Allen Stein with Garett Eckbo, when a Glass House was added to the garden near a British-period gateway, still being used as an entrance. The gardens surround four monuments of the Lodi dynasty — Mohammed Shah's Tomb, Sikander Lodi's Tomb, Sheesh Gumbad and Bara Gumbad. Bara Gumbad is a magnificent Lodi-period building, built in 1494. Shaped like a tomb, schol-ars nevertheless believe it to be a gate-way attached to a three domed Masjid. The building stands on a platform fur-nished by arched recesses, giving it an appearance of a two-storey building. Each of its sides has a typical Lodi en-trance, with an outer enclosing arch and a corbelled doorway. There is also a res-idence surrounding a central courtyard, where the remains of a water tank can

be seen. Sheesh Gumbad, which stands opposite the Bara Gumbad, was erected around the same time. This building, made of local stone, comprises a 10 square metre chamber covered by a dome. On the north, south and east sides are openings with a typical Lodi period gateway and niches. The tomb gets its name from the blue glazed tiles ornamenting the exterior, only some of which now remain; the ceiling of the dome is decorated with floral motifs and quotations from the Quran. Sikander's own tomb, an octagonal building very similar in style to Mohammed Shah's tomb but without the *chhatris*, was built by his son Ibrahim Lodi in 1517, the last Sultan of Delhi from the Lodi dynasty. It is the earliest surviving enclosed garden tomb in Delhi. It consists of a chamber surrounded by a verandah each face of which contains three arched openings. Arched recesses relieve the lower external and internal portions. The enclosure walls have two entrances in the centre of the south and east walls. Mohammed Shahs tomb is the earliest and most elegant octagonal tomb in Delhi. It was built in 1444 by Ala-ud-din Alam Shah in honor of Mohammed Shah. The architecture is characterised by the octagonal chamber, surrounded by a verandah, each face of which contains three arched openings. On the roof, the centre of each face is emphasized by a eight-pillared *chattris*. At each corner of the verandah is a sloping buttress used to strengthen the corner. A *chajja*, supported on heavy stone brackets, runs above the arches. This is topped by a parapet in each corner, on which is a *guldasta*. The dome springs from a 16-sided drum.

Jamali Kamali
Mosque and Tomb ⚐ ☈

015 I

Unknown (1528–1529)
🚇 Qutab Minar
Mehrauli Archeological Park

Jamali Kamali Mosque and Tomb is located in the Mehrauli Archeological Park in south Delhi, and comprises of two monuments adjacent to each other. Jamali was the pseudo name given to Shaikh Fazlu'llah, a great traveler and a poet in the time of Sikander Lodi. Kamali was an unknown person associated with Jamali, whose antecedents have not been established. The mosque stands in an enclosed court: the prayer chamber is entered through five arched openings on the south. The central arch is higher than the rest and is aesthetically carved with fluted pilasters flanking it. The western wall of the mosque has niches decorated with Quranic inscriptions. It also has a narrow gallery running around the mosque on the second storey with three oriel windows. The facade of the prayer hall is decorated by pendant lotus-buds that can be seen below the parapet. There are also octagonal towers at the rear corners of the mosque and only a single dome surmounts the central bay. The mosque has an adjoining graveyard with many unknown, unmarked graves. Here stands the square tomb of Maulana Jamali. The chamber is beautifully decorated with phenomenal stuccos in the interior and blue tiling on the exterior, including inscribed verses composed by Jamali. The mosque is considered to be a transition between the architectural styles of Moth-ki-Masjid and Sher Shah's mosque.

Purana Qila Ramparts

Purana Qila
Unknown (1538)
🚇 Pragati Maidan
Mathura Road

016 A

Purana Qila is the inner citadel of the city of Dina-panah, founded by the second Mughal Emperor, Humayun in 1533 and completed five years later. Purana Qila and its environs flourished as the sixth city of Delhi. Sher Shah Suri defeated Humayun in 1540, and renamed the fort Shergarh, and also added several more structures to the complex during his five-year reign. The fort is an excellent architectural example of a 16th century AD medieval fortress built with military precision to combat any attack from enemies. It has high walls with three arched double-storey gateways named 'Bara Darwaza' overlooking the west, 'Humayun Gate' overlooking the South, and 'Talaq Gate' which was a forbidden gate and is flanked by towers and bastions on either side inlaid with white marble and blue coloured tiles, ornate overhanging roofs and balconies, small windows (*Jharokhas*), pavilions supported by pillars and covered by cupols (*chhatris*) depicting a typical blend of Rajasthani and Mughal architecture. Only two of the many beautiful structures remain within the complex—the Qila-i-Kohna and the Sher Shah Mandal. The Qila-i-Konha mosque within the Purana Qila, was built by Sher Shah, and is one of his finest works and among the most elegant in Delhi. The mosque was constructed within a huge courtyard with a single dome shaped roof, which displays numerous pointed arches on its five doorways. Designed with a typical horse-shoe shaped opening on each arch, the mosque is designed in the Persian style, which predates the Mughal style of architecture. The special prayer hall within the Mosque is designed as a single aisle with five beautifully carved Mihrabs

Humayun Gate

Khairul Manzil

Sher Mandal, Purana Qila

placed on the wall to the west. The central Mihrab is seen with inscriptions embedded with red and white marble slates revealing the transition of its design from the Lodi style to the Mughal style. The Sher Shah Mandal monument was also built under the rule of Emperor Sher Shah Suri within the precincts of the Purana Qila during the 16th century AD.

It is a two-storey octagonal tower made of red sandstone with steps leading directly upto the top of the Mandal. Each face of the octagon is provided with a recessed arch. It is covered with an octagonal shaped cupola which is supported by eight strong pillars ornate with white marble. The interiors are decorated with plasterwork and shelves made of stone.

Qila-i-Konha mosque

Bara Darwaza

Humayun's Tomb

Mirak Mirza Ghiyath (1562–1566)
🚇 JLN Stadium
Nizamuddin

017 **A**

Inspired by Persian architecture, the tomb of Humayun reaches a height of 47 metres and a width of 91 metres, and was the first Indian building to use the Persian double dome on a high neck drum. The dome measures 42.5 metres and is topped by a six-metre-high brass finial ending in a crescent, common in Timurid tombs. The double or 'double-layered' dome has an outer layer which supports the white marble exterior, while the inner part gives shape to the cavernous interior volume. As a contrast to the pure white exterior dome, the rest of the building is made up of red sandstone, with white and black marble and yellow sandstone detailing. The simple, symmetrical design on the exterior is in sharp contrast with the complex interior floor plan of inner chambers, which is a square 'ninefold plan', where eight two-storey vaulted chambers radiate from the central, double-height domed chamber. It can be entered through an imposing entrance *iwan* (high arch) on the south, which is slightly recessed, while the other sides are covered with intricate jaalis. Underneath this white dome, in a chamber (*hujra*), lies the central octagonal

sepulcher, the burial chamber containing the single cenotaph of the second Mughal Emperor Humayun. Per Islamic tradition, the cenotaph is aligned on the north-south axis: the head is placed to the north, and the face is turned sideways towards Mecca. The real burial chamber of the Emperor, however, lies further away in an underground chamber, exactly beneath the upper cenotaph, accessible through a separate passage outside the main structure, inaccessible to visiting public. The marble and stone inlay ornamentation in numerous geometrical and arabesque patterns, seen all around the facade, is an important legacy of Indo-Islamic architecture.

The main chamber also carries the symbolic element, a *mihrab* design over the central marble lattice or *jaali*, facing Mecca in the West. Instead of the traditional inscription on the mihrabs, this one is just an outline allowing light to enter directly into the chamber, from the direction of Mecca, thus elevating the status of the Emperor. The building was the first to use a unique combination of red sandstone and white marble, and includes several elements of Indian architecture, like the small canopies, or *chhatris*, surrounding the central dome, popular in Rajasthani Architecture and which were originally covered with blue tiles.

Red Fort

Ustad Ahmad Lahori (1648)
🚇 Chandni Chowk
Netaji Subhash Marg, Old Delhi

018 A

The Red Fort was the palace for Mughal Emperor Shah Jahan's new capital, Shahjahanabad (present day Old Delhi). The layout of the Red Fort was organised to retain and integrate this site with the Salimgarh Fort. The fortress palace was an important focal point of the medieval city of Shahjahanabad. The fort lies along the Yamuna River, which fed the moats that surround most of the wall. The planning and aesthetics of the Red Fort represent the zenith of Mughal creativity, which prevailed during the reign of Emperor Shah Jahan. The artwork in the Fort is a synthesis of Persian, European and Indian art which resulted in the development of unique Shahjahani style which is very rich in form, expression and colour. The walls of the fort are smoothly dressed, articulated by heavy string-courses along the upper section. They open at two major gates, the Delhi and the Lahore gates. The Lahore Gate is the main entrance; it leads to a long covered bazaar street, the chhattar bazaar, whose walls are lined with stalls for shops. The chhattar bazaar leads to a large open space where it crosses the large north-south street that was originally the division between the fort's military functions, to its west, and the palaces, to its east. The southern end of this street is the Delhi Gate. Among other important structures within the fort there is Diwan-i-Aam and Diwan-i-Khas. The first is a large pavilion for public imperial audiences with an ornate throne-balcony (*jharokha*) for the emperor. The columns were painted in gold and there was a gold and silver railing separating the throne from the public. Diwan-i-Khas—the 'hall of private audience'—was used by the emperor for giving private audience to courtiers and state guests. The hall, with openings of engrailed arches on its sides, consists of a rectangular central chamber surrounded by aisles of arches rising from piers. The lower parts of the piers are inlaid with floral designs, while the upper portions are gilded and painted. The four corners of its roof are surrounded by pillared *chhatris*. Over the marble pedestal in its centre stood the famous Peacock. Through the centre of the hall flowed the *Nahr-i-Bihisht* or the 'stream of paradise'. Over the corner arches of the northern and southern walls, below the cornice, is inscribed the famous verse of the 13th century Sufi poet Amir Khusrau, exclaiming: if there is to be a paradise on the earth, it is this, it is this, it is this. The two southernmost pavilions of the palace are *zenanas*, or women's quarters: the Mumtaz Mahal (now a museum), and the larger, lavish Rang Mahal, which is famous for its gilded, decorated ceiling and marble pool, fed by the *Nahr-i-Bihisht*.

Fatehpuri Masjid ⌄

Unknown (1650)

⬀ Chandni Chowk
Chandni Chowk, Shahjahanabad

019 A

The third largest mosque in Shahjahanabad, Fatehuri Masjid is a 17th-century structure located at the prominent western end of Chandni Chowk. It was built in 1650 by Fatehpuri Begum, one of Mughal Emperor Shah Jahan's wives; the mosque at Taj Mahal is also named after her. The mosque is built with red sandstone on a large scale and is surmounted by a single fluted dome with *mahapadma* and *kalash* on the top. Flanked by towering minarets, the Fatehpuri mosque has a traditional design with the prayer hall having seven-arched openings, the central one being the highest. The centrally positioned Iwan is flanked by three arches on either side. Its pillared prayer hall is made up of multi-lobed arcades and columns. The Fatehpuri mosque in Delhi has single and double-storey apartments on the sides, used as shops and dwelling houses.

Jama Masjid ⌃
Unknown (1656)
🚇 Chandni Chowk
Shahjahanabad

020 A

The Jama Masjid of Delhi is one of the largest and finest mosques in India. Built between 1650 and 1656, the mosque is one of the last architectural works of the Mughal emperor Shah Jahan. The spacious courtyard of the Jama Masjid was designed to hold thousands of faithful. The mosque was built in red sandstone and marble by more than 5000 artisans. Originally called the *Masjid-i-Jahan-Numa*, or 'mosque commanding view of the world', the Jama Masjid stands at the centre of the erstwhile capital city of the Mughals, Shahjahanbad. Located on a mound in the heart of the old city, the Masjid projects beautifully into the Old-Delhi skyline. It stands ten metres above the level of the city with wide flights of red sandstone stairs leading up to it on the North South and East sides. The main East gate, facing the Red Fort, is the grandest of the entrances and was used by the Emperor to attend prayers. Between the gates runs a delicate arcade open on either side, allowing for stunning views of the city from within the courtyard. Three domes ornated with alternate strips of black and white marble and gilded pinnacles surmount the mosque. The main prayer hall is made up of 11 high cusped arches and marble domes; over these arched entrances are tablets of white marble inlaid with inscriptions of black marble. Two lofty minarets, longitudinally striped with white marble and red stone, mark the facade. The floor of the mosque is ornated in an imitation of the *mosalla* (prayer carpet). Relics of the Prophet, the Koran written on deerskin, a red beard-hair of the prophet, his sandals and his footprints, implanted in a marble block, are preserved in a room in the north-eastern corner of the court.

Jantar Mantar

Maharaja Sawai Jai Singh II
(1710)

021 D

🚇🚇 Rajiv Chowk
Sansad Marg, Connaught Place

The Yantra Mantra, popularly known as the Jantar Mantar, consists of 13 architectural astronomy instruments. Built by Maharaja Jai Singh II of Jaipur, it is one of five erected by him to complete the task of revising the calendar and astronomical tables on the instructions of the Mughal emperor Muhammad Shah. The primary purpose of the observatory was to compile astronomical tables and to predict the times and movements of the sun, moon and planets. There are four distinct instruments within the observatory of Jantar Mantar: the *Samrat Yantra*, the *Ram Yantra*, the *Jayaprakash*, and the *Mishra Yantras*.

The *Samrat Yantra*, or Supreme Instrument, is a giant triangle that is basically an equal hour sundial, and is built into a quadrangular excavation. The structure is 20.7 metres high. The essential parts are the inclined edges of the huge gnomon and the quadrants attached to it. The edges of the gnomon point to the celestial North Pole, ie they make an angle of 28°37′ with the horizon, equal to the latitude of Delhi. The quadrants are at right angles to the gnomon and therefore the circles of which they form a part are parallel to the plane of the equator. These quadrants have a radius of 49°6′ and are graduated on the each edge in hours, degrees and minutes. At the time of the *Samrat Yantra's* construction, sundials already existed, but the *Samrat Yantra* turned the basic sundial into a precision tool for measuring declination and other related coordinates of various heavenly bodies.

The *Ram Yantra* consists of two large circular buildings, each with a pillar in the centre. The height of the walls and pillar from the graduated floor is equal to the inside radius of the building, the walls and floor are graduated for reading horizontal (azimuth) and vertical (altitude) angles. To facilitate observation, the floor is cut into 30 sectors, with the spaces between them being of the same angular dimensions, i.e. six

degrees. The graduated sectors are supported on pillars 1m high so that the observer can place his eye at any point on the scale. The central pillar is graduated with vertical strips, each marking six degrees.

The *Jayaprakash Yantra* consists of two complementary concave hemispheres with markings on their concave surfaces. Theoretically only a single hemisphere is necessary, but to facilitate observation, pathways are cut into the surface and the second *Jai Prakash* is so constructed that the two instruments together show the complete surface. Cross wires were originally stretched across the hemispheres north to south and east to west, and the shadow of the intersection of these wires on the concave surface of

the hemisphere indicated the position of the sun. The pins to which the cross wires were attached can still be seen.

The *Misra Yantra*, or mixed instrument, is so named as it combines four separate instruments in one structure. The *Niyat Chakra*, in the middle of the building, consists of a gnomon with two graduate semi-circles on either side. The semi-circles correspond to meridians of the observatories in Greenwich, Zurich, Notkey (Japan) and on the east coast of Russia. On the either side of *Niyat Chakra* is half of an equinoctial dial constructed on the same principal as the large *Samrat Yantra*. On the east wall of the building is a graduate semi-circle called *Dakshinovritti Yantra* used to obtain meridian altitudes.

Saffdarjung's Tomb

Unknown (1753)

Jor Bagh
Intersection of Aurobindo Marg
and Lodi Road

022 A

Safdarjung's Tomb is a garden tomb with a marble mausoleum of emperor Safdarjung. Built in 1754 in the late Mughal Empire style, it was described as 'the last flicker in the lamp of Mughal architecture'. The garden, in the style evolved by the Mughal Empire that is now known as the Mughal gardens style was influenced by Persian gardens. The complex is enclosed by 6 m high walls, the corners of which are reinforced with octagonal tower. The only entrance to the enclosure is by a large ornate gateway in the centre of the east wall. In the centre of the wall on

the remaining three sides are pavilions, and living rooms built into the walls. The mausoleum stands on a lofty platform containing a series of arched recesses with the vault containing the grave of Safdarjung in the centre. The structure built in red and buff coloured sandstone over the grave measures 20 square metres and consists of a central chamber of 7 square metres with eight apartments surrounding it. These apartments are repeated on the upper floor. All the four facades of the tomb are treated similarly; their central feature being a cusped arch framed in marble and red sandstone. The building is covered by a triple dome, with the outer dome rising from a 16-sided red sandstone drum approximately 5 metres in height. Its facade is decorated with elaborate plaster carvings.

Shāhjahānābād

DELHI around 1850

Redrawn, by courtesy of the British Library, Oriental and India Office Collections,
from an original manuscript in the India Office Records. Archive reference: India Office Records X/1959
Printed with financial support by Deutsche Forschungsgemeinschaft (DFG)

Editors: E. Ehlers, Th. Krafft, J. Malik
Design and Cartography: G. Storbeck
Printing: Landesvermessungsamt Nordrhein-Westfalen
© Geographische Institut der Universität Bonn, 1992

1800–1947:
Colonial Architecture

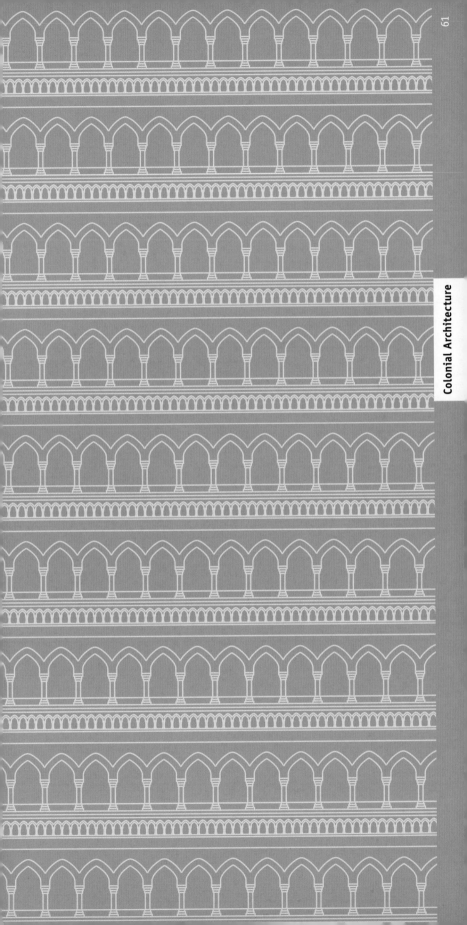

Colonial Delhi

Anupam Bansal

New Delhi was established in 1911 as the capital of British India. The British designed the new city as the political centre of the Empire on a historically strategic site. The city as conceived was a manifestation of power and supremacy of the British in India. Underlying the creation of New Delhi was the intention of the rulers to bring India under one administrative and political structure. New Delhi was precisely an architectural reproduction of the 'pyramid of power' existing in the city, in fact, in India. The British used their military tactics and technological advantage to extend control over the subcontinent, this was further helped by the weakening of the Mughal Empire. By the 1850s the British had gained control from Bengal in the East to Indus in the West, and from Kashmir in the North to Comrin in the South. As mercantile interests gave way to political ambitions, the primary objectives of the British shifted to internal unification and modernization. Growing nationalism and the first war of independence in 1857 precipitated

matters and the British Parliament passed an act transferring the company's rights in India to the British Crown. From then until India's independence in 1947, the subcontinent came under direct rule of the British Monarch. The British provided a rare instance of an all-India empire in the history of India. Never had there been an empire signifying unity of political control and administrative cohesion. Qualitatively, the process was unique in terms of principle and organization, in approach and mode of operation. Indeed the rise of the British power in its first phase during the eighteenth century was a result not so much of wars, conquests and annexations, as of peaceful penetration through the prevailing system which conferred rights to collect land revenue and administer justice, law and order.

The Native City

The existing capital of the Mughal Empire, Delhi (Shahjahanabad) was built in 1648 as a fortified city, with its walls running along the Jamuna river on the east, and below the slope of the Ridge along the north and west. The river and the ridge formed natural defenses. In fact it was the strategic location of Delhi which had made it a capital city of some empire or other during the course of its history. The reason for the persistence of the site throughout history was found not in its commercial or agricultural advantages but in its political and strategic importance. Delhi is set in the most northerly navigable point of the river Jamuna, and lies athwart the Punjab corridor which connects the northwest with the rest of India, and it is through the northwest passes from Persia and Afghanistan that many of India's invaders had come.

Having temporarily lost control of the city in 1857, the British regained it after a few months. The inhabitants of the city were expelled and the soldiers and the cantonment were moved from their existing location North-West of the city into the centre and the British army overtook the fort. The British occupied the former stronghold of the Mughals and the fort was converted into living quarters for the army. *'Where is Delhi asked Ghalib'* in 1858. *'By God it is not a city now. It is a camp. It is a cantonment. There is neither Palace, nor bazaar, nor the canal.'*

The basis for the emerging colonial culture and the capital city of New Delhi, was laid during the three imperial assemblies in Delhi. The first one held in 1877 proclaimed Queen Victoria as the Empress of India, followed by assemblies marking the coronations of King Edward VII in 1902 and King George V in 1911. These ceremonial assemblies were modeled after Mughal courts or durbars. Durbars had originally been used to sustain and validate the structure of society in Mughal India. By the eighteenth century, both Hindu and Mughal rulers had adopted the custom of holding these courtly rituals. Administrative and state matters were attended to, awards were bestowed and complaints were heard in these durbars. The entire ritual of audience was marked by a strict code of conduct and the precise observance of rules and regulations. Even the spatial arrangement of the durbars followed a well-established rule. The British adopted the durbar for similar purposes as a means of strengthening their ties with the people.

Imperial New Delhi

King George V announced the transfer of the Indian capital at the Durbar celebrating his coronation as Emperor in 1911. The viceroy at the time, Lord Hardinge, had supported the decision saying that Delhi was intimately associated in the minds of both the Hindus and the Muslims. By this time Delhi had developed the three essential component parts of the colonial city in India: the 'native city', which was the old part of the city largely inhabited by indigenous population, the 'cantonment', which housed the military establishment, and the 'civil station', which was largely inhabited by bureaucrats and officials of the government.

Edwyn Lutyens and Herbert Baker were commissioned to design the new capital as an expression of colonial power. The architecture drew both upon European classical styles and upon those of India's past, particularly those associated with the Mughal Empire.

Lutyens based the layout of the city on a geometrical plan made of a system of hexagonal grids and visual axes. In his layout reflection of the Imperial supremacy, Lutyens was influenced by other cities in the West: L'Enfant's plan of Washington, Haussman's plan of Paris and the contemporaneous creation of a new Federal capital at Canberra in Australia. Trained in the Classical style of architecture, he applied its principles to design the city not only because he found it interesting and most aesthetically satisfying, but also because it represented British sovereignty.

The plan established two major visual corridors: one with the Jama Masjid in Shahjahanabad and the other with Purana Qila, an even older fortification of Delhi, culminating in the Capital Complex. The circular Council Chamber (present Parliament) building marked the terminus of the axis towards the Jama Masjid. In the middle, along this axis was located Connaught Place, an

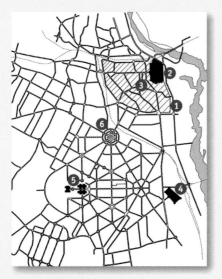

Lutyens' Delhi
1. Shahjahanabad / 2. Red Fort
3. Jama Masjid / 4. Purana Qila
5. Viceroy's House / 6. Connaught Place

The Canopy, India Gate

immense circular, colonnaded commercial node which remains to this day the nerve centre of Delhi's Central Business District. Along the Purana Qila axis, in the east-west direction, was the major ceremonial green called the Central Vista with the King's Way (present Rajpath) penetrating the Capital Complex between two major office blocks, and terminating in the Viceregal Palace. The integrated mass of the Capital Complex provided a visual climax to this dramatic linear open space, criss-crossed by lateral roads and punctuated by India Gate (a War Memorial to the Unknown Soldier built in 1923) and a small but ingeniously designed pavilion (referred to as the *Chhatri*) to shelter the statue of King George.

The King's Way or Rajpath, which ran in the middle of the Central Vista green, flanked by two shallow, linear water bodies on either side, was crossed in the middle by the Queen's Way or present Janpath. Queen's Way enjoyed a special status in Lutyens' plan by virtue of the fact that this was the only lateral road that directly interconnected the proposed railway station and the civic node with the Anglican Cathedral (unbuilt). The Cathedral was to be the focus of the residential areas of higher officials of the government, located south of the Vista. More significantly, the intersection of King's Way and Queen's Way was to form a cultural or intellectual plaza with the four symmetrical blocks of the National Museum, the Oriental Institute, the National Library and the Imperial Record Office. The visual linearity of the Central Vista was later considered more important and the four buildings were proposed to flank the Queen's Way on either side where it enters the Central Vista. Of these, a part of the Imperial Record Office (now known as the National Archives) was designed and built by Lutyens on the north of the green, and the National Museum was designed and built on the south of the Vista, by the Central Public Works Department of independent India.

Based on hexagons and equilateral triangles, the road network had a radial configuration and used roundabouts for directional change. Terminal vistas were established wherever possible, often using proposed public buildings or an existing Mughal monument. The geometry was used as a device to integrate the old and new structures into a coherent visual experience. As a general pattern in New Delhi, Lutyens adopted a technique where built form was defined by the space around it, generating on the whole a low-key urban fabric.

Lutyens' city was also deeply rooted in symbolism. The pursuit of a system of

Viceregal Palace/Rashtrapati Bhavan

geometry and symmetry was symbolic of Britain's efforts to impose order and unity in the Subcontinent, while the monumental scale of the avenues and the buildings implied the stability and permanence of the Empire. Irving states, 'the domes and the towers fashioned by Lutyens and Baker rose on Raisina Hill, bright against the sky above city and plain, they had seemed to proclaim the success of British discipline and power.'

Hierarchical City

Symbolism was further reinforced by the hierarchical nature of the plan. The plan was a translation of the hierarchy of the power existing in New Delhi. Every event, symbol and building was a part of a greater design, a subcomponent of the stage setting and role assigning crucial to the administration of the colonial city.

Atop Raisina hill, the highest point in the city, stood the Viceregal Palace. East of the Viceregal Palace were two large offices accommodating the Imperial bureaucracy, the North and South blocks of the 'Secretariat'. The remaining area was allocated entirely to the residential and institutional needs of the government and its accompanying network of roads. In 1919 the circular 'Council Chamber' was integrated in the acropolis. The Viceregal Palace formed the centre of the whole spatial layout. It became the origin of all-important

axes and the radials. 'Every single building and vista reflects the hierarchy of the society which built it and at its centre stands the focus of the entire city, Viceroy's House, the supreme fount of political, cultural and social patronage.' In the British Indian hierarchy, the viceroy, as representative of the Crown, was located prominently on the highest knoll; on his left, i.e. to the north of the Viceregal Palace was located the head of the religious system, the church; on his right, i.e. to the south of the Viceregal Palace, was located the head of the military institution, the commander-in-chief. Thus the triangle connecting the heads of these three primary institutions of civil government, the military organization and religion occupied the key positions in the capital.

Residential areas were allocated according to occupational rank, race and socio-economic status. Five areas were created accordingly: first for 'gazetted officers', consisting mainly of the European elite; second for European 'clerks'; the third for indigenous 'clerks' and the lower ranking officials; the fourth for members of the indigenous elite, the nobility of the Indian states; and the fifth area was a non-official space, reserved for those with insufficient rank or status. Plot sizes were also allocated according to status: the ruling princes received between four and eight acres, gazetted officers between two and three-and-a half acres, and Members of the Legislature, one-quarter acre. Residences of members of the Viceroy's Council lined the ceremonial avenue while heads of Government departments were placed within the inner ring and the finer parts of the city.

Architectural Character

Even though the New Delhi plan was alien in spirit to indigenous planning practices, Lutyens & Baker attempted an interesting mixture of architectural styles blending Indian and European vocabularies. Innovative detailing using Buddhist, Hindu and Islamic elements abound in these buildings. Aware of the fact that local labourers had to be employed in the actual construction process, the design adopted a vocabulary using materials and techniques familiar to them. Lutyens and his team of architects borrowed freely from Indian architectonic elements using them not only as appropriate building components, but also to create a contextual continuity. The adaptation of *chhatri* in the Capital Complex and, more dominantly, in the structure sheltering the statue of King George along the main axis, provides an example of how a simple architectonic element was used by Lutyens to create symbolic and physical continuity.

Apart from the *chhatris*, stone trellis-work, sunshades (called *chhajja* locally), balconies supported by brackets, characteristic door and window details, cornices, mouldings, etc., were executed in combinations of red and pink sandstone in the Central Vista buildings. In Lutyens' own buildings, masonry structures are often clad with stone, or stone is used directly as structural material. However, the scale of structures is broken by the use of carved stone depicting European and Indian symbolic elements such as elephants, snakes, shells, bells, fruit forms, leaves and so on at appropriate places. Compound walls, benches, lampposts and other urban furniture elements are also used to create textures and rhythms, which break down the scale to a human level.

The consistent use of sandstone, with the visually heavier red stone at the base of buildings and lighter pink stone on the upper parts, was another dominant factor that lends visual cohesion to the entire group of buildings. The warm hues of stone complemented the vast green background in the Central Vista. The sandstone, readily available even today, was a versatile material traditionally used for structures and easily amenable to ornamentation. In post-independent India, major government buildings were erected on either side of the Central Vista and most conform to this general colour scheme.

New Delhi was an enormous political, strategic and also ultimately logistical undertaking. 700 million bricks, 100,000 cubic feet of marble, 3,500 stone dressers for the sandstone, all of these under harsh local conditions of heat and dust, irregular supply of resources and finally the numerous and often conflicting directions from various sources of authority. A world war intervened and slowed down construction. After 17 years of continuous work, New Delhi was ready to be inaugurated in 1931. This was a celebration of grand receptions with dances and cocktails, all celebrating the British Empire's greatest architectural achievement. The impeccable geometry and order imposed by the Delhi plan on the site was emblematic of the order imposed on the world by the British Empire. What irony though: by 1931 it was already clear that the British rule in India was drawing to a close. Like the Raj, New Delhi was already the symbol of an age that was ending — an age of splendor, an age of kings.

References

· Irving, Robert Grant. *Indian Summer; Lutyens Baker and Imperial Delhi.* Yale University Press; New Haven & London. 1981, p. 2
· Ghalib, Mirza. 'Military Security and Urban Development: A Case Study of Delhi 1857–1912'. By Narayani Gupta, *Modern Asian Studies*, 5, I, 1971, p. 77
· Irving, Robert Grant. *Indian Summer; Lutyens Baker and Imperial Delhi.* Yale University Press; New Haven & London. 1981, p. 72, 73
· Davies, Philip. *Splendours of the Raj*, John Murray; London, 1985, p. 227

St. James Church ⚟ »

Major Robert Smith (1836)
⊜⊝ Kashmere Gate
Kashmere Gate

023 A

St. James' is an Anglican church and was the first one to be built by the British in Delhi. Commissioned by Col. James Skinner, the church is designed in a Renaissance Revivalist style on a cruciform plan with three porticoed porches, elaborate stained glass windows and a central octagonal dome, similar to that of the Florence Cathedral in Italy, which was the first Renaissance structure to be built in the world. Porches on the north, south and the west provide the building with three entrances. The central portion of the church is an octagon with circular columns supporting the dome.

St. Stephens Church ⌣

Anglican Missionary (1862)
⊝ Chandni Chowk
Fatehpuri, Chandni Chowk,
Shahjahanabad

024 A

St. Stephens Church is located on Church Mission Road in Delhi. The church was built by the Anglican Missionary in the Italian Romanesque style. It is a part of the Church of North India, Diocese of Delhi. A high bell tower rises from the north-eastern end. The central hall is separated from the sides by impressive semi-circular arches. Apart from its ornate walls and ceilings, it has a unique stained glass rose window, the only one of its kind in Delhi. Arched windows allow ample sunlight to brighten the interiors, which is designed with motifs, pictures, carvings and beautiful furniture. A series of fine plasters form an arcade on either side lined with beautifully carved sandstone columns.

Old Delhi Railway Station

Unknown (1867)
Chandni Chowk
S.P. Mukherji Marg,
Shahjahanabad

025 A

Old Delhi Railway Station was among the earliest railway stations built in India by the British. It was built in 1900 and was open for public in 1903. Started with just two platforms and 1,000 passengers, today Delhi Railway Station handles more than 180,000 passengers and 200 trains daily. Built in red stone in a Gothic style, the two-storey building has deep verandas on its two floors. It has six clock towers, of which tower four is in use today as a water tank. Though the original building is in good conditions, many modifications and additions have been done. Semi-octagonal turrets rise from the corners of the building. Until the opening of New Delhi Railway Station in 1926, ahead of the inauguration of the New Delhi city in 1931, this served as the main station for the city of Delhi, hosting four junction railways. When first built, the building known today as the Old Delhi Railway Station was the most powerful symbol and harbinger of the changes that would transform the city after 1857. For several months after the British regained control of the city following the revolt of 1857, they had debated whether to keep the city or destroy it completely. There was a suggestion for Jama Masjid to be replaced by a cathedral, for example. Even after such

drastic plans were abandoned, European troops continued to occupy much of the walled city, Daryaganj and the Palace (the Lal Qila), which was now called the 'Fort'. Further, the military decision to clear a 500-yard space around the Fort led to some of the loveliest buildings of the city being destroyed—Kucha Bulaqi Begum, the Haveli Nawab Wazir, the Akbarabadi Masjid, the palaces of the Nawabs of Jhajjar, Ballabgarh, Farrucknagar and Bahadurgarh. Alongside this planned urban destruction, however, came a spate of construction at the core of which was the railway. The railway embankment created in the 1860s divided the city in half, cutting right through the central residential areas. The railway was built along an east-west axis, distorting the concentric structure of Shahjahanabad, and running between the now-military bastions of Salimgarh and the Fort, which provided the British complete assurance of security and military access in case of a rising in the city. The entry to the city, which until then had been either by river or from Ghaziabad, after crossing the bridge of boats, changed completely. Where until the mid-nineteenth century travellers were greeted by a view of minarets, the post-1870s visitors got off the train and emerged through the Italianate arches of a railway station into a new Victorian-style city centre, including a Town Hall, a Clock Tower and soon after, a Fountain. It was hard to visualise the crowded mohallas that had once stood in their place.

Old Secretariat ⩗

E. Montague Thomas (1912)
🔁 Civil Lines
Shamnath Marg, Civil Lines

026 A

National Archives ⩗

Edwin Lutyens (1926)
🔁🔁 Central Secretariat
Janpath (north of Rajpath)

027 F

The construction of the Old Secretariat building was undertaken by the British when they decided to transfer their capital from Kolkata to Delhi. It was built with the purpose of housing the Legislative Council of the Central Government. The Old Secretariat is a stately building with a long front line and two lateral structures, the portion facing the Alipur Road curving gracefully in the centre like a half moon. The central doorway connects with the main chamber. There are two minarets at each end and small towers decorate these corners with domes. A colonnaded verandah with square archways runs all along the building. The building now houses the Delhi State Assembly.

The National Archives was one of the most iconic buildings of the new capital. It was part of four museums and archives building planned by Edwin Lutyens at the interaction of King's way and Queen's way, known as 'Point B'. But eventually, only the record office was erected. The building was different from others in terms of its facade which, as Andreas Volwahsen writes in his book *Imperial Delhi*, reflects 'the two most important architectural clichés of the late neoclassical building style in India, namely the hall with columns and the verandah with capitals of the Delhi Order'. The building features red and buff-coloured sandstone with the lower storey in red stone and the upper floor in buff stone.

Parliament House

028 E

Herbert Baker (1927)

Central Secretariat
Sansad Marg

The seat of Indian Parliament was designed by Baker, under the supervision
of Lutyens, in response to the need for
additional space to house the expanded Indian participation in Government.
Lutyens envisioned a coliseum like structure, favoured by the decision-making
committee, forcing Baker to change his
original idea of a three-pronged building. The structure is 174 metres in diameter and about one-third of a mile in
circumference. Each the semi-circular
house chambers is connected via large
lobby spaces to the Central Chamber,
which is where Nehru made his 'tryst
with destiny' speech on the eve of India's
independence. The central chambers are
surrounded by offices and service rooms,
all accessed from the continuous open
corridor on the first floor, fringed with a
colonnade of 144 creamy sandstone pillars. The central chamber is topped by a
dome, which, due to budget constraints,
is too small for the scale of the building, and looks rather out of place. The
interiors are very plain, and the exteriors
finished in painted plaster rather than
stone, as a result of the limited budget.

Hyderabad House ☆

Edwin Lutyens (1928)
🚇 Mandi House
Ashoka Road,
India Gate C Hexagon

`029` F

The interior was very richly decorated. It is located to the northwest of the India Gate. The Hyderabad House is an amalgam of the Mughal and European styles of architecture.

Hyderabad house is the former princely residence of Osman Ali Khan, Nizam of Hyderabad state. The need for a residence in Delhi arose because the most important traditional rulers (maharajas) of Indian states were inducted in 1919 into a Chamber of Princes and, therefore, had to come to Delhi to attend the Chambers meetings of the British. It is currently used by the Government of India for banquets and meetings for visiting foreign dignitaries. It has also been a venue for joint press conferences and major government events. Hyderabad House is the largest and grandest of all palaces that were built during the period 1921–1931 to house various state rulers. The plan was a butterfly shape with a central domed entrance hall from which symmetrical wings radiated at 55°. Arcaded verandahs, prominent cornices and Dholpur stone *jaalis* articulate the facade of the building.

St. Martin's Garrison Church »

Arthur Shoosmith (1929)
🚇 Dhaula Kuan
Church Road, Delhi Cantonment

`030` A

St. Martin's Church marks the culmination of the British architectural ventures in India. A monumental, solid brick building with very few openings or ornamentation, Shoosmith abstracted Lutyens' method of geometric design and massing into something timeless and uncompromising in its austerity. The monolithic appearance of the church is accentuated by the fine brick work with very narrow joinery. The main entry on the west is the only decorative opening, with receding brick arches. The high square tower and deeply sunken window ledges are reminiscent of Dutch and German architecture. The bays inside the church are articulated with plain arches, while the walls are plastered and painted.

Teen Murti Bhavan ⮡

Robert Tor Russell (1930)
🚉 Race Course
Teen Murti Marg

031 A

The Teen Murti Bhavan is the former residence of the first Prime Minister of India, Jawaharlal Nehru. It was designed by Robert Tor Russell, the British architect of Connaught Place and of the Eastern and Western Courts on Janpath during the British Raj. Teen Murti Bhavan was built in 1930 as part of the new imperial capital of India. The Bhavan was originally known as Flagstaff House and was the residence of the Commander-in-Chief of the British Forces in India. Situated in a large estate, the building is constructed of stone and stucco, and faces the south side of the Rashtrapati Bhavan. The rather long building has a central porch on the ground floor. It has a very Colonial facade, marked by semi-circular arches, pediments, bold plaster lines and typical moldings. The central portion of the first floor at the rear has a deep verandah overlooking the lawns. On Nehru's death in 1964, the house was converted into a national memorial comprising a library and a museum. A room on the ground floor of the house has been refurbished to recreate Nehru's office in the Ministry of External Affairs with the original furniture, objects and manuscripts used by Nehru during his time in office. The Nehru Memorial Library is one of the finest for information on modern Indian history.

India Gate

India Gate

Edwin Lutyens (1931)
🚇 Central Secretariat
Rajpath

 `032 F`

The India Gate is the national monument of India. Situated in the heart of New Delhi, it was designed by Sir Edwin Lutyens, inspired by the Arc de Triomphe in Paris. Originally known as the All India War Memorial, it is a prominent landmark in Delhi and commemorates the 90,000 soldiers of the Indian Army who lost their lives while fighting for the British Raj in World War I and the Third Anglo-Afghan War. It is composed of red and pale sandstone. The 42.35 metres high arch has a 10 metre wide main opening with smaller openings on the sides which relieve the massiveness of the north and south sides. Giant pine cones stood in urns beneath the smaller arches. A flame is constantly lit in the centre of the arch. The word 'INDIA' is boldly visible at the top, giving the arch its name. Originally, a statue of George V of the United Kingdom stood under the now vacant canopy in front of the India Gate, but it was moved to Coronation Park together with other statues. The canopy is set in a raised circular basin in a square pool. There is a deep concavity in each side reducing the size to a slender white marble pedestal.

The canopy is 22.25 metre high. Following India's independence, the India Gate became the site of the Indian Army's Tomb of the Unknown Soldier, known as *Amar Jawan Jyoti*. The shrine itself is a black marble cenotaph surmounted by a rifle standing on its barrel and crested by a soldier's helmet. Each face of the cenotaph is inscribed in gold with the words 'Amar Jawan' (Immortal Warrior). Standing behind the gate is an empty canopy made out of sandstone, also designed by Lutyens, and inspired by a 18th century Mahabalipuram pavilion.

Rashtrapati Bhavan
Sir Edwin Lutyens (1929)
Central Secretariat
Raisina Hill

033 E

Built as the residence for the British Viceroy, the Rashtrapati Bhavan is a vast mansion with four floors and 340 rooms, spread over an area of about 330 acres. The plan of the building is designed around a massive square with multiple courtyards and open inner areas. The plan called for two wings; one for the Viceroy's residence and another for guests. The focus of the building is the great dome in the centre of the main building. The dome sits directly on top of the Durbar Hall, known as the Throne Room during British rule, and is now the room where the President hosts all official functions. Essentially a two-storey building, the ground floor appears as a monumental platform of red sandstone with minimal perforations. A grand colonnade of cream sandstone linking sections of solid cream wall forms the facade on the upper levels. A wide sweeping stair leads up to the main entrance, which takes directly to the *Durbar* Hall. The interiors of the Hall, like almost all the rooms of the palace, are bare, relying on stonework and shapes to show austerity rather than intricate decoration. The Durbar Hall, Ashoka Hall and the pillars are all excellent examples of traditional Indian art and engravings. The circular stone basins on the top of the palace, statues of elephants, fountain sculptures of cobrasin the gardens, and the *jaalis* made from red sandstone are well known for their unique Indian designs. The beautifully built Jaipur Column, a gift of the Maharaja of Jaipur, stands in the middle of the main court in front of the Rashtrapati Bhavan. Lutyens stated that the dome is inspired by the Pantheon of Rome. Noticeable are also Mughal and European colonial architectural elements. Overall the structure is distinctly different from other contemporary British Colonial symbols.

Eastern and Western Courts ⌄ 034 D

Robert Tor Russell (1932)

Patel Chowk
Janpath

The Eastern Court and Western Courts were designed by Robert Tor Russell as a hostel for legislators. The Western Court still serves the original purpose for which it was built and retains the same look. The Eastern Court now houses the Central Telegraph Office and a host of other government offices. The two elegant buildings were part of the masterplan built for New Delhi by Edwin Lutyens and flank Janpath (Queen's Way) leading towards Connaught Place. The structures are three-storey blocks in stuccoed plaster. The two floors above the massive arcaded ground floor have been treated as a single continuous verandah with giant Tuscan columns.

St. Thomas Church ⌃ 035 A

Walter Sykes George (1932)

Ramakrishna Ashram Marg
Mandir Marg

Originally built as a place of worship for Indian Christian sweepers, this building designed by Walter George has considerable architectural merit. The church is entirely built of brick without the use of steel or reinforced concrete. The plinth is in local Delhi quartzite. The facades have few windows and the entrance is through a round arched portal with splayed jambs. The rainwater spouts at different levels are very pronounced.

Eastern Court

Western Court

North and South Block
Herbert Baker (1930)
♻♻ Central Secretariat
Raisina Hill

036 E

The Secretariat building is where the Cabinet Secretariat is housed, which administers the Government of India. Built in 1929–1930, it is home to some of the most important ministries of the Government of India. Situated on Raisina Hill, the Secretariat buildings are two blocks of symmetrical buildings (North Block and South Block) on opposite sides of the great axis of Rajpath, flanking the Rashtrapati Bhavan. The Secretariat Building was designed in the Indo-Saracenic style of architecture. Both the identical buildings have four levels, each with about 1,000 rooms designed around a series of inner courtyards. Some space for expansion was incorporated into the layout. In continuation with the Viceroy's House, these buildings also used cream and red

sandstone from Dholpur, with the red forming the base. Together the buildings were designed to form two squares. The elevations are strongly articulated with light and shade resulting from deep recessions and projections. A dome marks the centre of each building, and each wing terminates in a colonnaded balcony. Much of the building is in classical architectural style, but was incorporated with traditional motifs from Mughal and Rajasthani architecture. These are visible in the use of *jaalis*, perforated screens, and deeply shadowed and ornately decorated openings. Another feature of the building is a dome-like structure known as the *chattri*, a design unique to India, used in ancient times to give relief to travellers by providing shade from the hot Indian sun. In front of the main gates of the buildings are four 'dominion columns', given by Canada, Australia, New Zealand and South Africa.

Regal, Rivoli Buidling

Walter Sykes George and
Robert Tor Russell (1930s)

`037` `D`

Rajiv Chowk
Outer Circle, Connaught Place

Built mostly in the 1930s, many of these theatres survive today as some of New Delhi's most popular commercial cinemas: the Regal, the Rivoli, the Odeon, and the Plaza. The four cinemas were all designed by British architects, who were inspired by Victorian architecture. The Regal, designed by Walter Sykes George, was influenced by some Mughal elements, such as the pietra dura decorations, including floral motifs that were strikingly similar to those of Safdarjung's Tomb. The cinema was popularly called the 'New Delhi Premier Theatre,' when it first opened in 1932. Following the Connaught Place curve, the building is very distinctive with two sloping roofs over the central portion. The building has a large central porch, the original character of which is partly disfigured due to a large number of hawkers. The Regal building, which houses the Regal and the Rivoli, looked like a prototype of a mall. Conceived by Sir Sobha Singh, the real estate tycoon, the building had shops, restaurants and cinemas under the same roof. The Rivoli cinema, the smallest in Connaught Place, was completed in 1934. The hall had minimalist architecture and was designed with 'Western' sensibilities in mind: the interiors were a striking blend of black and white marble. The Plaza, designed by Robert Tor Russell, had a two-storey foyer, velvet curtains and a heavy chandelier hanging over the hall. The walls were embellished with plaster of Paris decorations and floral art, while large paintings and cylindrical pillars adorned the cinema's lobby. The cinema was completed in 1940. The Odeon, completed in 1939, was also designed by British architect Tor Russell in an opera house style and owned by builder Sobha Singh until 1953. In the late 1990s and early 2000s, all Connaught Place cinemas with the exception of the Regal were leased out to multiplex giants. While most cinema halls have been refurbished over the last decade, Regal has retained traces of its cultural identity.

Connaught Place
Robert Tor Russell (1933)
🚇🚇 Rajiv Chowk
Connaught Place

038 D

Connaught Place is one of the largest financial, commercial and business centres in Delhi. It was developed as a showpiece of Lutyens' Delhi featuring a Central Business District. Named after the Duke of Connaught, the construction work was started in 1929 and completed in 1933. It was renamed as the Rajiv Chowk after the late Indian Prime Minister Rajiv Gandhi. Connaught Place is one of the most vibrant business districts of Delhi. Connaught Place's Georgian architecture is modelled after the Royal Crescent in Bath; however, while the original Crescent is a largely

residential, semi-circular and three-storey structure, Connaught Place features only two floors, makes an almost full circle and was planned to have commercial establishments on the ground with a residential area on the first floor. The circle was eventually planned with two concentric circles, creating Inner Circle, Middle Circle and the Outer Circle and seven radial roads, around a circular central park. As per the original plan, the different blocks of Connaught Place were to be joined from above, employing archways, with radial roads below them, but the circle was 'broken up' to give it a grander scale. The blocks were originally planned to be 17.2 metres high, but later reduced to the present two-storey structure with an open colonnade.

Sacred Heart Cathedral

Henry Medd (1934)

039 D

🚇 Patel Chowk

1 Ashok Place, Near Gol Dakhana

The Cathedral Of The Sacred Heart is a Roman Catholic cathedral and one of the oldest church buildings in New Delhi. The structure is in red brick with contrasting bold lines of cornices and string courses binding the whole building together. The west side was originally designed with a single central tower but needed to be changed, resulting in an Italian influence much more delicate than the rest of the building. A facade of white pillars supports the canopy, and circular arcaded turrets rise above the roof on each side of the Cathedrals entrance porch. The absence of light at the entrances emphasizes the massive quality of the building. The altar is domed, and the church has a huge barrel vaulted ceiling and polished stone floors in its interiors.

Cathedral Church of Redemption

040 E

Henry Medd (1935)

Central Secretariat
1 Church Road, North Avenue

The Anglican church, designed by Medd, is built with coarse rubble white Dholpur stone, with a roof and plinth of red sandstone. Polished Ashlar was used for the moulded courses and the elegant columned porches. The church is erected on a cross plan with the main entry on the west and the altar on the east. The most striking feature is the central high tower, to which the building rises in levels. On each side of the central tower are pediment windows that let in streams of sunlight and strong surges of breeze, keeping the interiors cool and serene even in the hot summers of Delhi. The Church's solemn and austere exteriors lead to a magnificent interior, which has a wonderful play of arches. The entire interior is white stone except for the vaulted ceiling. Besides the main entrance on the western side, there are two additional entrances to the North and the South. The high altar in the East is topped with a half dome above it. On two sides of the high altar are the Chapel of Ascension and the Children's Chapel. The choir gallery over the main western entrance has a unique William Hill and Norman and Beard pipe organ. With Lady Willingdon's help funds were raised to battle bad acoustics and the vaulted ceiling and the dome were sprayed with asbestos mixed with adhesives and colouring matter to successfully lessen the 11-second reverberation.

Free Mason's Hall ⌃
Unknown (1935)
🚇🚇 Rajiv Chowk
Tolstoy Marg, Connaught Place

041 D

A few likeminded members of Lodge Raisina thought it proper to secure a suitable site and build a Masonic Temple at Raisina, as New Delhi was then known. The foundation stone was laid by the Earl of Willington, the Viceroy and Governor-General of India, in April 1935. The large, exposed brick building is entered from the east by an imposing entrance way. The entry lobby has a large winding staircase leading to the upper

floor. To the west is a hall, both north and south sides of which have arched openings. Amongst other things which complemented and supplemented the Masonic temple was the Library which, erected thanks to the joint efforts of all the Masonic bodies. The library houses various examples of Masonic literature, books and periodicals, which now form the collection of the Grand Lodge of India for the brethren to benefit from. An incongruous addition has been built to the north of the building.

Jaipur House/National Gallery of Modern Art ⚲

Sir Arthur Bloomfield (1936)
🚇🚇 Central Secretariat
Justice SB Marg

042 F

Jaipur House, now the National Gallery Of Modern Art, is situated near India Gate. The building, formerly the residential palace of the Maharaja of Jaipur, was inaugurated as the Delhi National Gallery of Modern Art in the year 1954. Similar in layout to the other residences built for kings of princely states, Jaipur House has a butterfly shaped plan with a prominent central dome. Despite the numerous restrictions on the layout and face controls, the building exhibits a distinct Indian character. The building itself is seated on a plinth with bands of red sandstone. The red sandstone *chajja* is also a very prominent feature of the building.

Sujan Singh Park ⚲

043 A

Walter Sykes George (1945)
🚇 Khan Market
Subramaniam Bharati Marg,
Near Khan Market

The Sujan Singh Park apartments were one of the first private residential colonies built in Delhi. Designed in a style similar to his PWD project at Lodi Colony—apartment blocks set around communal gardens—the complex, which presently features the Ambassador Hotel as a focal point, has elements of twentieth century British housing juxtaposed to art deco. Like all typical twentieth century British style housing, the buildings have high ceilings and punctured arched main entrances. Its curved facades, on the other hand, are a subtle nod to art deco. Two exact plans are placed on opposite sides of Subramaniam Bharati Marg: they mirror each other and closely resemble the European model of identical styled houses built around garden squares in cities such as London. It was the first time that two parts of a housing complex were built identically in Delhi. The architecture and plan are also in keeping with the 'Garden City' idiom that was heavily prevalent in Delhi at the time. The architecture, with its uniformity and small garden squares, creates a sense of community, a feature not easy to find in the capital's neighbourhoods. The overall effect is that of a very charming and scenic complex.

1948–1970:
Post-Independence

Post Independence Architecture of Delhi

Anupam Bansal

Post-independence Indian politics till the 1990s was largely dominated by the Congress party, each time with a representative of the Nehru-Gandhi family at the helm. Principally backed by Nehru and his coterie of advisers, India with its five-year plans embarked on a socialist model of development that featured a top-heavy State with minimal delegation of power to the regions or to district-level representative bodies. This socialist-industrial model called for massive state-controlled investment in heavy industry and associated activities.

While this model of governance may possibly have been the only viable solution at a time when India was struggling to become a cohesive political unit, it was also subsequently criticized for encouraging and entrenching endemic corruption and propagating a multilayered bureaucracy that continues to this day. The state, as the biggest actor in the country, controlled almost everything — including information flow, social development and, most importantly, became also the biggest client for architectural and urban development projects.

Just as in 1911 the Viceroy had taken the initiative to change the face of Delhi, it was the Prime Minister of India who in the 1950s became the moving force behind the idea that the city should be managed and planned through a government propelled masterplan. By 1956, Nehru had decided that there would be a central authority to control and regulate the expansion of Delhi and that this authority would draw up a detailed plan for this purpose. In 1957, institutions which *Dilliwallas* today associate with the planning, upkeep and problems of their city were created. The Municipal Corporation of Delhi (MCD) and the Delhi Development Authority (DDA) were set up that year, with the DDA's objective being 'to promote and secure the development of Delhi according to Plan'. Work on the masterplan for Delhi began even before this and was prepared by a team

of Indian planners, most of who were educated in the U.S., and assisted by consultants of the Ford Foundation.

Since Independence in 1947, Delhi has seen many explorations of architectural ideas as architects have sought inspiration from a number of sources. They and their clients have provided a rich legacy of buildings and urban designs. During this era of 1947 to 1990 spanning almost 45 years, Delhi experienced unprecedented change and growth.

Delhi underwent massive expansion following the influx of refugees from Pakistan as a result of the Partition of India. From 1947 onwards, refugee housing areas were built on the peripheries of New Delhi by the New Delhi Improvement Corporation, the CPWD and, later, the Delhi Development Authority (DDA). The building of housing colonies throughout the Nehru years attempted to keep pace with the migration of people to Delhi.

The immediate architectural response to independence was a major revivalist phase throughout India. Official government architecture was most susceptible to this phenomenon. Public Projects built in New Delhi by Government agencies under the Chief Architects of these various departments were generally constructed in Indo-British Style or revivalist styles derived by a combination of Mughal, Hindu and Buddhist architecture.

As a counterpoint to these approaches, young intellectuals and architects returning from Europe and North America proposed Modernism as being more relevant to the spirit of the period. Modernism to them was perceived as the natural approach for expressing the new nationalism; it was unhampered by historical or cultural restraints and reflected the optimism of a free nation.

Indian architects in the 1950s and 1960s struggled to make Modernism work — not only in regard to their existing traditions, but also in how they would situate their modernity within a cultural context. As a result, this period and the subsequent decades saw numerous attempts by Indian architects to reconcile Western forms and local issues, using ideas and lessons from the past.

Implicit in the work of the Neo-Modernists is a recognition of both the strengths and weaknesses of the work of the Modern Masters. Instead of seeking alternative approaches to design they have continued to work within the Modernist fold but have adapted the basic tenets of Modernism to deal more empirically with the problems at hand. There is a paradox: How to be modern and return to sources; how to revive an old dominant civilization and take part in universal civilization. The Neo-Modernists in India retain an admiration for the skills of the modern master and the precision with which they detailed their work but also recognized that Modern architectural ideas have to be adapted to India.

Independence

On regaining its independence on 15th August 1947, New Delhi was retained as the capital of the newly formed nation. The Government of India adopted the Imperial city as the capital for all practical purposes. The Viceroy's House was converted to the residence and office of the Governor General and later the President of the Indian republic. The Secretariat Buildings were converted into the offices of all the important government ministries including the office of the Prime Minister. The circular Council House became the Parliament House of India. The city continued to remain the bureaucratic centre and the ceremonial centre of the nation. National rituals like the 'Republic Day Parade', and the 'Beating of the Retreat', are still held here. The new independent nation, so much in need of symbolic construction, of creating a sense of unity and a sense of identification with the

new abstract entity, the nation, capitalized well on the city for this purpose. In the course of time various other ministries and offices were added in this part of the city. These included the headquarters of all the armed forces of the nation. It slowly evolved as a centre of national and international politics. All the embassies of foreign countries were built to the South of New Delhi. The houses representing all the states of the nation were also located nearby.

Housing Colonies

More than Independence, it was the partition of India that had the most profound impact on the growth of Delhi. In the turmoil that followed the partition of India, Delhi experienced an unprecedented refugee influx from West Pakistan (it is estimated that 15 million people crossed both ways) post-1947. This meant that Delhi's population underwent a sudden, substantial increase, as displaced persons from what was now Pakistan poured in across the border. The city's infrastructure — in some places already taxed to its limit — was simply not prepared for a massive population increase — Delhi's population went from 700,000 in 1941 to nearly 2.5 million people in 1961. In the absence of sufficient housing, refugee camps sprang up all over the city. As an emergency measure, the government set up the Ministry for Relief and Rehabilitation, which had as its primary task housing the immigrants, and then absorbing them in viable occupations. Hectic building activity occurred because millions had to be re-settled in Delhi. Among the many new colonies planned and built for this purpose were the localities of Lajpat Nagar, South Extension, Karol Bagh, New Friends Colony, Malviya Nagar, Kaka Nagar and Bapa Nagar. Some of these settlements were erected at the site of refugee camps, and others clustered around existing villages and gradually absorbed

Multi-Storey Housing at R.K. Puram, Habib Rahman (1965)

them into their midst (Hauz Khas being among the better-known examples). These colonies were either 'plotted' developments or built by a governmental agency. A typical governmental agency plan (1947 to 1955) consisted of units built on a site of 60 to 70 square metres. This size — compared to 150 to 200 square metres during the late British period — shows the difference between the imperial and vernacular spatial orders and also, more simply, the impact of upward spiralling land values.

Laxmibai Nagar, built in the 1950s by the CPWD for government employees, is typical of the period. Located south of Safdarjang Airport, it consists of two types of housing units: 756 three-room flats for gazetted workers and 655 two-room units for non-gazetted staff. A central area contains schools, while a market is located in one corner.

Over time, each area becomes a symbol of the status of its inhabitants, depending on the size of unit and often the ethnicity of the people who lived there. Names of areas give identity. Chittaranjan Park in Delhi, named after Chittaranjan Das, for instance, was developed for Bengali refugees from East Pakistan (now Bangladesh).

Role of Government Agencies

The design efforts of the architects of the CPWD in New Delhi have made a major impression on the city. The CPWD designed architecture of 50s and 60s transformed Delhi. Though finances were severely limited, Nehru encouraged a vast building programme for urgently required offices, hotels and housing, with very little participation of architects in private practice. CPWD was the major builder along with various other government departments with architectural wings such as the Railways, Post and Telegraphs, Municipal Corporation, New Delhi Municipal Corporation and so on. They were responsible for much building work, in their capacity as ex-British institutions in charge of government buildings.

It was a mix of institutional buildings (schools, colleges, public offices) and large housing projects for the refugees

Claridges Hotel (1950)

Ashok Hotel, E. B. Doctor (1955)

that gave Delhi its unique character, and continues to define the image of the city even today. Colonies like Kaka Nagar, Bapa Nagar and Sarojini Nagar were among the first large-scale experiments in mass urban housing, and the experience of these generated many valuable lessons for the future.

New Delhi required several buildings to complete its main esplanade, and also to provide for the new institutional buildings that were needed. The challenge here was a vocabulary that would be sufficiently indigenous, and yet also dovetail with the built form of New Delhi's British buildings. Thus the Supreme Court (1952), Krishi Bhavan and Udyog Bhavan (both 1957) and the Rail Bhavan (1962), while serving very different purposes, were marked by certain strong similarities. The imperial style of Lutyens and Baker was considered worth emulation and repeating even after more than three decades of the making of New Delhi. While few architects concentrated on the spread of Indo-British style or the continuance of Lutyens' and Baker's architectural style, others propagated revivalism based in traditional pre-colonial styles. These architects borrowed more elements from Mughal and Hindu architecture than from the colonial era, and fused them with a modern building vocabulary. In E. B. Doctor's Ashok Hotel and the Vigyan Bhavan (1962) revivalist styles were seen at full power.

First Generation of Indian Modernists

Just as architects were beginning to size up to the enormous challenges of construction that lay ahead, the old debate on style erupted. The central question in the debates on style was: how much indigenisation of style could a newly

independent nation afford without appearing backward. Nationalism sought to be expressed through Revivalism in all forms of cultural expression, including architecture. Ranged on the other side were a handful of intellectuals and architects who argued that monuments should be viewed in the context of their times, that they were not to be imitated, and that modern India required modern architectural symbols and forms to express the dynamism of a free nation on their march to economic development.

Foremost amongst this group of Indian Modernists were the first batches of Indians to receive their architectural training in America: Habib Rahman, Achyut Kanvinde and Durga Bajpai. They were later joined by the American architect Joseph Allen Stein. Young and idealistic, this generation was exposed to Le Corbusier and other European masters via their American education. They were also influenced by masters of the American Modern Movement.

Though Habib Rahman worked on a large number of government projects all over India, the greatest concentration of his work is in Delhi, some 15 large office complexes including the 21-storey Vikas Minar, several hundred units of innovative government housing, the Delhi Zoo, and three exquisite memorials—the Mazhars of Maulana Azad, Zakir Hussain and Fakhruddin Ali Ahmed. Rahman's early work was marked by an emphasis on western ideas and forms. The turning point came in Rabindra Bhavan where Rahman was at his creative best: sensitive site planning, an intuitive approach, innovative structural solutions and great care in detailing was apparent. It was inspired by the philosophy of Tagore who advised him that modern creative work should neither blindly copy India's past

Hindustan Times, Habib Rahman

Rabindra Bhavan, Habib Rahman
(1961)

heritage nor blindly imitate the modern West. Two further works exemplify this philosophy: Indraprastha Bhavan (1963–1965) and the Administrative building for Pragati Maidan (1971).

In Delhi's Oberoi Hotel by Durga Bajpai and Mody, there was a clear recognition that a new tourism required new functional forms, which could economically integrate structure and services.

Achyut Kanvinde attended Harvard Graduate school of Design in 1945 becoming the first Indian architect to have studied in America. It was Kanvinde, and not as is widely believed Le Corbusier in his work in Chandigarh, who first introduced Modernism and the aesthetics of Function into the dormant Indian Architectural scene. What Kanvinde introduced was the Modern legacy of rational and 'pure' structure. One of his first buildings to come up in Delhi was the CSIR Headquarters completed in 1953. Kanvinde has often been referred to as a 'modern Indian' architect.

The work of American architect Joseph Allen Stein added considerably to Delhi's architectural palimpsest. In New Delhi, Stein continued his search for refined, expressive forms in a garden setting, elaborating on ideas developed in his first Indian works. This was reflected in a succession of major buildings for cultural, humanitarian and environmental institutions that he designed at Lodi Estate adjacent to the Lodi Gardens. These included the India International Centre (1959–1962), Ford Foundation Headquarters (1968), Ford Foundation Guest House (1972), UNICEF Headquarters (1981) and India Habitat Centre (1993), contributed to the growing vocabulary of modernist design in India (Stein labeled his style 'Regional Modernism') by mixing local stone with concrete and Mughal-inspired grand courtyards and decorative tile flourishes with covered walkways and rational, rectilinear angles. The designs of the India International Centre and Ford Foundation,

Indraprastha Bhavan, Habib Rahman
(1965)

Sri Ram Centre, Shiv Nath Prasad
(1972)

Oberoi Hotel, Bajpai and Piloo Mody (1958)

India International Centre, J. A. Stein (1962)

situated next to each other, are Stein's subtlest achievements, notable for their simple layouts of buildings, garden and water, enriched by Stein's adaptation of the traditional north Indian jail and the inclusion of local building stone. Steins interest in structural expression as a generator of form also led him to explore a variety of shell forms with structural engineer Vishnu Joshi from the late 1950s. The American Embassy School was characterized by vaulted and domed steel lattice roof. Steins most widespread and dramatic use of steel lattice shells had been in a series of industrial buildings constructed for Escorts Ltd. in Faridabad on the outskirts of Delhi. Here steel lattices in a variety of configurations — domes, vaults, hyperbolic paraboloids and prismatic roof forms have created an uplifting atmosphere for workers employed in various industrial processes. The coming of Le Corbusier left a lasting impression on Indian architects. It was a definitive influence on the minds of young evolving architects to experience the versatility of the master ranging from city planning to architectural detailing and also extending to art and sculpture. Indian architects wanted to emulate the plastic forms of Le Corbusier. A pioneer amongst the architects inspired by Le Corbusier was Shiv Nath Prasad. In his design for Sri Ram Centre, the full potential of reinforced concrete is used to express distinct platonic forms and volumes growing out of clear functional needs. Though the work of the young generation shared bold articulation of structural elements and form, the resulting visual expression varied considerably according to each architect's personal handling of scale, materials and

detailing. The pioneering work here was the Design Group's Y.M.C.A. Staff Quarters. The treatment of exposed brick and plain shuttered bands of concrete, the staggered terraces, all combined to produce a precedent of sorts.

The heart of New Delhi, as many town centres in India, experienced a burst of utilitarian high-rise construction in the 1960s and 1970s. The architects of early high-rise buildings, such as the Bank of Baroda and the Hansalaya building, were fascinated by the structural potential of reinforced concrete. The buildings repeated a similar style of vertical lines of columns or sunshades ad infinitum highlighting the exuberance of their sky-scraping proportions. Though only about 20 floors high, they borrowed liberally from much taller prototypes in the USA. The NDMC Civic Centre, designed by Kuldip Singh, echoes the forms of the Jantar Mantar.

Learning From The Past

By the mid-60s, signs of discontent began to surface among the architectural avant-garde. These were the first signs of the evaluation and questioning of identity. Architects began to question the use of modern forms and vocabulary not adapted to India. To more honest and inquiring minds, what had begun as a stimulus now seemed increasingly rigid and not suited to the Indian context. By the end of the 60s, a number of architects had already started to re-examine existing towns and villages in India. They reviewed the rationale of traditional Indian rural as well as urban architectural heritage. A new architecture attempting to create a modern idiom learning from these

Bank of Baroda

Hansalaya Building

traditional examples was being explored. Some began to look at our old heritage with new eyes. A new search began for appropriate solutions based on the traditional experience of town-planning, neighbourhood clustering, and climate control. Delhi Architects like Ranjit Sabhiki, Kanvinde, M.N. Ashish Ganju, Vasant Kamath along with other architects from other parts of the country wrote on the relevance of tradition. They looked to the vernacular architecture created by the common men and women of India over the ages as a source of socially and economically relevant design ideas. Since 1970, architects have increasingly looked at traditional urban design and building types for inspiration. They have looked at the way light, massing and siting have been handled; how decorative features form part of the architecture; the materials used; and the construction process.

The architects of Northern India have been particularly anxious to explore neo-vernacular possibilities. The old

Sheikh Sarai Housing, Raj Rewal Associates (1982)

State Bank of India

Ashoka Estate, Achyut Kanvinde

towns of Rajasthan, such as Jaisalmer and Udaipur, provide the intricate environments and territorial hierarchies that stand in strong contrast to the urban design and building patterns of Utilitarian Modernism that so pervade India. The use of these patterns is seen as a response to the critical studies of Chandigarh, Gandhinagar and Bhubaneshwar.

The use of traditional forms has been explored in Raj Rewal's Asian Games Village (1980–1982), his National Institute of Immunology building (1984–1988), and in the Sheikh Sarai Housing (1982) in New Delhi, as well as in the Design Group's Yamuna Housing Society (1973–1980) and the Tara Housing (1975–1978) by Charles Correa. All these schemes stress the street as a meeting place, reflecting the recent world-wide urban design response to Modernist Architectural Ideology—the rediscovery of the street as a seam rather than an edge.

Raj Rewal explored the use of Urban Patterns from Jaipur and Jaisalmer in both the Asian Village and Sheikh Sarai.

Asian Games Village, Raj Rewal Associates (1982)

Malviya Nagar Housing

The site design is based on the system of streets and chowks of traditional housing areas in Rajasthan. Vehicular movement and parking are thus on the periphery. In Kuldip Singh's Malviya Nagar Housing, a playful cross typology was adopted to generate terraces at all levels and pedestrianized streets resembling shaded *galis* of traditional towns. It was the first housing layout to consciously simulate, on a large scale, the traditional rhythm of a pedestrian street punctuated with squares.

In the new Modern School designed by Sachdev and Eggleston, an older vocabulary of exposed brick (extensively used by Walter George in Delhi) is used to create deep arched recesses for sun protection, and exposed concrete is used where it is most effective: in interior columns and ramps protected from rain.

Satish Gujral, a renowned painter, sculptor and muralist who had turned to architecture, conceived the Belgian Embassy as a monumental geological formation of earth banks and brick vaulting, with associations and images recalling domes, lingams and various other tantric artefacts.

Trade Fair 1980 and Asian Games 1982

The trade fair in 1980 and the Asian Games to be held in 1982 propelled building activity in Delhi in the late 1970s. The Pragati Maidan complex, built on the eve of the Asian Games, provided a space for many innovative architectural experiments and cemented the careers of a whole generation of professionals. The most ambitious section of this complex was the construction of huge exhibition areas christened the Hall of Nations and the Hall of Industries. Designed by Raj Rewal in association with structural engineer Mahendra Raj, it was a stunning expression of structural and technological aesthetic, which ironically was constructed using labour intensive techniques.

The Asian Games in 1982 provided a massive fillip to construction, especially in Delhi. Also constructed for the Games were a series of stadia, the most prominent being the Jawahar Lal Nehru Stadium by CPWD, Indraprastha Indoor Stadium by Sharat Das and the Talkatora stadium by Satish Grover. The Indraprastha Stadium was an imposing structure with bearing walls of concrete and roofing of steel trusses, marked by its rapid construction with movable shuttering on the bearing columns ensuring continuous activity on the site. Apart from all the facilities constructed for the games, Delhi underwent a massive facelift with the construction of 7 flyovers, widening of 30 roads and construction of 10 hotels and electrification of the Ring Railways. The Asian Games Village, designed by Raj Rewal for the athletes visiting the capital, was a cluster of interlocking housing

Talkatora Indoor Stadium, NDMC (1982)

units that takes its formal inspiration from the streetscape and scale of towns in Rajasthan, particularly Jaisalmer. Rewal claims to have used these spatial references to create a series of courts and 'streets' through the complex and even to use finishes and material that correspond to their original inspiration.

Conclusion

Most of the architectural production of any significance till the 1990s was marked by a certain commonality of factors: firstly it was sponsored or commissioned by the State and its organs, and secondly the search for an appropriate aesthetic varies between two extremes — that of a completely 'international' vocabulary of Modernism (such as Prasad's Akbar Bhavan) and an attempt to reinterpret the vernacular on the other (exemplified by Correa's Crafts Village).

Many of the questions being raised in India today by indigenous architects are the same the world over; it is only their specific manifestations which are different. The 1980s, in particular, saw a strong search for what remains a highly evasive regional character in architecture based on the spiritual and craft heritage of Indian Tradition. With some exceptions, the Gandhian approach to design, with its emphasis on austerity and economy of means, had been lost. Nehru's message has been largely lost too, again with some notable exceptions. There has been little effort to marry the two, although the austerity of a pure Modernism suggests how it might be done if its patterns were Indianized — made culturally and climatically appropriate.

References

1. Chaterjee, Malay. 'The Evolution of Contemporary Indian Architecture', *Architecture in India*, Electra Moniteur, 1985
2. Grover, Satish. *Building Beyond Borders — Story of Contemporary Indian Architecture*, National Book Trust of India, New Delhi, 1995
3. Lang, Jon. Desai, Madhavi & Desai, Miki. *Architecture & Independence — The Search for Identity — India 1880 to 1980*, Oxford University Press, 1997
4. Mehrotra, Rahul. *Architecture in India since 1990*, Pictor, Germany, 2011
5. Nangia, Ashish. *Post Colonial India and Its Architecture — III*, www.boloji.com
6. Nangia, Ashish. *The Beginnings of an Architectural Culture: Delhi — Post Independence Challenges*, www.boloji.com
7. Sharma, Ram. 'The search for Roots and Relevance', *Architecture in India*, Electra Moniteur, 1985

University Grants Commission 044 A
Habib Rahman (1954)

Pragati Maidan
Bahadur Shah Zafar Marg

The building is designed to house all the offices of the University Grants Commission, New Delhi. It was the desire of the UGC authorities that the building have the maximum floor area permissible according to the existing Corporation rules on the 1.6 acre plot of land allotted. The shape of the plot is an irregular pentagon. The effort, therefore, was to locate the building on the plot in such a way that it fits into the plot logically. Offices are planned on two sides of a central corridor, in a building consisting of two wings parallel to the two sides of the pentagon with the service core (staircase, lift and toilets) where the wings intersect. The southern wing is six storeys high and the northern wing is partially six and partially five storeys high. The ground floors of both wings are occupied services and stores, etc. A portion of the ground floor area of the northern wing has been allotted for parking of cars, cycles and scooters. The chairman's office, the conference room and the rooms of most senior officers are located on the first floor. The canteen and recreation rooms are on the fifth floor of the northern wing, which has a roof terrace. A couple of suites have been provided on the fifth floor of the south wing with bathrooms and kitchen facilities, to serve as guest rooms for visiting Vice Chancellors. A free standing open RCC staircase has been placed at the end of the north block. A small block has been placed at the rear end of the plot, which accommodates closed garages and residential quarters for essential staff. To reduce the need for air conditioning, *chajjas* and louvers have been planned to control the levels of direct sunlight coming into the rooms and to protect the walls from the summer sun. Conventional local materials such as brick, wood and concrete have been used.

Vigyan Bhavan » 045 F
Ramprakash L. Gehlot (CPWD) (1955)

Udyog Bhawan
Maulana Azad Road

Vigyan Bhavan, centrally located on Maulana Azad Road, is a premier convention centre of the Government of India in New Delhi. Built in 1956, over the years it has hosted conferences of national and international stature, seminars and award ceremonies attended by distinguished world leaders and dignitaries, including the Commonwealth Heads of Government Meeting (CHOGM) in 1983, the 7th Summit of the Non-Aligned Movement (NAM), held on 7–12 March 1983, and the SAARC Summit. It is managed by the Directorate of Estates under the Ministry of Urban Development, Government of India. It is strategically located in one of the most beautiful areas in Delhi near the President's Estate

and India Gate. Overlooking lush green lawns, it is within walking distance from the Gallery of Modern Art, the National Museum and other sites of touristic interest. The main building was designed in 1955 by R.L. Gehlot of Central Public Works Department (CPWD), incorporating elements of British Raj architecture, evident in the nearby buildings of the Central Secretariat, and of Lutyens' style, along with Hindu and Mughal and ancient Buddhist architecture, especially the Chaitya arches of the Ajanta Caves. The overall style of the building remains modernistic with revivalist elements. The large entrance is of black marble and glass and is shaped in the form of a *Chaitya* arch of the Ajanta Style. The floor-to-ceiling windows on each side are spanned by similar *Chaitya* arches. The roofline is accentuated by a perforated *jali* railing below which is a long *chhajja* stretching the whole length of the facade. The main feature of the complex is the plenary hall, with a seating capacity of over 1,200 delegates, besides which there are six smaller halls with capacities ranging from 65 to over 375 delegates. The building also has a VIP Lounge, an office block for on-site offices, a secretariat and a documentation centre, a studio, a business centre and an exhibition hall. The adjacent building, called the Vigyan Bhavan Annexe, was added later on and features four committee rooms and a separate media centre.

Dak Tar Bhavan ⌃ ⌄ 046 D
Habib Rahman (1955)
🚇 Patel Chowk
Patel Chowk

Ashok Hotel » 047 A
E. B. Doctor (1955)
🚇 Race Course
50-B, Chanakyapuri

Designed in 1954 to house the General Post Office and the Posts and Telegraphs Directorate, this building has a facade which flows with the curve of Patel Chowk. The main lobby level contains the public post office area with one long curved counter. The roof of the back section of the building has open verandahs and covered terraces with lunch rooms, a library and recreation hall for the staff. The inner courtyard made it possible for all offices and cubicles to have their own windows.

Nehru's idea of India was of a dynamic, new nation-one that was modern while retaining an Indian soul. It was a vision that he extended to architecture and, although he invited many of the great modernist architects from Europe and USA to build in India and teach her young generations, he also admired his country's more traditional style. One building where Nehru was able to let his stance on modernized architecture take a revivalist drift was the Ashok Hotel designed by E. B. Doctor (1900–1984). Although the extent of his involvement is unclear, it is believed that he was insistent that the architect add traditional (in this case Rajasthani) features to the building. The Ashok, which was India's first 5-star hotel, was meant to symbolize India's grand past by showcasing ancient symbols on a modernist structure. The large Mughal styled *chhattris* that embellish the roof,

the *jaalis* that take on many patterns on the balconies, the ornate eaves, the massive cantilevered *jharokha*, the rose pink kota stone walls and the turreted contours all add to the facade's synthesis of the old planted on a modern building. Such an obvious use of traditional features on a quintessentially modern structure has had its detractors. However, for over 50 years, the Ashok has given tourists a taste of the romanticized days of the grand Rajasthan and its now diluted kingdoms. No surprise then, that the project was partly funded by princely states. Although this is a not a building for purists, the structure is an exaggerated effort to deal with the architectural quandary of the appropriate definition of Indian post-Independence architecture. Over the decades, the Ashok has gone through various changes, awful paint jobs and tasteless renovations, losing most of its historical sheen. In its heyday, it was the place of choice of visiting dignitaries chose and such was the pride associated with this new creation that some princely states gifted various artefacts to the hotel. To mark its 50th anniversary, the government issued a stamp of this 25-acre property.

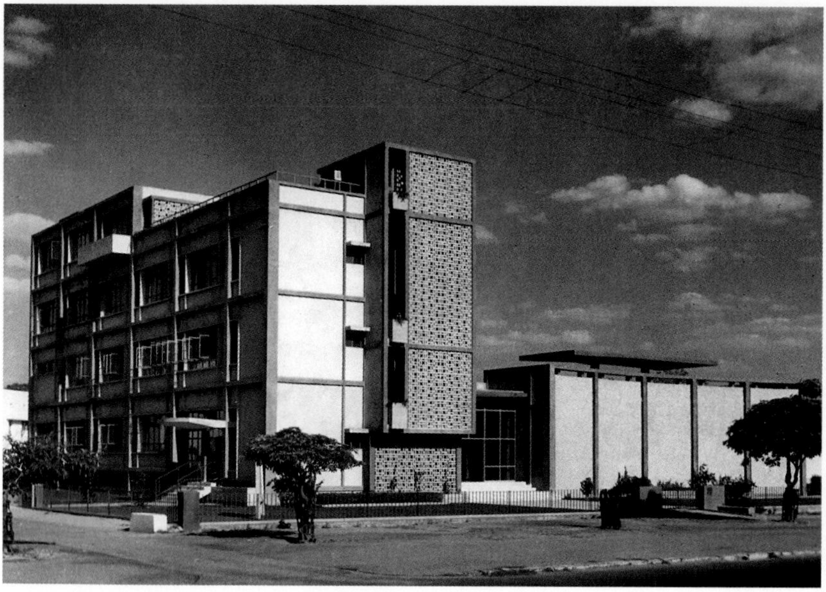

Triveni Kala Sangam 048 A
J. A. Stein (1957)
Mandi House
205, Tansen Marg

The Triveni Kala Sangam was founded in 1952 as an academy of dance, music and painting with the aim to reintroduce traditional forms of expression into Indian life. From its humble beginnings in quarters above a coffee shop in Connaught Circus, Triveni's scope has grown considerably over the years since it expanded into its new facility, the first phase of which was built in 1957. Triveni's offerings have come to include the teaching of sculpture, pottery and ceramics, and photography, with a separate section of art for children. Additional classroom and studio spaces were added in 1977. Each of the functional units of the complex — its theatre, classrooms, studios and galleries — is individually articulated in the building's massing. The centre is organized into a four-storey classroom block with a canteen and shaded dining/tea terrace to the north and a ground floor gallery block with a shaded roof terrace above to the west. Opposite the gallery is a covered stage opening onto an outdoor garden theatre which is the heart of the complex. Plants draping down from planter boxes placed between *jaalis* on the face of the classroom block and tea terrace, and flowering bougainvillea on the pergola fronting the gallery form a backdrop for performances and make the space a garden oasis away from the heavily-trafficked intersection outside. The three-storey extension to the north houses additional classrooms, an indoor auditorium and instructors' apartments, while also creating shaded outdoor spaces for painting and sculpture classes. Triveni's buildings are composed of a clad reinforced concrete frame structure with several infill materials: *jaali* panels along the classroom block corridor and stair, concrete block with a plastered finish on most elevations, and rough-cut stone facing presented to the street from the gallery block. Extensive areas of *jaalis* and planting boxes arranged into vertical gardens are prominent elements at Triveni. The *jaali* panels were assembled from small pre-cast concrete units of three different sizes. They create a cool, light-filtered space with an ever changing pattern of light and shadow along the corridors of the classroom block.

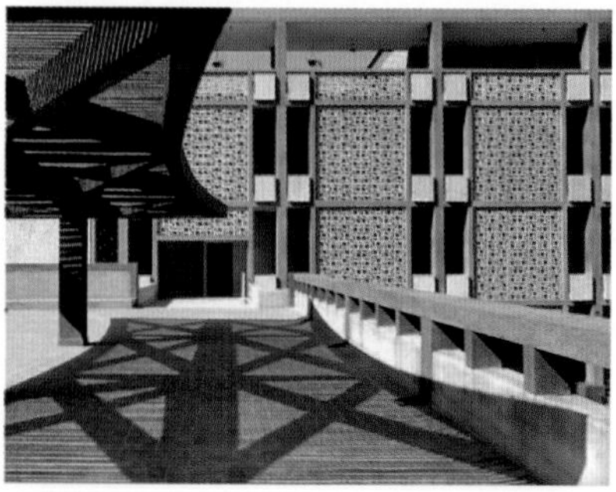

Supreme Court of India ⌃ 049 A

CPWD, Ganesh Bhikaji Deolalikar (1958)

🚇 Pragati Maidan
Bhagwan Das Road

The main block of the Supreme Court building was built on a square plot of 22 acres and was designed by the first Indian to head the CPWD, Ganesh Bhikaji Deolalikar. The building is shaped to project the image of the scales of justice with the Central Wing of the building corresponding to the cental beam of the scales. In 1979, two new wings—the East Wing and the West Wing—were added to the complex. In all there are 15 court rooms in the various wings of the building. The Chief Justice's Court is the largest of the courtrooms located in the middle of the central wing, with a large 27.6-metre-high dome, and two court halls on either side. The right wing of the structure consists of the bar room, the offices of the attorney general and other law officers and the court library. The left wing houses various administrative offices.

Maulana Azad Memorial » 050 A

Habib Rahman (1959)

🚇 Chandni Chowk
Jama Masjid,
Meena Bazaar Street

Maulana Azad, a close associate and friend of Mahatma Gandhi, was buried in the historic setting between Shah Jahan's Jama Masjid and Red Fort. In keeping with the requirements set down by Jawaharlal Nehru, the design does not conflict with the neighbouring historic monuments and befits the humble personality of Maulana Azad. The Mazaar was designed in direct consultation with Jawaharlal Nehru, who wanted a simple tomb that complemented the historicity of the site. Set in a 67 metre × 67 metre enclosed Mughal garden, the memorial structure consists of a delicate, white marble *chattri* over the grave. Rahman's design derives from the central arch of the mosque. The *chattri* is a cross vault 7.5 centimetres thick, supported by four slender L-shaped columns. The treatment of white marble used in the construction of the *chattri*, the flooring and the low *jaalis* surrounding the grave was inspired by Mughal designs. The concrete was a mix of white cement and crushed white marble, slightly polished by hand. A pool on three sides beautifully reflects both the *chattri* and the Jama Masjid.

The American Embassy
Edward Durell Stone (1960)
🚇 Race Course
Shantipath, Chanakya Puri

051 A

Edward Durell Stone's (1902–1998) design for the American Embassy marked the start of New Delhi's impressive embassy architecture. It has been one of the most widely published embassy buildings in New Delhi. Built at a cost of 2.5 million USD in a little over two years, the American embassy was one the first of a number of notable embassies erected in the Chanakyapuri area of South Delhi over the years. The American Embassy in New Delhi stands as an example of Indian-American collaboration in design and craftsmanship, symbolic of the long friendship between the two countries. In designing the Embassy complex, the architect sought to capture the best in South Asian architecture and blend it with modern Western concepts. Planning of the Embassy complex began in the early 1950s with allocation of a 28-acre site in Chanakyapuri. The Embassy complex includes the Chancery, the Roosevelt House (official residence of the U.S. Ambassador), office space and living accommodations. On 1 September 1956, the Chief Justice of the United States, Earl Warren, laid the corner stone and wishing that the structure would become

'a temple of peace'. The building was formally opened on 5 January, 1959 in the presence of Prime Minister Jawaharlal Nehru and other distinguished guests. The Embassy is a modern classical building. The whole white rectangular composition with its slender gilded columns has a classical appeal but does not rely on classical features. It also features elements that relate to its Indian context — an internal courtyard, elevated platforms and pierced walls — with a different purpose. While the traditional use of these features in India was dictated by the climate, Stone's purpose was largely aesthetic. The facades combine elements of traditional Mughal architecture and European classicism. These two opposing elements have been handled with great dexterity and balance. The Indian touches come in the form of *jaali* style cladding across the outer walls of the building and the internal courtyard, while there are slim Greco-Roman columns on the exterior of the building. Architect Frank Lloyd Wright called it one of the finest buildings of the past hundred years. The internal courtyard of the building evokes the feeling of finest Indian architecture. The building is full of air and light yet assures privacy for all the occupants. It was considered as one of the supreme achievements of modern architecture.

Rabindra Bhavan
Habib Rahman (1961)
🚇 Mandi House
35, Feroze Shah Road

052 A

Rabindra Bhavan was built to mark the birth centenary of Tagore, who in addition to being a poet and novelist was an artist, playwright and composer. The building houses three National Academies: Lalit Kala (Plastic Arts), Sangeet Natak (Dance, Drama and Music) and Sahitya (Literature). Set up by the government with the objective to encourage and promote these art forms, the site, measuring three acres, is located at the corner of Copernicus and Ferozshah Roads, and has a frontage on both of them. The requirement stated that the administrative offices of the three academies had to be accommodated on site, in addition to a gallery for the exhibition of paintings and sculpture and a moderate-sized theatre. The design solution as it finally emerged consists of an administrative block with three wings of more or less equal length at an angle of 120 degrees to each other, and a pentagon shaped exhibition block which follows the curve of the traffic island. The theatre was never realised. Each four storeyed wing of the administrative

block houses an academy, the Lalit Kala being in the wing nearest to the exhibition block to which it is connected by a covered walkway. The main entrance into the administrative block is where the three wings meet. The entrance hall, lift and staircase are placed here, though each of the three wings has their own staircase for internal vertical circulation. A large library is provided on the ground floor of the Sahitya wing opening out to the garden. The exhibition block has a basement and two upper floors. Of these two, the ground floor is on two levels, the floor above being reached by a freestanding spiral staircase. The long walls of the administrative block are load bearing in brick masonry, whilst the end walls of the wings are in random rubble stone masonry. RCC sun-shade in two continuous rows over all the windows have been provided, the lower row in each case being placed on cantilevered brackets so that it is away from the wall and is no obstruction to breeze. The angle of the sun-shades is designed to eliminate the strong morning and afternoon sun. The roof slab projects six feet beyond the walls on all sides. The administrative block is an RCC frame structure with filler walls.

Shiela Theatre

053 A

Habib Rahman (1961)
🚇 New Delhi
Deshbandhu Gupta Road

Habib Rahman was commissioned to create the design for Sheila Cinema. Since this was a public entertainment venue, he developed a scheme that was colourful and joyous. He collaborated with Luc Durand to do murals and a colour scheme to liven up the overall ambience. The structure of the rake was kept exposed from below and incorporated into the lobby space. The stairs and the railings were carefully detailed and proportioned, recalling the details at Rabindra Bhavan, designed during the

same period. The theatre has been carefully maintained in its design and colour scheme by the owners. It is still one of the most entertaining cinema lobbies in Delhi and is an expression of the modernist ethos of the early 1960s.

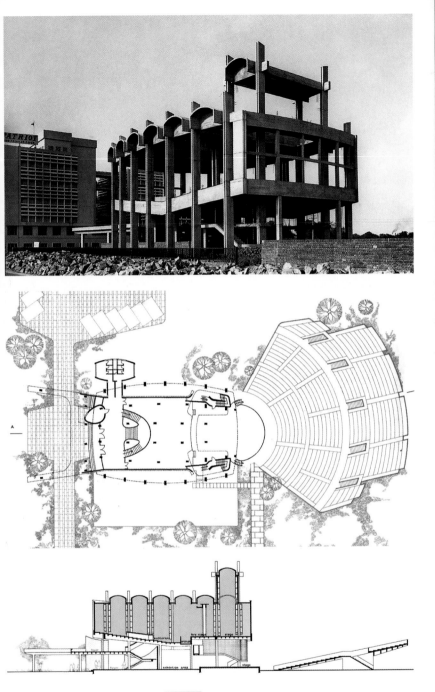

Gandhi Memorial Hall

Achyut Kanvinde (1961)

🚇 Pragati Maidan

Pyarelal Bhavan,
2 Bahadur Shah Zafar Marg

054 A

The project of the Gandhi memorial hall has been sponsored by the Pearey lal Bhavan association to fulfill the cultural needs of the citizens of Delhi in activities pertaining to fine arts, literature, dance and drama. An exposed reinforced concrete structure with concrete shell roof over the main theatre designed in the form of a cylindrical form, the building has been designed for exhibition areas with both indoor and outdoor spaces integrated with landscaping. A small library is provided near the entrance to serve the literary demand of the people, while the main theatre, which is located at the first floor level, is destined to fulfil multipurpose activities including lectures, dramas and film shows.

Indian Council for Cultural Relations (ICCR)

Achyut Kanvinde (1961)

055 A

⊜ Indraprastha/Pragati Maidan

Azad Bhavan, Indraprastha (I.P.) Estate

Maulana Abul Kalam Azad, the first education minister of independent India, founded the Indian Council for Cultural Relations (ICCR), on 9th April 1950. ICCR was established as an organization that would foster and strengthen cultural relations and mutual understanding between India and other nations and peoples. It sought to fulfill this objective by a two-way cultural flow process, on the one hand by promoting and widening knowledge and appreciation of India's cultural heritage in other countries and, on the other, by encouraging the dissemination in India of the knowledge of the culture of other countries. To fulfill its varied activities satisfactorily, the ICCR envisaged premises which would not merely serve as an office for the council, but were designed to become a centre for exchange of cultural activities. An auditorium, exhibition halls, a museum for the collection of manuscripts, lecture rooms, a library and connected reading room with their research facilities, were all designed to

be integral parts of the building. The 1.5 acre site earmarked for the building was located in the Indraprastha Estate near the central Board of Revenue building, flanked on two sides by 60'-0' wide roads and on the other two by the proposed buildings for the Audio-Visual wing and the National academies. The entire activities have been resolved into two different building blocks. The Main Block houses the Administration offices mainly on the two upper floors, while the ground floor is occupied by the Library, the Reading room with specific areas for research workers, the Museum and a Cafeteria. The Auditorium block has a seating capacity of 450 and has been provided with green rooms etc. to accommodate diverse types of performance. The site conditions favoured the main block to face East-West, which in turn involved the problem of sun protection. Consequently, the openings on the West facade were kept small and shielded by a panel of hollow block *Jaalis* to mitigate any heat gain. Close co-operation with the painters and sculptors was envisaged. A sculpture on the facade of the main block, a mural on the free standing wall in the Auditorium and a mural on the large wall surface in the interior of the entrance hall were some of the prominent works specifically commissioned for the project. The structure was visualized mainly as a reinforced concrete frame with walls of masonry, glass or other lightweight partition materials. External walls were brick partly exposed and plastered with rough texture. The outside facade was covered in cement paint while the inside was painted in pastel shades. At the request of the client, Kanvinde incorporated some Indian motifs onto the design of the Azad Bhavan. A *jaali* was used at the entrance as a screen, windows were protected with overhanging concrete eaves to suggest *chajjas*, and the entrance canopy and dome have Rajasthani qualities. The Azad Bhavan represents a rare departure from his firm conviction that buildings are expressions of their time and that the resolution of programmatic requirements and the tectonic issues should be expressed in the universal language of abstraction.

India International Centre ⩗

J. A. Stein (1962)
🚇 Jor Bagh 🚇 Khan Market
40, Max Mueller Marg

The India International Centre (IIC) provides facilities for a variety of artistic and scholarly activities, conferences and symposia organized by national and international groups. The centre was originally conceived in the late 1950s by Dr. S. Radhakrishnan of India and John D. Rockfeller III of the United States along the lines of other 'International House' facilities built in Tokyo and New York in the same period and equally funded which like IIC, were founded with support from the Rockfeller Foundation. The functional scheme is characterized by the careful relation of outdoor and indoor spaces, and finely detailed, expressive construction. The centre's 18,600-square-metre site at Lodi Estate was designed so that the grounds of the IIC and the adjacent Lodi Gardens could function as a single entity. The Centre is composed of individually articulated Stein blocks: 46 guest rooms, a lounge and dining room, a programme block of library and offices and a domed auditorium are all grouped around two great courts and connected by porticoes and ground level and rooftop verandahs. All the main rooms (offices, library, and guest rooms) face approximately north-south, the preferred orientation of the Delhi latitude, while the dining rooms and lounge enjoy an exceptional view of the Lodi Gardens. The height of the buildings has been kept below the base of the domes of the nearby tombs. The materials used in construction have been allowed to assume their natural colours and textures as a result of climate and ageing. The construction methods and procedures employed in the building of the IIC were typical of the techniques and skill levels available in India at the time of construction (1958–1959). The attention to detail in the design and construction at the IIC has resulted in an extraordinary variation and finesse. The IIC is regarded as Stein's finest work in India. It is also considered as one of the best examples of Modern architecture not only in Delhi but in the entire country. A new block consisting of a multi-purpose hall and exhibition spaces as well as an additional recessed floor on the existing guest room block were added in a recent addition by the Delhi based architectural firm Sumit Ghosh and Associates.

Syrian Orthodox Church
The Design Group (1962)
🚇 Green Park
C-3, Safdarjung Development Area, Hauz Khas

057 B

Built in 1962 in HauzKhas, the Syrian Orthodox church was commissioned by the Malankara Orthodox Church of Kerala.

The church was designed specifically to cater for the growing numbers of Syrian Christians migrating to Delhi from the southern Indian state of Kerala, in search of opportunities of employment. The Syrian Orthodox Church is a rare example of a modern minimalist aesthetic being engaged for a religious building. Externally the building is finished with rough rendered plaster and painted in white. The church is approached by a grand flight of steps leading up to its entrance. Devoid of the ornamentation and fenestrations normally associated with churches, the Syrian Orthodox church relies on a more monolithic massing and appearance, with the central aisle accentuated by a simple tower rising above the rest of the mass.

World Health Organization (WHO)

058 A

Habib Rahman (1962)

🚇 Indrapratha

Indraprastha Estate, Mahatma Gandhi Road

Habib Rahman's building for the WHO Headquarters consists of two major blocks: a low slung auditorium-cum-conference block connected to a six-storey office building. The composition is effective and develops a very synergetic relationship between these varied blocks. The auditorium block has a distinctive facade with a graceful light staircase in the centre leading directly from the ground level to the first floor level of the building. The main facade facing the Ring Road also consists of vertical concrete fins. The office block on the contrary emphasizes the horizontal lines of each floor by cantilevered projection bands above and below the window fins. Spanning between these horizontal bands are vertical concrete fins or louvers which form the distinct identity of the building. By means of the cantilevered projections and vertical louvers Rahman was able to give the facade a skin independent of the structure as if it were freely floating from the outside. The office block thus consists of same facades on all the four sides and appears as a box featuring a game of light and shadow on different facades at different times of the day. Amongst all the chaotic development around the site and in the Indraprastha Estate area as a whole, Rahman's WHO headquarters stands out for its clean lines, clarity and fine proportions.

Y.M.C.A. Staff Quarters

The Design Group (1963)

🚇 Shivaji Stadium
Bangla Saheb, Jaisingh Marg,
Connaught Place

059 D

YMCA Staff Headquarters is a complex of four secretaries' apartments and four junior staff quarters. The clients brief insisted on the physical separation of the two categories of apartments and this was achieved in the form of a separating street. The basic system of planning on a square grid with a system of alternating terraces on each floor ensured an overall unity of concept. Alternating terraces ensured that all large openings to the outside were adequately protected from the harsh summer sun. A system of internal courtyards and the separating street were in keeping with traditional planning systems providing both comfortable climactic conditions and the much needed privacy to each apartment. Building blocks are pushed to the periphery, giving rise to central free areas. The access staircase in each block forms important design elements. These staircases wind around a central wall panel but at each half landing have an independent flight leading directly to the front door of an adjacent residential unit. This solution not only gives the staircases a sense of gracefulness but in addition attributes them a considerable importance as transitional spaces between the common areas and the private spaces of each unit.

Multi-storey Flats

Habib Rahman (1965)

AIIMS

R.K. Puram, Ring Road

060 B

The need for a multi-storey dwellings arose from the rapid urbanization of Delhi to accomodate an ever increasing population. Soon the government agencies in charge of development started to realize that it was no longer feasible or pragmatic to continue with two-storey flats for government employees. Rising land values made it necessary to plan high-rise housing schemes particularly in central Delhi area. Several multi-storey housing projects were thus planned by Habib Rahman while he was the Chief Archiect at CPWD (Central Public Works Department). The complex at Ramakrishna Puram and the Curzon Road Hostels are prominent amongst many such projects. The complex at RK Puram consisted of Type V, Type VI flats along with other amenities like shopping centre, restaurant etc. Type VI flats are Y-shaped in plan so as to allow maximum radial bifurcation of each wing and at the same time to enable wings to be served by common lifts, staircases, etc. The central core contains an entrance hall, lifts, staircase and other services on each floor. Type V blocks are T-shaped in plan with each of the three wings being served by common lifts and staircase.

A compact plan was evolved for each flat. With large open spaces between blocks, a feeling of openness with good air and light and considerable privacy for each flat is established in the entire complex. The structure consists of RC frame with 9" external walls and 4-1/2" internal partition walls. External walls have had or have exposed brickwork to add texture and interest on the external facades. In the layout plan six blocks of Type V quarters and ten blocks of Type VI quarters were planned. The distinctive feature of these buildings is the balconies that cantilever out alternatively in two directions so as to benefit from the maximum solar exposure.

Kanvinde's Residence ≈
Achyut Kanvinde (1967)
🌐 Jasola-Apollo
Maharani Bagh

061 C

This house was envisaged for a family consisting of husband, wife and two children, with a provision for guests and study. Since the house is designed for a medium sized plot and provides space for garden and landscape, it was felt desirable to organize spaces in two levels — living areas on the ground floor and bedrooms at the upper floor level. The basic design has been organized to provide the ground floor space integrated with the garden and sky. As the weather in Delhi varies between extremes in summer and winter, the house responds to two kinds of living needs, exploiting both indoor and outdoor areas. The building has been planned on a structural system to create conditions of sub-division of spaces into living and service areas. Storage, bathrooms, kitchen etc. fall into service areas, whereas the rest of the space is dedicated to living and movement areas. The entire inner space has been organized as one continuous area around a traditional court-like zone which is covered at a higher level.

Ford Foundation Headquarter

062 G

J. A. Stein (1968)

🚇 Jor Bagh 🚇 Khan Market

55 Lodi Estate

The Ford Foundation is a private, non-profit philanthropic organization chartered in the United States. Dedicated to the advancement of human welfare, the Foundation offers funds for educational, developmental research, and experimental efforts designed to produce significant advances on selected themes. The Foundation's headquarters are in New York, with additional overseas field offices in Asia, Central and South America, the Middle East and Africa. At the invitation of Prime Minister Nehru, the Ford Foundation came to India in 1952. It was the Foundation's first programme outside of the United States, and the New Delhi office remains the largest of its overseas operations. The Foundation had the good fortune to have been granted a spacious site with delightful views of the nearby Lodi Garden with its historic tombs of the Lodi Emperors. As these rugged yet stately structures are among the most interesting of the many ancient monuments of Delhi, the Foundation's buildings have been designed in careful relationship to both the adjoining tombs and the neighbouring India International Centre. The rhythm of the building design is established by the regular spacing of the large stone piers in the walls. These massive vertical elements are tied together with blue tile faced concrete horizontal bands, which express the floor and roof levels. Projecting, they give protection to the windows as well as form the tiers of planting boxes creating a vertical garden, a feature of both the north and the south elevations of the building. The materials emphasize the beauty and natural quality of local resources as the main theme of the design. The same local stone which forms the outer walls is exposed in the interior while the exterior concrete is continued into the coffered ceilings of the interior. In contrast to these heavy materials, teak, the noblest and, until recently, a relatively easily available wood in India, is used throughout.

Vikas Minar

Habib Rahman (1969)

Indrapratha
Indraprastha Estate

063 A

Vikas Minar located in Indraprastha Estate is the head office of Delhi Development Authority (DDA) and was built in 1969. Among the tallest buildings in the city, and also the seat of the Planning department of the DDA, this showpiece structure is 82 metres high and consists of 23 floors. At the time it was built, one could easily view the River Yamuna from the upper floors of the building. The Vikas Minar was a point block tower consisting of a structural central core with shear walls. Two sets

of double columns appeared on each facade. The corner of each floor slab was cantilevered. As the building is a square in plan, all the four facades are identical and expressed in three parts. While the structural columns provide continuous vertical lines, the horizontal strip windows make the typical element only to be broken by recessed windows after every 5–6 floors. For the DDA, often defined as the builders of Delhi, Vikas Minar is the keeper of its glory. However, the building no longer boasts the impressive structure it once used to be. Years of neglect and poor maintenance by the DDA, compounded by thoughtless additions and modifications, have left the building falling apart at the seams.

Akbar Bhavan
Shiv Nath Prasad (1969)
🚇 INA
Chanakya Puri

064 A

Akbar Bhavan was designed for the New Delhi Municipal Committee. Shiv Nath Prasad was heavily influenced by the layout principles of Le Corbusier's *Unité d'Habitation* for the design of the hotel. He also demonstrated that the texture of exposed reinforced concrete (Prasad's preferred material throughout his career) can be moulded and handled by the untrained local craftsmen of the city. The building constructed in beton brut (rough cast concrete) is inspired after the Brutalist style of architecture. Akbar Bhavan can be seen towering above the tree line from all directions. Its visibility is one of its most striking aspects. What is worth noting and quite apparent is Prasad's homage to *Unite d'habitation*. Le Corbusier's five points of architecture such as the use of *pilotis'* are also on display. Other similarities include the service floor which closely resembles the Unite's shopping floor, the public areas which are placed on the roof, much like the communal facilities on the

roof of the Unite. The hotel is on a two-hectare rocky site and forms part of a commercial complex which includes a cinema, shopping arcade and office buildings. Post-tensioned shallow girders of 18-metre span carry the upper ten floors, containing 171 bedrooms, leaving the lower two floors column free for public areas. A 2.44-metre service floor separates the open lower floors from the bedroom floors. Two-storey curvilinear blocks on either side of the compact rectangular main structure house restaurants and lounges and are approached by curved ramps. On the thirteenth floor one can find a terrace garden, a restaurant and a small open air theatre. On the east face of the building, an exposed staircase descends to a natural depression, which holds the swimming pool and sun-bathing terrace. Akbar Bhavan is not as original as Prasad's Sri Ram Centre, but nonetheless remains an important building of the period. Today the building looks slightly jaded due to the many changes to the original design. Currently government offices occupy the building and a few floors have been given to the upcoming South Asian University.

Nehru Memorial Library ⌃ ⌄

Man Singh Rana (1969)

♻ Race Course

Teen Murti Marg

065 A

Teen Murti House is a classic, quintes-sentially colonial, Lutyens-style build-ing, designed by Robert Tor Russell. Originally called Flagstaff House, it was built for the commander in chief of the Indian Army and it became Jawaharlal Nehru's residence when he was prime minister. This historic setting with its manicured lawns and colourful landscap-ing is also the site of Nehru Memorial Li-brary. After Nehru's death, a Memorial Museum and Library were proposed on the grounds of Teen Murti House. A new structure was required for the Library. Indira Gandhi in her brief to the archi-tect wished the new structure to reflect Nehru's love for books and be a 'contem-porary complement to the beautiful ex-isting environment'. Having had the op-portunity to train and work with Frank Lloyd Wright at Taliesin in Arizona, Man Singh Rana's design for the memorial li-brary was heavily influenced by Wright's philosophy. Wright pioneered the idea of organic architecture, where nature and man's built habitat could be in har-mony with each other. This included use of materials from the site, so that the architecture would grow from the site itself. The two-storey building was de-signed to allow the reading areas an un-restricted view of the trees in their sea-sonal moods. An important aspect of the design is the manner in which the building relates to the existing envi-rons of the site and to Teen Murti House in particular. A landscaped entrance at

the main podium level leads into an exhibition space linked to the auditorium foyer. A small tea-house overlooks the central courtyard. The stacks in this library, designed to accommodate 1,750,000 volumes, are devoted to the modern India of Nehru's dreams. The seminar room on the upper floor is a tree-top meeting place for undisturbed discussions. Rana composed the exterior as a sequence of curvaceous forms that make the structure seem 'cornerless' and without any 'ends'. The facade with its subtle curves and off-white tones blends with the landscape and the Teen Murti House nearby. Inside, in the reception, is Sir Jacob Epstein's sculpture of Nehru. The Nehru Planetarium, also designed by Rana, is steps away from the library and completes this beautiful complex.

Gandhi King Memorial Plaza ♿ ♿ 066 G
J. A. Stein (1970)
Ⓜ Khan Market Ⓜ Jor Bagh
40, Max Mueller Marg,
Lodi Estate

The Memorial Plaza at the Lodi Estate commemorates the twentieth century's two foremost proponents of non-violent social change, Mohandas K. Gandhi and Martin Luther King Jr., and acknowledges the principles and ideals which unite the Ford Foundation and India International Centre as parallel organizations, creating a shared public space between them. The design of the plaza accomplishes several objectives in addition to its serving as a profound memorial. It establishes a relationship between buildings, expressed in the form of a pleasant walled garden. The central feature of the Plaza is a grouping of four large blocks of south Indian granite, which commemorate the themes, 'Man's Quest for Equality through Non-violence' by carrying quotations from Gandhi and King inscribed both in Hindi and English. Flanking the inscribed blocks are two ficus trees, planted by Stein. Other features of the design include an illuminated pool, benches, areas of grass and other plantings including the now full-grown trees. The plaza was completed in late 1969, twenty-one years after the assassination of Gandhi, and one year after the assassination of King, and dedicated early in 1970.

American International School

 067 A

J. A. Stein (1970)

⊜ Race Course

Chandragupta Marg, Chanakya Puri

The American International School in New Delhi was initially founded in 1952 by a group of Americans living and working in Delhi, who joined together on a co-operative basis to provide education on the American model for their children. Starting with only one room and one teacher, the school expanded throughout the 1950s to the point where its mail-order curriculum and quarters in renovated World War II barracks were no longer thought satisfactory in order to sustain the education of its growing number of students, who ranged from the first through to the twelfth grade. The school's courses of study follow American curricula, and graduates are prepared for college and university entrance. The institution became known as the American Embassy School in the late 1970s. Joseph Allen Stein began designing new facilities for 750 students in 1960, at a boulder-strewn site in New Delhi's diplomatic enclave. It was agreed between the school community and Stein that highly flexible buildings with an informal, inviting atmosphere were necessary to further the aims of the educational programme. Buildings were developed in three phases in what was conceived of as a 'garden school'. Primary, middle, high school and administration blocks were included in the first phase (completed 1963). The initial design featured classrooms and common spaces under vaulted and domed steel lattice shells in each of the classroom buildings. Garden classroom extensions and shaded outdoor walkways open out from the buildings, linking them together. The second phase (completed 1966) added a large central building containing the school library and music department, and a gymnasium which is convertible into an auditorium. The gymnasium/auditorium seats 600 under the cover of a hyperbolic paraboloid steel lattice roof. Student hostels built with a rectilinear geometry were added in the third stage (completed 1970).

YMCA University of Science and Technology

068

The Design Group (1970)

Badarpur

NH2, sector 6, Mathura Road, Faridabad

Located in the Industrial Suburb of Faridabad, South of Delhi, this was an early project in campus planning. Though small in scale, it had all the ingredients and concerns of contemporary campus planning. The academic component is planned in the centre with housing for staff and students on either side. The entire campus was done in exposed brick, then an enviable building material. The central complex which houses a variety of activities was conceived as a kind of pinwheel structure allowing the expansion of different wings in due course depending on future needs. Within the complex all the different elements were connected by a system of covered corridors and verandahs that even bridged across the road to link with the auditorium, the conference complex and the sports pavilion adjoining the playing fields. The four hostel blocks together defined a strong enclosed space that formed a major focal point for students on the campus.

Industrial Buildings for Escorts Limited
J. A. Stein
⊜ Badarpur (for 069/070)

Escorts I
069
Westinghouse X-Ray Plant

(1962)
Faridabad, Haryana

Escorts II
070
Motor scooter Assembly Plant
(1964)
Faridabad, Haryana

Escorts Motorcycle
071
Assembly Plant

(1988)
Surajpur, Uttarpradesh

In an association that goes back to the late 1950s, Joseph Allen Stein designed over three million square feet of factory floor space, spread over several sites in Northern India for Escorts Limited, a diversified industrial company and one of India's leading manufacturers of tractors, motorcycles and scooters. Stein's designs for the Escorts Factories near Delhi feature four different shell configurations which were developed with structural engineer Vishnu Joshi: barrel vaulted lattice shells for the Escorts I plant (completed 1962), hyperbolic paraboloid lattice shells for the Escorts II plant (completed 1964), concrete domes for storage facilities (completed 1965), all in Faridabad, Haryana; and octagonal

steel lattice domes for the Motorcycle Assembly plant at Surajpur, Uttar Pradesh (completed 1988). The varied resolutions of various technical issues, involving the use of daylight and construction methods, are a highlight of the works for Escorts. The resolution of detail has had a direct effect both on the forms of the individual shells and on their modular arrangements.

Controlling the heat and natural light — both serious problems in the Indian climate — have been the shared determinants of the various forms. All the systems were developed to allow the minimum of heat by limiting glass to the smallest possible area while providing natural light of a sufficient quality and uniform distribution. Stein's research into the optimum natural lighting arrangements began in the early 1960s in order to guide the development of modular roof systems, where the desired overhead glass is always shaded, and where factory workers should not have to look directly at large glass areas.

Due to stringent economic conditions, it was necessary to build with a limited range of materials and minimum amount of steel. The subsequent need to rely upon 'strength through shape' for spanning, rather than on material depth, resulted in a thinness and purity of form of the shell elements at Escorts that provides a rigorous, spartan quality to the factory workspaces.

On the History of the German Embassy

Jörn Düwel

Ambassador's residence of the Thai Embassy in New Delhi (1956)

The German embassy complex in New Delhi, built in the second half of the 1950s according to plans prepared by Johannes Krahn and the Federal Building Office is a *Gesamtkunstwerk* of national significance for Germany. Undoubtedly, there is great public interest in the preservation and continued utilisation of the building complex for which there are good historical, aesthetic and scientific reasons. At any rate, not only is the German embassy building in New Delhi held in high national esteem in Germany, it is also much honoured in India. India's interest in Germany's handling of its embassy renovation does not come as a surprise as there has been a growing consciousness in the subcontinent over the last couple of years that seeks to value and cherish architectural heritage from the 20th century.

The preservation of such buildings is a challenge for architectural conservationists, clients and architects alike, in Germany as much as in India. External appearances can in many cases unfortunately not be met when uses are to be changed. Therefore, what is needed is a careful assessment of the justifiable and highly different expectations and possibilities.

The Historical Significance of the German Embassy Complex

The founding of the Federal Republic of Germany in 1949 was initially not accompanied by the country's diplomatic sovereignty. Bound by the conditions of the occupation statute, its foreign diplomatic representation was solely in the hands of the Western allies. Although the Federal Republic of Germany was soon allowed to open consular offices abroad and the country's ministry of foreign affairs was founded in 1951, it was only in 1955 that the western allies removed the occupation statute whereupon the limitations that had initially been imposed on the Federal Republic

Johannes Krahn: German Embassy New Delhi; entrance to the chancellery shortly after completion in 1959

Ambassador's residence of the Japanese Embassy in New Delhi (1956)

The Vatican's Nunciature in New Delhi (1956)

ceased. In the following years, the country resumed diplomatic relations with a number of countries. In many cases, it was able to house its diplomatic missions in buildings that had already been used as embassies by the German empire or the Weimar Republic. The situation in India, however, was special. In 1947, the drive for independence led to the founding of the largest state on the subcontinent, the Republic of India. From independence up until 1964, it was prime minister Jawaharlal Nehru who largely determined the course of the young independent democracy with his Congress party being highly influential up until the early seventies. Under his leadership, India intermittently sympathised with the Soviet Union, something which was viewed suspiciously by the West. The resumption of diplomatic relations between Germany and India, together with its spatial representation, obtained a high public profile in this atmosphere. The Federal Republic of Germany was among the first countries to plan and construct a new embassy building in New Delhi. In doing so, West Germany saw it as the country's special mission to exemplify its adherence to the western block of states during the height of the Cold War, in a country that had declared itself non-aligned. The architectural design of the embassy thus also became a matter of symbolic importance as distinctive perspectives and outlooks were also evident in the sphere of culture. The relentless antagonism between the two differing systems, observable in all spheres, also came to affect the sensitive area of architecture. The architectural arm-wrestling came to be carried out on a compact building site in New Delhi. The Indian government had created a new city district

to house diplomatic missions. In the south-western part of the city, undeveloped areas were allocated as part of an urban masterplan. The new district was planned in the prominent location of *Chanakyapuri*, underlining its close proximity to the president's estate in the north. On the eastern side, the embassy district borders on the Nehru Park as well as on the museum of the Republic of India's founder, Jawaharlal Nehru.

A grid of orthogonal axes forms the spatial basis of the diplomatic enclave, with the transverse axes being shorter compared to the longitudinal ones. The German embassy lies on the southern end of the eastern side of the main axis, the *Shanti Path*. The largest embassies are those of the United Stated of America, Great Britain, Australia and Russia, the largest member of the former Soviet Union. In comparison to these embassies, the German embassy buildings seem rather modest, being roughly equally large as the embassies of Canada, the Netherlands and Japan, located directly next to the German embassy complex.

The Architectural Design Competition

Five years after the founding of the Federal Republic of Germany, the Federal Building Office announced the first competition of its kind for the construction of a German embassy building abroad. In the spring of 1954, six architects were invited to participate in the competition to design and build the German embassy in New Delhi. In their own different ways, each of the six candidates had already had experience in working with the western occupying powers as clients and even with various public buildings already

German Embassy New Delhi; model of the competition design (1954)

built in the young Federal Republic. The candidates were Fritz August Breuhaus de Groot from Honnef, Wilhelm and Dirk Denninger from Bonn, Johannes Krahn from Frankfurt am Main, Rudolf Lodders from Hamburg, Helmut von Lülsdorf from Berlin and Friedel Steinmeyer from Offenbach. Under the chairmanship of Werner March, a jury was to commission one of these architects in August 1954. After the results had come in, it became clear that a first prize could not be awarded as the jury felt that none of the six submitted designs fully satisfied all functional requirements. The second prize was awarded to Johannes Krahn. Other awards went to Breuhaus, Denninger and Steinmeyer. Apart from having had the choice of settling for a design submitted in the competition, the jury could also decide to choose the design of the Federal Building Office's workgroup. The result of the competition was published in September 1954 in 'Die Bauverwaltung', the journal of official architecture and civil engineering projects by Karl Badberger, the head of the Federal Building Office. Badberger, who had been a member of the jury, called attention to the challenge Germany faced, namely the appropriate appearance for a German diplomatic mission abroad. Apart from finding an answer to the question of whether or not the architectural language should reflect the aesthetics of the host nation or should rather display those of the home country, the political iconography of the design was of paramount importance. 'It does not

befit the Germans to build a pretentious building after a lost war, while it would also be inexcusable to upset the host country with a rather indifferent attitude', Badberger wrote, representing the official position of the federal government. The difficulty thus lay in striking the right balance between the required representative qualities and the assumed modest appearance. Without making the fact public, the jury had apparently not seen this balance to be evident in any of the six competition designs. All designs proposed symmetrical buildings aligned along axes, inspired by traditional elements of embassy buildings.

However, symmetries had fallen into disrepute in the Federal Republic's political and public architecture projects and had to be dropped for this prominent building assignment. Although the jury praised the degree of architectural detailing in Johannes Krahn's design, remarking that it 'corresponds to the contemporary perception of architecture', it objected to the grouping of the individual buildings within the complex. Krahn's design called for a gently curved main office building placed on stilts behind which the ambassador's residence was located. In the record of the jury, it was critically remarked that both buildings had been placed too close to each other. The real reason for the criticism appears to have been the office block's rigorous symmetry, which, in effect, had prevented a more agreeable spacing of the individual buildings. All the more remarkable is the design of

German Embassy, main entrance (1959)

the Federal Building Office that stood outside the competition. It appears to have fulfilled all the requirements: the positioning and spacing of the individual buildings didn't allow symmetries to emerge anywhere. The office block and the ambassador's residence are clearly disconnected from each other, while the latter opens up towards a park. The accommodation for local employees is located at the western limit of the site, behind a row of plants that also served as optical separation. The head of the Federal Building Office concluded in somewhat complicated terms that 'it is definitely desirable that the building agency responsible for the implementation of the building vis-à-vis the client does not limit itself to just carrying out delegated tasks but that it becomes accountable to itself as to how the task at hand is to be best solved.'

As such, it comes as no surprise that Johannes Krahn and the Federal Building Office formed a project-based partnership following the competition for the construction of the German embassy. The arrangement of the individual buildings and their relationships with each other are taken from the design of the work group of the Federal Building Office. However, no noteworthy suggestions of Johannes Krahn for the basic conception of the embassy ensemble seem to have been included. The names of individual persons who were active in the Federal Building Office's work group are unknown. The German Architecture Museum in Frankfurt houses Johannes Krahn's

archive. Here, many drawings of the design for the German embassy are kept which have, in most cases, been signed by Johannes Krahn himself, while the seals recall the cooperation between Johannes Krahn and the Federal Building Office. The numerous drawings showing elevations, sections and details are proof of the fact that a good number of design decisions were taken while the building was already under construction. The architects were initially overcome by a sense of helplessness. The client's stipulation that the embassy should be a symbol of German architecture on the

Post-Independence

Cover of the German journal
'Die Bauverwaltung',
issue 9 (September 1954)

Laying of the foundation stone in 1956: Ambassador Dr. Meyer; Mr. Ollenhauer, member of the Bundestag and Mr. Wetzel, project manager

Contact architect Karl Malte von Heinz (3rd from left) with project manager Mr. Wetzel (3rd from right) and other members of his office (1958)

one hand, reflecting 'the current state of German architecture', while simultaneously avoiding 'unnecessary sensationalism, with the design expected to be modest and restrained' on the other, did not make it easy to imbibe strong representative qualities into the design. It was decided to undertake an educational trip to India to help find a way forward. Johannes Krahn and the architects of the Federal Building Office explored various new buildings in New Delhi together with their architect contact Karl Malte von Heinz following their appointment as architects of the German embassy. The photographs that were taken and the freehand sketches of Heinz that were made during this trip show that crucial suggestions concerning the design were only put forward following the exploration of buildings in the city, instantly making their way into the final design. This particularly applies to the design of the facade with its shading louvers for the windows as well as decorative elements. Exactly which buildings were studied during the trip is not

clear as the architects were more concerned with finding exemplary and general architectural details rather than naming actual buildings. The captions of the photographs concern themselves with design-related or technical questions while the individual buildings are only described in general terms. As such, the Court of Audit in New Delhi which was under construction at the time is simply labelled as 'a new administrative building'. What the architects from Germany found interesting in this building were the box-like sun-shading louvers placed in front of the facade on the fourth floor. With a view to explore local building techniques, the architects from Germany studied the Ashok Hotel which was just nearing completion at the time. Not only did the architects explore new buildings being erected on the numerous sites of the city, they were also particularly interested in what was being constructed in the diplomatic enclave. The issue that presented itself before them was how to balance the relationship between appropriately representing

Construction sign of the German Embassy in New Delhi (1956)

Object of study Hotel Ashoka in New Delhi (1956)

Chancellery with residential wing, 1st building phase; view from Shanti Path (1959)

Germany and negotiating Indian conditions and sensibilities. The record of the observations is evidence of the measure in which a neat balance was woven into the building design.

To a large extent, New Delhi's climatic conditions alone determined the external appearance of most embassy buildings as the architects observed. A simple transfer of Johannes Krahn's design for Bonn on which he had collaborated with Hans Schwippert was thus inconceivable. Large glazed surfaces would have been impossible to realise with the technology available at the time and inappropriate for a subtropical climate. Two buildings form the focus of the complex: the four-storey office block and the ambassador's residence that opens up towards a park. The office block or chancellery which included the official residence of the chancellor of the embassy and of other employees was provided with a separate driveway along the main axis of the complex. The ambassador's residence was aligned to a by-road.

The chancellery with its adjacent residential building was constructed using a reinforced concrete frame, while the facades were shaped by fixed sunshading louvers that offered protection from intense sunlight. The windows of the residential building are protected by thick box-like frames. The open ground floor also facilitates good ventilation and serves as shaded parking space for official vehicles. The ambassador's residence, the official residence of employees and the front side of the chancellery have all been clad in Indian marble. The choice of materials was not only determined by aesthetic factors but also by the fact that excessive monsoon rains and sand storms have a lesser effect on marble than they do on other cladding materials.

The ambassador's residence consists of two parts: firstly, the stately wing on the ground floor which houses an entrance hall and a roughly 110-square-metre-large reception hall, a dining hall, as well as further spaces; and secondly, the two-storey residential wing. At the junction of the two wings, at an exposed location and accessible from the hall, there is a room reserved for the the ambassador where semi-official visitors can be received. The kitchen complex is set around an originally semi-covered courtyard, corresponding to local typologies. The entrance to the ambassador's residence is shaped by a spectacular canopy made of concrete. This expressive gesture contrasts with the otherwise calm and modest appearance of the complex. The dramatic flying roof that seems

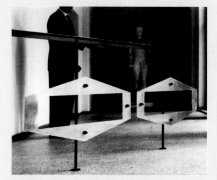

Sample of balcony railing before
installation (1958)

Construction of interior walls and
natural stone slab (1958)

to be full of energy and movement recalls the image of Le Corbusier's pilgrimage church in Ronchamp. He had
also planned the much-noticed city of
Chandigarh during those years.

Chandigarh, the provincial capital in the
north of the country, had been designed
as a modern ideal city. It was to assume
a model role based on the most current
scientific insights. Undoubtedly, it exud-
ed a suggestive power which was stronger than the physicality of the city itself. It had a unique reputation though
few people actually seem to have made
the trip to the remote city. Chandigarh's
symbolism, however, was strongly felt
not least due to the numerous publications on it, including in the popular media. The architects from Germany, however, indeed saw Chandigarh with their
own eyes and translated some of the visual ideas into their own design.

The appearance of the ambassador's residence is largely determined by compar-
atively small windows, covered terraces and balconies, aluminium and rolling
bamboo blinds. Unlike the chancellery,
the ambassador's residence was built of
brick. Increased wear and tear as well
as modified user requirements meant
that some of these elements have been
changed over the last decades, leading
to a substantial alteration of the original appearance. Already during the competition phase, the client had included provisions for extending the original buildings which the architects
were required to consider. Even before
the completion of the initial construction phase, the chancellery was extended to include four further axes. The laying of the foundation stone took place

two years after the design competition,
on 4th December 1956. The first building phase was, to a large part, complete by 1959. After having been under
construction for six years, the extended embassy complex was inaugurated
in 1962 in the presence of the Indian
prime minister, Jawaharlal Nehru. For
thirty years, the embassy building per-
formed smoothly without the need for
substantial renovations or alterations.
Between 1992 and 1997, the Federal Office for Building and Regional Planning
for the first time carried out a comprehensive renovation and extension of
the complex. A four-storey office building and a multi-purpose hall were constructed at the southern end of the site.

The Aesthetic Interpretation of
the Chancellery Building

A reappraisal of the German embassy
complex in New Delhi took place in 2008.
The Berlin architecture firm Meuser, on
behalf of the Federal Office for Building and Regional Planning, took over the
task of renovating the building's facade
while gently reinterpreting it. Meuser
Architects sensitively respected the aesthetics of the existing building while incorporating their own aesthetic details.
The result is impressive: the distinctive
colour scheme meaningfully relates to
local preferences for colour with colour-
fulness being evident in much of Indian
architecture.

On the other hand, the design represents
a confident and somewhat ironic reference
to the ubiquitous model of Chandigarh
from the 1950s. Le Corbusier's design for
the provincial capital in northern India

Ongoing demolition work to make way for the chancellery extension (1994)

Federal Building Office: model of the chancellery extension (1992–1997)

was at the time perceived to be seminal for Modernism. Both the ideal theoretical principles of urban planning and the sculptural buildings not only found many enthusiastic supporters but also led to a whole range of imitations. Chandigarh didn't just become a model for the young democracy of India. Its urban design, along with Le Corbusier's other designs assumed exemplary importance in the spheres of architecture and planning on the subcontinent. Likewise, the young German democracy which was, for its part, also looking for urban and architectural idioms to express its liberal outlook, found Chandigarh exemplary too. As such, it is not surprising that the German architects formally recalled aspects of this new provincial capital city in their design for the German embassy. For this reason, it was rather self-evident for Meuser Architects to take up this early design and reinterpret it in a contemporary fashion.

The Artistic Significance of the German Embassy in New Delhi

The building ensemble's historical dimension is inextricably linked to the artistic significance of the complex. For ages, architecture and city design have transcended their purely functional aspects. A subtle system of signs that goes beyond the pure functionality of spaces conveys a multitude of meanings. During the Cold War, architectural vocabulary played a very special role. It made both a foreign-policy statement and a cultural statement in an atmosphere charged with political tensions. The encounter between diverging cultural perceptions

determined German politics to a large extent, and this in two ways. The close proximity of the two German states conjured up a sense of mutual fixation and simultaneous rejection between them. Government architecture, as stipulated by Bonn, was to be open and cheerful. Ever since the architect Hans Schwippert had torn open the walls of the Pedagogical Academy in Bonn in 1948, installing two ceiling-high glazed walls in the plenary hall of the German *Bundestag* which had been under construction by the banks of the Rhine River, the Federal Republic's symbol to the outside world became a glasshouse. The new open spaces were a far cry from the bunkers, burrows, and air raid shelters of the past. Schwippert's 'house of openness and of dialogue' was not only intended to try to heal a mass psychological trauma. His architecture was more than simply a cheerful aesthetic gesture. Schwippert's purpose was to enlighten and educate, in the best sense of the terms. Together with his clients, he translated the German Basic Law prescribing transparent parliamentary debates quite literally into the transparency of glazed walls. The plenary hall was to become the central space of democratic discussion. 'Politics is dark and obscure. Let us bring some light into it', the architect had said. From that time on, the glazed transparency of public and political buildings in West Germany came to be considered as good architectural practice. Almost all buildings that served to represent the Federal Republic were consciously designed to represent democracy in aesthetic terms, following the maxim 'transparent buildings are democratic buildings'.

Meuser Architekten: German Embassy New Delhi, Design proposal
for the facade renovation (2008)

Though simple, this maxim was indeed taken seriously, representing a formula for reaching consensus on a day-to-day level, and creating the smallest common denominator for public buildings in the republic right from the very start. The interpretation of architectural forms was, of course, not arbitrary. On the contrary, it followed a certain political classification. The iconographic programme was laid down in conjunction with the cultural perceptions of the different occupying forces which later became protector states. The increasing hostility between the occupying powers not only led to a severe political and economic segregation between the Soviet and the three Western zones after the end of the Second World War, it also led to a polarisation of culture. As early as a few weeks after the founding of the German Democratic Republic, its Ministry for Reconstruction launched a high-profile campaign that was directed at West Germany in particular. What was explicitly demanded was a model of 'German architecture' for the 'beautiful German city'. The hope may have been to reanimate old resentments: in the 1920s, conservatives in Germany had undertaken a campaign against Modernism and had defamed the Bauhaus calling it the headquarters of 'architectural bolshevism'. This kind of intensified politicisation of architecture also contributed to

the fact that public buildings constructed under national socialism were mostly designed in a neo-classicist idiom while regionalist elements were overlaid onto everyday architecture. Building officials of the GDR seemed to believe that the national socialist propaganda against the 'nomad building method' of the new era of architecture had been effective enough to reconnect with the old prejudices in a campaign against the 'cosmopolitanism' found in West German Modernism. East Germany forcefully rejected the light and transparent architectural forms of the West that smacked of the continuing influence of the former Bauhaus architects and that was now being effectively re-imported from the United States. East Berlin attacked this alleged 'American cultural imperialism' and called on all 'honest architects in the Western part of our fatherland' to oppose this. By partly basing its 'cultural struggle' on national socialist propaganda, the GDR placed the ball in the West's court. After all, the leadership of the GDR had laid claim to a new German architecture by introducing catchy images as early as 1950. Following the motto 'national in shape, democratic in contents' it campaigned for an all-German reconstruction concept. In doing so, the actual origin of the slogan had been neatly disguised: nothing ostensibly suggested that its origin

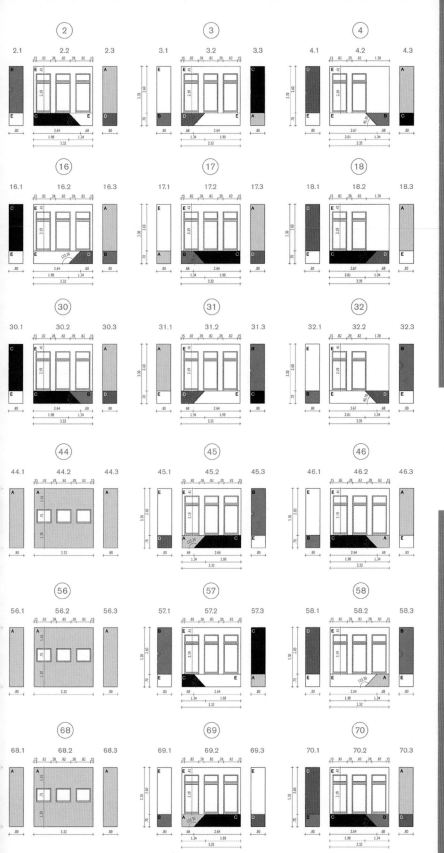

Meuser Architekten: German Embassy New Delhi; facade design (2008)

Edward D. Stone: Embassy of the United States of America in New Delhi (1958); facade (left) and entrance to the chancellery (top)

lay in the Soviet Union. In reality, this maxim had already been applied in the USSR since the 1930s, both in architecture and urban planning. It was the link to Stalinist rule which intended to apply the doctrine of 'socialist realism' to the reconstruction of the destroyed cities in Germany, exemplifying Stalin's claim to shape an all-German post-war policy. Apparently, the objective was to preserve national, regional and local identities in a multiethnic state. However, while certain building vocabularies were developed from regional traditions to refer to identity formation and

historical consciousness, below the surface entirely new political structures were taking shape, dictated by Moscow, that only served to strengthen authoritarian rule. It was to this proven and tested pattern that the Soviet Union turned after the Second World War to reinforce its influence in Europe: the official turn to cultural heritage and national building culture can be understood in this context. It was hoped that by emphasising national moments, domestic political support would be generated and propagandist advantages secured with regard to the West. One of the main

Heritage conservation strategy 'preservation': Kaisersaal of the Hotel Esplanade in Berlin by Helmut Jahn (1995–2000)

Heritage conservation strategy 'continuation': Kolumba art museum of the archbishopric Cologne by Peter Zumthor (2003–2007)

goals was to counteract the increasingly successful western integration of the Federal Republic which was being felt at the beginning of the 1950s.

However, the results achieved an effect opposite to that intended. The GDR's push and the reinterpretation of national building vocabularies to serve certain political goals unavoidably led the Federal Republic to an even stronger appraisal of Modernist idioms which were also used by the United States and other western countries. After all, the GDR had laid claim to the architectural vocabulary of the past and hence any involvement with it would have been taken to mean the Federal Republic's acquiescence with the political objectives of the GDR. The maintenance of distance towards the political adversary in the East necessitated West Germany to stylise the modernist idiom as its own model. The forms of architecture and city planning were thus placed in the service of political iconography. However, the rejection of traditional symbols and architectural vocabularies not only served to distance the Federal Republic from the East, it also served to distance it from national socialist design. This rejection, however, could only take place by demonising certain building typologies which mainly belonged to the sphere of public building. By focussing its accusations in a single direction, the breadth of building activity and architectural vocabularies used under national socialism became more manageable for the Federal Republic in two

ways: it became superfluous to take inspiration from models of national building culture because the GDR had already successfully capitalised on this. It was therefore self-evident that a similar architectural repertoire in national socialism was declared to be the national socialist style per se. Although even national socialism used Modernist vocabularies, this paved the way for a fundamentally new interpretation. By claiming that neo-classicist architecture was a frozen ideology, certain architectural details could be successfully stigmatised with the result that columns and ornamentation came to be treated with suspicion in the Federal Republic. Cubes, columns, sequencing and axial arrangements were, and still are, associated with a celebration of power and contempt for human beings. The positioning and segregation of certain forms deemed to be part of a national socialist style only took place after the war. A clear classification and double segregation, firstly of the most recent past, i. e. of national socialism, and secondly of the GDR seemed inevitable to unmistakably demonstrate a new social beginning. This is the reason why the relationship between architectural form and its alleged meaning played such a significant role that even served to legitimise the state in the early years of the Federal Republic. Almost all building assignments adhered to this principle. What applied domestically was even more valid when it came to shaping the Federal Republic's image abroad. It was here that German architecture was expected to display its proficiency while avoiding 'unnecessary commotion, preferring to be modest and reserved'. With these words, the building administration illustrated the expectations that were placed on new foreign missions. Quite directly, architecture took on a metaphorical role. Building designs became manifestoes of a reformed and refined Germany, a demonstrative confession of adherence to the liberal values of the West. In this respect, the demand for floating buildings with facades typical of contemporary western European standard can be understood to exemplify a particular affiliation. Behind this lay the obsession that foreign countries were avidly watching Germany's every move, speculating whether the horrors of the past would re-emerge in the guise of architecture. It was the desire for recognition and respect that was a significant factor in Germany's decision to enforce American and western European patterns.

What becomes apparent immediately is the fact that Johannes Krahn and the Federal Building Office did not design the German embassy in New Delhi without having had models and conditions to stick to. The embassy buildings refer to certain shapes and forms that the architects discovered during their visit to new buildings in New Delhi and Chandigarh. As such, the three upper floors of the chancellery consisting of a mesh of vertical and horizontal elements and facing both the street and the garden, recall the facade grid of Le Corbusier's court of law in Chandigarh. In a refined way, the architects made an aesthetic virtue out of the climatic challenges they faced in the design. They designed and built sun shades arranged in a concrete grid and created a rhythmic and taut horizontal pattern. However, it is not the formal analogies to the provincial capital of Chandigarh that dominate the embassy building. While Le Corbusier stressed the grand gesture and declaredly created sculptural freestanding monuments, an entirely different spirit pervades the embassy complex. It is the power of calm that is evident in these buildings. Monumentality seems completely alien to them. With its deep terraces and balconies, the ambassador's residence is reminiscent of the pavilion-like villas of classical Modernism built in Germany in the 1920s.

Without resorting to boastful metaphors, the architects succeeded in creating a ceremonial yet casual atmosphere in their architecture. The client's objective to produce a building that would represent Germany while equally respecting India was, by all means, implemented in an impressive manner. The architectural interpretation of the aesthetic vocabulary is unique: local motifs were sensitively imbibed and infused with a contemporary western European iconography to create a self-contained whole. This architectural self-containment distinguishes the German embassy complex in New Delhi. While the Federal Republic of Germany accepted India's offer to construct an embassy in the new diplomatic enclave, the GDR chose a non-descript, former residential building as its embassy, taking it on rent. It was in North Korea which had just emerged as a sovereign nation following a war that the GDR constructed a new embassy of exceptional symbolic significance.

The Refurbishment of the German Embassy in New Delhi

The prospects for professional and successful heritage conservation at the German embassy in New Delhi are good. Compared to other noteworthy buildings that equally satisfy similar criteria for heritage conservation while offering little source material leading to speculations in the conservation approach, the German embassy has a wealth of source materials. The German Architecture Museum in Frankfurt houses a few hundred drawings of the partnership between Johannes Krahn and the Federal Building Office. This archive alone provides detailed knowledge, from the early designs of the embassy to the final built version. Furthermore, the archive of the Federal Office for Building and Regional Planning houses a few dozen excellent photographs that plug certain gaps in the archive of the German Architecture Museum.

It is obvious that the German embassy buildings in New Delhi do not constitute a cultural monument according to formal law. As such, no special conditions or restrictions necessarily apply when it comes to structural maintenance, renovation or constructing extensions. Nevertheless, the owner and the client have a particular responsibility to bear which results from the historical and cultural significance of the embassy. For this reason, an appropriate heritage conservation approach is desirable, not least because Germany has been campaigning globally for a respectable handling of cultural heritage. What is at stake here is the reinforcement of this claim's credibility. With respect to administrative law, cultural heritage conservation in Germany does not have deep historical roots. It emerged out of the romantic yearning for all things old and ruinous in the first third of the 19th century. It was in Hesse that a systematic listing of 'old art monuments' took place for the first time. By around 1900, heritage conservation had established itself as a separate field. During this period, Georg Dehio, doyen of heritage conservation in Germany, was able to push through his manifesto which became the proof of avowal for the profession: the motto was to 'preserve, not restore'. In this way, the profession of heritage conservation successfully countered the prevalent practice of boldly extending historical monuments as a sort of purifying act.

It condemned the demolitions that went with this practice, calling them 'restoration vandalism', and demanded that old and new parts should be clearly distinguishable from each other. In doing so, Dehio greatly influenced the prevalent conceptions on heritage conservation as they had been codified in the Charter of Venice. This document, passed in 1964, had significant influence on the perception of heritage preservation in Germany for several decades.

The Charter of Venice laid down basic rules for handling historical monuments. Although they were not legally binding, they had a considerable influence on architects and planners. Special attention was paid to the issue of identity. This meant that, under all possible circumstances, the original building stock was to be preserved. The rules that the Charter propagated were not always practicable.

In many cases, they just served the purposes of an indoctrinating dogmatism. In the last few years, the basic tenets of heritage conservation have become more varied in shape and form without resulting in a change of the legal framework. Simply put, a dualism has emerged: on the one hand, the rules and values of the half-century old Charter of Venice continue to live on, being increasingly described as representing a more conservative approach. On the other hand, the perception that such an absolute approach does not in itself represent a priority has gained ground. This has to do with claims of a more holistic understanding of existing buildings as seen in their contemporary environments, opening up the possibility for adapting to contemporary uses. In this view, there is no hierarchy between functions, construction and aesthetics. All elements are equally important. What lies at the basis of this perception is the view that the image should be preserved without necessarily insisting on authenticity of contents.

This more contemporary understanding of heritage conservation can be appropriately applied to the conservation of the German embassy building in New Delhi. Without conforming to a rigid set of rules, it would be sensible to carefully analyse every detail and every decision within the context of the ensemble as a whole while considering changed user requirements. Today, the sensitive handling of architectural heritage is supported by a large section of the public.

Ensuring appropriate care for existing buildings naturally also concerns extensions and additions that do become necessary with changed uses. Put simply, it is basically irrelevant whether or not a certain building qualifies as a historical monument in legal terms. As such, the appraisal of the proposed building measures for the German embassy finally rests with the state and its institutions. The political, cultural and historical significance of the German embassy building in New Delhi demands path-breaking solutions. The embassy complex has the chance to become a future model for implementing similar tasks on other official German sites abroad.

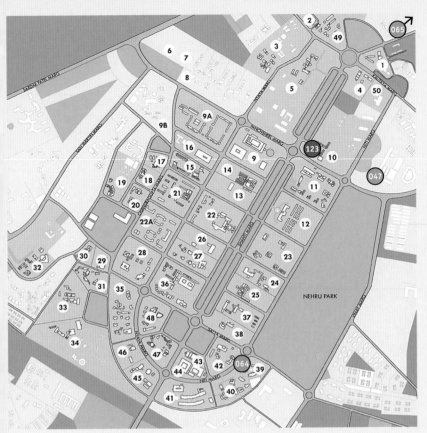

Street map of the Diplomatic quarter in Chanakyapuri district.

1. Indonesia
2. Vietnam
3. Lebanon
4. Norway
5. China
6. Angola
7. Portugal
8. Latvia
9. United States of America ········ `051`
9a. USA's Embassy Housing
9b. American Embassy School ········ `067`
10. Great Britain
11. Australia
12. Pakistan
13. Mynamar
14. France
15. Finland ········ `098`
16. Switzerland
17. Austria
18. UAE
19. Bulgaria
20. Oman
21. Sweden
22. Russia
22a. Russian Embassy Housing
23. Serbia and Montenegro
24. Sudan

25. Japan
26. Afghanistan
27. Netherlands
28. Italy
29. Qatar
30. Mauritius
31. Korea
32. Uzbekistan
33. Singapore ········ `165`
34. Nigeria
35. Thailand
36. Canada
37. Germany
38. Ethiopia
39. Egypt
40. Hungary
41. Czech Republic + Slovakia
42. Malaysia
43. Kuwait
44. Poland ········ `083`
45. Turkey
46. Philippines
47. Belgium ········ `093`
48. Ghana
49. Sri Lanka
50. Vatican City

1971 – 1990: Regionalism

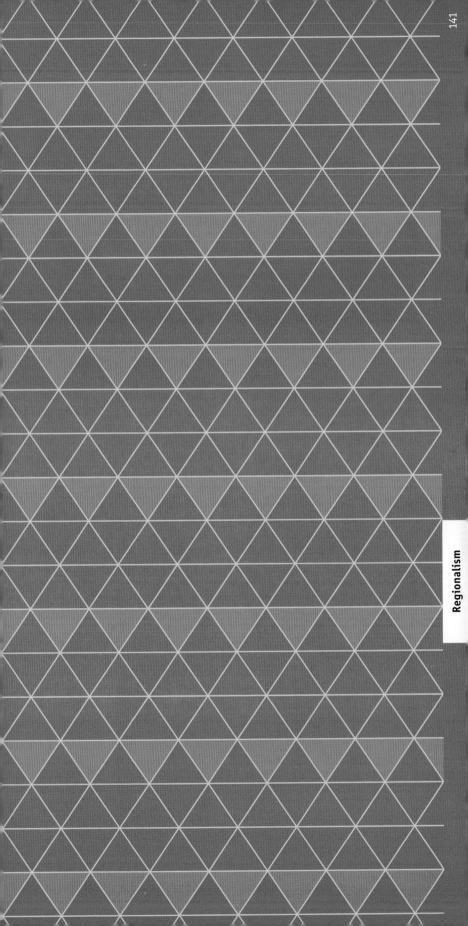

Regionalism

Jawaharlal Nehru University [072] [B]
C. P. Kukreja Associates
(1970–1995)
⊜ Hauz Khas
New Mehrauli Road

Masterplan (1970)
In 1970, a national design competition was organized to develop the masterplan for Jawaharlal Nehru University in Delhi. The programme called for the development of an Academic Complex consisting of seven schools, a library, administrative offices, a Residential Complex for both the faculty and students and other facilities for the residents. It also underlined the necessity for the creation of a flexible environment. The 400-hectare site for the campus is on undulating, boulder-strewn land in South Delhi. Its development was planned in three phases to meet the needs of an ultimate population of 10,000 students and 1,240 faculty members. Kukreja's proposal shows a deep concern for site characteristics and use of materials. The Academic Complex features a main central plaza with buildings grouped around it. The structures rise along the natural contours. The Library, at the highest level, imparts a monumental scale to the plaza. The Academic Complex is encircled by an arterial loop road from which links are provided to all important buildings. The residential sectors consist of sixteen hostel clusters and faculty housing grouped around them.

Hostels at JNU (1976)

The students' hostels of Jawaharlal Nehru University form a part of the residential sector of the masterplan which visualizes accommodation for 10,000 students. The masterplan includes sixteen hostel clusters. Each cluster consists of three hostel units grouped around a courtyard. Housing for faculty is provided on the periphery of hostel clusters to help overcome traditional hierarchical barriers between faculty and students. Each hostel unit consists of two parallel rectangular blocks linked by bridges to a community dining room, lounge and common room. Each block houses a hundred students and two faculty members. Every student has been provided rooms with open balconies. Following the natural configuration of the land, these three-to four-storey structures in exposed brick are built around semi-enclosed courts, which provide shaded spaces for interaction and promote cross-ventilation in hostel rooms.

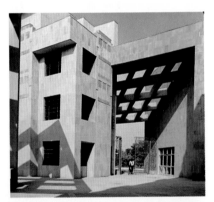

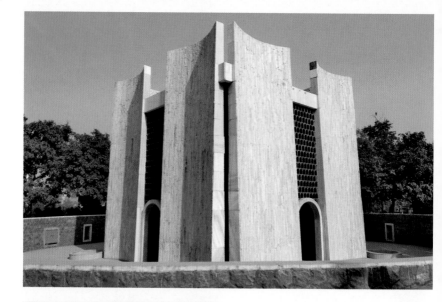

Mazaar of Zakir Hussain 073 C

Habib Rahman (1971)

Jasola-Apollo

Jamia Milia Islamia, Jamia Nagar

The tomb was built to commemorate India's third president, Dr. Zakir Hussain, who served from 1967 to his death in 1969. It is located within the campus of Jamia Milia Islamia University, where Dr. Hussain was a teacher. The museum on site displays some personal belongings, including his collection of geological specimens. The tomb is inset into the top of a raised mound. The inward sloping walls were inspired by Tughluq period tombs in Delhi. The sloping concave walls, arranged in a square, do not meet at the corners and support a shallow concrete dome. The facing of these walls is of rough cut marble pieces mounted on their edge.

Hall of Nations and Hall of Industries (Permanent Exhibition Complex) » 074 A

Raj Rewal Associates (1972)

Pragati Maidan

Pragati Maidan

The permanent exhibition complex forms the focus of the fifty-two hectare Pragati Maidan where several trade and industrial fairs are held each year. The complex consists of two main structures: the Hall of Nations and the Hall of Industries. The buildings are connected at the mezzanine level by means of ramps and they enclose an area for open-air exhibits. A limited competition was held in 1970 for the design of permanent exhibition spaces for the International Trade Fair two years later, and Raj Rewal's proposal was selected. The present buildings are the result of a subsequent alternative design which was evolved to meet the constraints of time, availability of materials and labour, but above all to reflect symbolically and technologically India's important place in the modern, industrializing community of nations. While the programme set forth by the government simply stated the number of square feet of exhibition space required, it was the architect who opted for a structure that would allow for vast, unobstructed areas; with the aid of a celebrated engineer, Mahendra Raj, the space-frame solution emerged. The plan of these pavilions is square with chamfered corners,

providing eight anchoring points. The chamfered corners were inspired by the plans of the tomb of the Mughal Emperor Humayun and the Taj Mahal. The main pavilion of the Hall of Nations has a clear span of 78 metres and a height varying from three metres to 21 metres, thereby providing a vast capacity for items to be exhibited, from books to bulldozers. The Hall of Industries, on the other hand, is a combination of four smaller pavilions connected by ramps enclosing a central area for open-air exhibits; utilities, toilets and other services are located under the ramps. Although each of the halls was initially conceived as a full pyramid, the truncated form was ultimately adopted in order to avoid unnecessary construction. The technological statement made by the architect and the engineer, and the circumstances of the actual execution, are most informative. The steel for this space-frame construction was expensive in India and not always available in the strengths desired. Labour, however, is not expensive and contractors have experience with reinforced concrete construction. As a result, the system was conceived, analysed by computer and built in the latter material. Octahedra measuring five metres from joint to joint were employed as the basic three-dimensional unit of the space frame, which rests on eight points around the essentially square plan and allows 11 metre-wide openings between the supports. An effective system of

environmental control inside the building was another outcome of the three-dimensional structure, as solid triangular panels at regular intervals provided sun-screens — a modern equivalent, according to some authors, of the traditional *jali* in Indian architecture. It was originally intended that the halls should be constructed of pre-cast elements but this had to be abandoned when all the contractors tendered for in situ concrete construction.

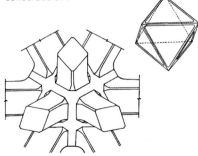

Nehru Pavilion
Raj Rewal Associates (1972)
Ⓢ Pragati Maidan
Pragati Maidan

075 A

The Pavilion was built to house the exhibition on Jawaharlal Nehru designed by the late Charles Eames. The pavilion was conceived as a two-level structure buried within a grassy embankment. This created architecture without pretentions, a departure from monumentality, and resulted in a concept in keeping with the exceptional qualities of the man it was designed to honour. At the upper level, the circulation is based on the traditional *parikarma*, a circumambulatory passage around an object of veneration. Rising from the centre of the pavilion is a truncated pyramid which forms a stepped roof over the lower level. Along the periphery of this are enclosed spaces for audiovisual presentations. At this level the visitors can have overviews of the display material at the lower level or can sit and listen to the speeches of Nehru, or see films on his life. The central stepped roof incorporates glass bricks which provide subdued light. The lower level is approached by a central flight of steps providing the visitor a total view of the hall below where exhibits are arranged in four sections. The enclosures at the corners are of double height for display of large objects.

Sri Ram Centre
for Performing Arts
Shiv Nath Prasad (1972)
🚇 Mandi House
4, Safdar Hashmi Marg

The Sri Ram Centre was sponsored by a private trust active in promoting dance, drama and music. The 0.25 ha site is in the heart of New Delhi, adjacent to other cultural institutions. The client's needs were extensive considering the small site available. This provided an opportunity to express individual functions at different levels, using distinct forms supported by independent structural supports. These diverse functional expressions in exposed concrete are woven together to work in harmony. Prasad, inspired by Le Corbusier, realized that he was essentially copying Le Corbusier's design patterns rather than the design process that led to them in his earlier works. In his later works he responded to this self-awareness. The Sri Ram Centre can be regarded as an example of the work resulting from the second phase of Le Corbusier's influence. In a true Rationalist manner Prasad explored the use of pure forms — the cylinder and rectangle — to create a piece of sculpture in reinforced concrete. The forms are by no means arbitrarily used: they express the different activities housed. The theatre is a cylindrical form and the rehearsal spaces are located in the rectangular mass. Other spaces are open-ended in character to meet the needs they serve. At the ground floor level, space enclosure is kept to a minimum so that the entrance hall and ticket foyer can also be used for exhibitions, and spaces flow out to encounter grass, trees and sunshine. A coffee shop opens off it for use by various art groups. Above the cloakrooms is a mezzanine floor containing the manager's flat and offices. In the basement is a small experimental theatre. The main theatre, seating 550 persons, is at the first-floor level and is 21 metres in diameter. It is supported on circumferential and radial beams cantilevering out from six columns. Above the cylindrical form of the theatre is the top floor, a large rectilinear mass supported at four cross-shaped columns placed at 19 metres centres with 6-metre cantilevers all around. This floor provides spaces for rehearsals, dancing, dormitories for visiting performers, and a small circular auditorium for puppet shows and films.

N.C.D.C. Office Building
Kuldip Singh (1973)
🚇 Hauz Khas
4, Siri Institutional Area,
Hauz Khas

077 B

The N.C.D.C. Office Building houses 78,000 square metres of office space
in an innovative building form. Two inclined nine-storey high wings join with
the central core at the top to create an
open atrium. Each typical floor is 11 metres × 25 metres of column-free space.
Alternate floors are tied together with
post-tensioned cables. The whole building is finished in exposed concrete with
bronze anodized window frames and
double-glazing.

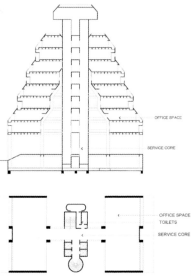

Tibet House
Shiv Nath Prasad (1974)
🚇 JLN Stadium
1, Institutional Area, Lodi Road

078 G

His Holiness the Dalai Lama founded The Tibet House in 1965. It was established to preserve and disseminate the unique cultural heritage of Tibet and to provide a centre for Tibetan and Buddhist studies. It has since widened its horizons. Before occupying this building in 1974, The Tibet House was located in the nearby residential locality of Jor Bagh. From

1959 onwards, Tibetans have been fleeing from the political upheavals in their homeland, travelling the difficult paths across the Himalayas into India. Many brought with them precious objects and books of religious and cultural significance. This formed the seed of the museum and the library. Located in the heart of New Delhi, the five-storey facility houses a museum of valuable Tibetan art and artefacts as well as a library with nearly 5,000 volumes of manuscripts and books, a resource centre, a conference hall, a gallery and a bookshop. Located on a small site in the Lodi Institutional Area and accessible from the main Lodi Road, the building bears a striking resemblance to Prasad's earlier work; the Sri Ram Centre for Performing Arts. The Tibet House though is smaller in scale and volume compared to its predecessor. The Tibet House has a similar use of geometric shapes, the upper cuboid perched over the lower cylindrical base. The upper storeys have an evenly partitioned brise-soleil adapted and inspired by Le Corbusier's architecture. The interiors of the building are also in concrete with a coffered ceiling in the small reception area on the ground floor. Recently the building facade has been painted with the Buddhist palette of yellow and red paint, thus diminishing the structure's original exposed RCC finish.

Mazaar of Fakhruddin Ali Ahmed

079 E

Habib Rahman (1975)
Central Secretariat
Parliament House

All three tombs that Rahman designed in Delhi were a conscious addition to the hundreds of tombs around the city. This tomb for President Fakhruddin Ali Ahmed is situated in the garden of a small old mosque next to Parliament House. Here, the design has been sensitive to the existing building. In this case the concept of the open linear forms — almost like a line drawing in space — was carried out to fruition. This form was an ongoing experiment for Rahman. Freestanding screens with an onion-dome silhouette enclose the tombstone mounted on a modest plinth. First sketched and then

conceived in cardboard cutout models, the proportions of this tomb and its *jalis* were finally refined in a full-scale plywood mockup. To achieve the thin frame members in marble, an unusual engineering solution was devised. All the structural elements are made in thin steel around which were clamped two C sections of carved marble, fixed with internal pins.

Yamuna Apartments

The Design Group (1975)

080 C

Govind Puri
Alaknanda, G. K. – III

Yamuna Apartments was one of the first co-operative group housing schemes to be completed in New Delhi, and although it was built within the same constraints applicable to other housing developments in the city — including DDA's own housing — it presented a refreshing contrast in concept and design. The layout of the complex is in the form of four radial streets converging on an asymmetrically placed central square that forms the focus. Staircases are used as an extension of the street. Building blocks are pushed to the periphery, giving rise to central free areas. The access staircases in each block form important design elements. These staircases wind around a central wall panel but at each half landing have an independent flight peeling off to lead directly to the front door of an adjacent residential unit. This device helps not only in giving the staircases externally a sense of gracefulness but in addition imbues each staircase with considerable importance as a transitional space between the common public areas and the private areas of each unit.

Malviya Nagar Housing
Golf View Apartments
Kuldip Singh (1976)
Ⓜ Malviya Nagar
Press Enclave Road, Saket

081 B

In a landmark of its kind, for the first time, the public agency DDA appointed a private architect in 1970 to plan and construct housing units for the Middle Income Group at Malviya Nagar. A unique concept of housing units was conceived, comprising two types. One was a three-storeyed unit, which linked up with the next to form a chain. The other was a four-storeyed cruciform unit with

services at the four corners and the main living spaces in the arms of the cruciform. The dwelling units are composed of varying modifications and combinations of a basic cruciform module. On elevation, these rectangular blocks reveal staggered terraces, balconies and rooms. Four of these modules are clustered to enclose an internal court. The problems of privacy and sleeping terraces for every dwelling unit, considered essential for the Delhi climate more than 40 years ago when A.C.s were almost nonexistent, have been successfully tackled by providing different sized units in each block rather than by limiting each block to a

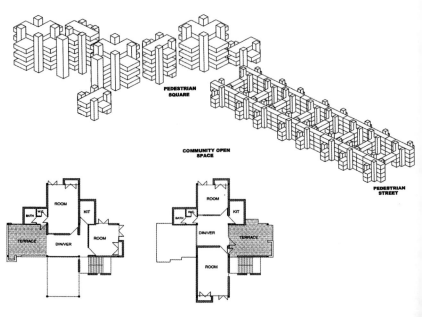

particular sized unit, and giving terraces to each unit, with high parapet walls having slits so that the breeze could penetrate the terraces but they still retained their privacy. The units linked up to form a 'Gully'—a pedestrian space leading to entrances of various houses, with open spaces alternating with covered spaces at various levels, where neighbours could meet, children play etc. The 'Gully' in turn formed a partial ring around a large open green space. The entire housing development was done in exposed brickwork. A majority of the clusters are arranged in a row linked by a pedestrian street through a series of hard paved courts, each framed at the entry, providing a pleasant rhythmic sequence. Vehicular access is provided through a series of culs-de-sac off a peripheral road, leaving undisturbed large central spaces for recreation. A prototype of 32 dwelling units was first built at Hauz Khas on a site of an acre and the development was called 'Usha Niketan'. 1,200 units were then constructed development at Malviya Nagar. Unfortunately the entire housing at Malviya Nagar was plastered over a few years after it was built at the insistence of the residents. Only a few blocks have retained the original exposed brick finish.

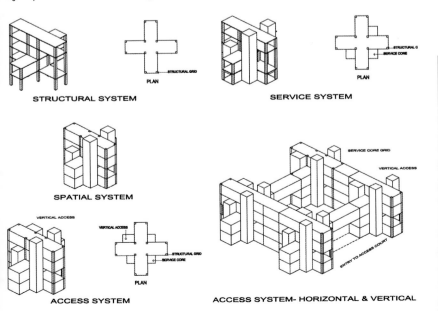

STRUCTURAL SYSTEM

SERVICE SYSTEM

SPATIAL SYSTEM

ACCESS SYSTEM

ACCESS SYSTEM- HORIZONTAL & VERTICAL

Tara Housing
Charles Correa (1978)
🚇 Govind Puri
Alaknanda, Don Bosco Road

082 C

Over 160 units (of two and three bed-rooms each) had to be accommodated at a density of 125 units per hectare. This could have been achieved in a pat-tern of low-rise high-density configura-tions (in which each family would have its own garden), except for the fact that the municipal code in Delhi does not al-low a building footprint to cover more than one third of the site. Thus, in or-der to use the full amount of floor ar-ea available on the site, the built form had to be at least four stories, or high-er. In order to avoid expensive solutions involving elevators, etc., it was decid-ed to build two decks of narrow double-storey units, stepped back in section so that the roof of the lower ones form terraces for those of the upper level.

This configuration creates a central land-scaped area, a kind of humidified zone, which provides both circulation as well as major community space for all the families. Stacked this way, the units protect each other against the hot dry climate of northern India — a centu-ries-old energy-saving pattern found in other parts of the world as well. Hu-midity to cool dry winds is provided by the trees and running water in the cen-tral community space. The two-bedroom units have an area of 84 square metres. They are 3 metres wide, 6 metres high and 15 metres long. The three-bedroom units cover 130 square metres and in-terlock in an L-shape, using one bay width on the lower level and two bays on the upper (or vice-versa). Every unit has an open-to-sky terrace of 10 square metres, partially protected by a per-gola, for sitting out during the morn-ings and evenings, and for sleeping out at night.

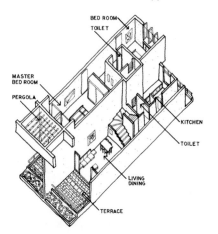

Polish Embassy »
Witold Ceckiewicz (1978)
🚇 Race Course
50-M Shantipath, Chanakyapuri

083 A

The result of a national competition, the complex of the Polish Embassy in New Delhi is a vast, open expanse of space, light and water. Situated opposite the Belgian Embassy, the Polish Embassy is one of the city's best examples of the usage of pilotis. Ceckiewicz's (b. 1924) structure, which he designed in asso-ciation with Stanislaw Denko, is raised through a series of columns, providing an underpass for parking, shade and cross-ventilation, as well as the structure's visual impact. Internally, the design is focused on a series of two picturesque semi-roofed courtyards. The architects' aim was to combat the harsh, hot Delhi summers; greenery, water and shade were the three elements they played with. The water features in the courtyards cooled the complex while the concrete sun breakers shielded the horizontal windows. The double elevation of the principle building and the shade it provides allowed the architects to use the surrounding greenery in an effective and flexible manner. NK Kothari assisted the architects in the design relating to construction. Today, the complex houses the International Finance Centre apart from the departments of the Polish Embassy.

National Institute of Public Finance and Policy ↗
084 B

Raj Rewal Associates (1979)
⊜ Hauz Khas
18/2, Satsang Vihar Marg,
Special Institutional Area

The NIPFP is primarily an academic institution, engaged in both research and training programmes in the realms of public finance and fiscal policy. Economists, administrators and the public all use these facilities for seminars and study, many coming from outside Delhi for a short intensive stay. The design concept takes into account the necessity for three different components: academic spaces, hostel facilities and residences. The three functions have been integrated into a complex that has a hierarchy of internal and external open spaces. First of all there is the three-storey academic building with its lecture halls, offices, auditorium, library and canteen. Secondly, a hostel building with adjoining common facilities for approximately 35 research scholars is located next to the teaching building. Finally, there is residential accommodation for the Director and the teaching staff in a separate wing. The entire complex has been built utilizing a concrete structural frame, with concrete slab floors; the ceilings of rooms have been left without rendering in order to make the texture of the wooden shuttering visible. However, all of the exterior wall surfaces have been covered with a buff-coloured sandstone. To enrich this exterior texture, the knobs which serve to tie the sandstone to the wall panels have been left visible and covered with sandstone grit.

Press Enclave Housing
Cooperative Group Housing

085 B

Ashish Ganju (1979)
Malviya Nagar
Press Enclave Road, Saket

Located in a suburb of Delhi, this site of 1.7 hectares accommodates 180 apartments of three basic categories: 65 square metres, 100 square metres, and 120 square metres for members of the Press Association of India. The grouping is in modules of five apartments, each three and a half storeys high with units interlocked on the ground floor. This module generates compact spaces, which encourage social interaction, enable easy maintenance and allow for variety in layout. The resultant open spaces are structured according to a hierarchy of functions: private courtyards and terraces; semi-private entrance porches; and public garden courts shared by six or seven modules. These are linked by paths across vehicle-free pedestrian zones. The structure is of load-bearing brick masonry with RCC slabs for floors and roofs. Service areas are stacked vertically to promote efficiency and economy in plumbing. The orientation of the apartments and their spatial and volumetric design, tunnels monsoon breezes through rooms. The structure is formed by parallel load-bearing brick masonry walls supporting a short-span reinforced concrete slab which significantly reduces the cost of construction. The parallel walls also generate deep plan houses with major openings on north and south faces allowing only the winter sun to enter the rooms. The long east and west walls are either shared between houses or have kitchens, bathrooms, and private open courts/terraces attached which provide mutual shading from the summer sun and protection from the hot winds. The buildings function as passive solar engines to provide maximum environmental comfort by natural means. The siteplan allows adequate penetration of sunlight into garden courts, enabling vegetation to flourish for a comfortable micro-climate.

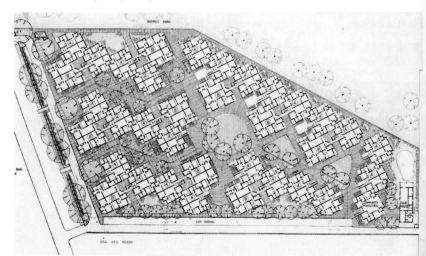

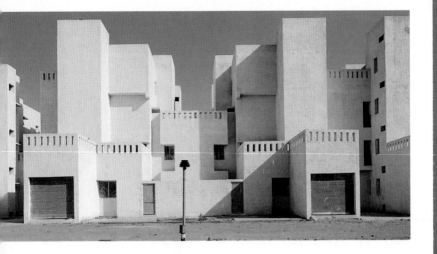

Sheikh Sarai Housing

086 B

Raj Rewal Associates (1982)
Malviya Nagar
Phase I, Sheikh Sarai

This low-rise high-density scheme for 550 units is designed on the basis of a self-financing scheme for the Delhi Development Authority. It segregates pedestrian and vehicular movement and provides for interlinked squares of varying scales for community activities. All the units have been provided with courtyards or rooftop terraces. The programme for 550 apartments was based on the norms in force for self-financed housing in south Delhi. Six different types of units, ranging in area from 70 square metres to 120 square metres, were organized into two distinct clusters, three and four storeys in height. Density is approximately 100 apartments per hectare. An important aspect

of this solution is the pattern of interrelated squares of an intimate scale that has been created. While there is a clear demarcation between pedestrian and vehicular spaces within these, the movement of people within the enclosures has been closely aligned with the access points for vehicles on the periphery. The scale of the various squares has been adjusted to encourage and to serve different community activities. All the units have been provided with a courtyard or rooftop terrace, the walls or parapets of which have narrow slits ensuring both privacy and good ventilation. Although the structure is of reinforced concrete posts and beams, the walls are of brick infill covered with roughcast plaster. This is customary for economical mass housing in the region, and allows for some modification by the users. All the units have been provided with courtyards or rooftop terraces.

Regionalism

Asian Games Village

Raj Rewal Associates (1982)

🚇 Green Park

Khel Gaon Marg

The 'Village' is located in South Delhi on a fourteen-hectare site adjacent to the ruins of Siri Fort, an erstwhile medieval capital city. The village was built to house the participants of the Ninth Asian Games and contains 700 dwelling units: 200 townhouses and 500 apartments. The layout simulates the traditional urban morphology of North India,

incorporating as its basic unit the typical urban neighbourhood: the *mohalla*. This concept is translated into a sequence of spaces interlinked with narrow pedestrian streets. The spaces are enlivened through a careful mix of recreational and commercial uses. The pedestrian streets are consciously broken up into comprehensible lengths and often defined by gateways. So, there are pauses, points for rest, and changing vistas. The creation of this traditional pedestrian street network—narrow and shaded by cantilevered projections from the apartment buildings—link all the housing units and promote intimate encounters between people. The squares serve clusters of twelve to thirteen dwelling units and encourage a sense of belonging. A distinct hierarchy of such landscaped squares climaxes in a central square. A complementary road network, along the periphery of the site, provides vehicular access to cul-de-sac parking squares, and to individual garages or car porches attached to the townhouses and apartment blocks. The floor plans of the housing units have been so designed that they can be linked together to form a street, create squares or generate clusters. The townhouses are grouped on the periphery with private courtyards screened by high walls. These are double storeyed structures with double-height living rooms to facilitate natural ventilation. In contrast, the apartments are located along the inner pedestrian network and vary in size from 90 to 200 square metres. Each unit has its own open-to-sky space in the form of either a courtyard or a private terrace. Concern for colour, texture and durability guided the selection of building materials and finishes: Delhi quartzite stone for the courtyard walls, white or red sandstone for pathways, and stone aggregate finish for exterior walls. Gates, doors and windows have different colours to give a sense of identity to dwelling units.

Le Meridien Hotel ⩙ 088 F
Raja Aederi (1982)
Rajiv Chowk
Connaught Place, Outer Circle

The first hotel in India with a large atrium going up to 70 metres high, the 420-key hotel features large public areas and a commercial complex, covering a total built-up area of 7,00,000 square feet. This was also the first curtain wall building in India and the first with capsule elevators. The swimming pool is located at a height of 18 metres above road level and is cantilevered beyond the building. 67 metres above the lobby is a restaurant suspended like a chandelier and accessed from four diagonally placed plate girder bridges. A restaurant at terrace level gives a magnificent view of Parliament House, Rashtrapati Bhavan, and Raj Path.

National Dairy Development Board

089 B

Achyut Kanvinde (1982)

🚇 Green Park

Safdarjang Enclave, Near Kamal Cinema

The National Dairy Development Board office building is located in the South Delhi area on a plot of land measuring about 3,500sqm. It has a floor area ratio of one hundred and a height limitation

of 26 metres. Most of the office buildings generally under planning control tend to result in a rigid and regimental block-like expression. Therefore, effort was made by the architect in this project to evolve a structure system that allows receding setback. This allows areas of green spaces to be planted around work areas to create an intimate humanistic environment. This also helped the building establish its identity. The

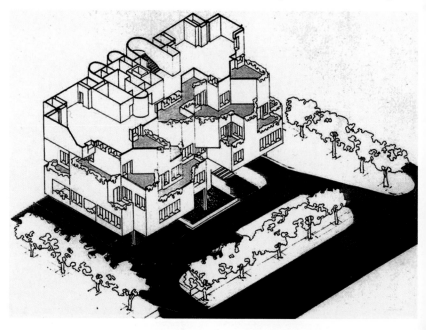

structure is mainly oriented to take advantage of southern and eastern orientation. Service areas are located mainly along the western face of the building. With its irregular terracing and hanging roof gardens, this six-storeyed structure assumes a modest, almost domestic character befitting both its immediate residential surroundings and New Delhi's garden city character. The building is an alternative to conventional office planning in India. The socialistic emphasis on office-worker amenities and an environmentally sensitive workspace is reminiscent of Dutch architect Hermann Hertzberger's works. The building sets back from the street in receding, irregular terraces. Vertical services — fire escapes, main stairs and elevator towers — are concentrated at the rear of the structure as clearly expressed shafts. The pyramidal effect of terracing on the floor areas of the upper storey is appropriately exploited. More exclusive functions such as private offices for the chairman and director, and meeting rooms for the board and other committees, are grouped at the top of the building. The larger, more public spaces, including reception and the various departmental offices, comprise the lower floors. The exterior is finished with a rough plaster composed of white marble grit plaster; interior walls are plastered and whitewashed. Extensive built-in wooden shelving provides for storage of a large quantity of documents. The floors are of polished grey-green sandstone; terraces are paved with scrap pieces of the same stone. The quality of execution and finishes reflects the architect's attention to detailing and an experienced yet exploratory attitude to design.

Centaur Hotel ⌄

Airports Authority of India (1982)
🛪 IGI Airport
Indira Gandhi International Airport

090 B

Centaur Hotel is a five-star hotel located close to the Indira Gandhi International Airport and the national highway. Due to its convenient location it is easily accessible from different parts of Delhi. This hotel is a perfect blend of traditional and modern architecture. It was built in 1982 and completed within 18 months, just in time to welcome business and leisure travellers who visited Delhi for the Asian Games held in 1982. It is constructed of white and red Jaipur stone. It has a typical fort-like appearance with a swimming pool right in the middle. The hotel has a unique star-shaped design with four arch-shaped guest room wings pointing in four directions. The guest room wings enclose a very large atrium space, which accommodates all the public functions of the hotel.

New Delhi Municipal Council Palika Kendra Building

091 D

Kuldip Singh (1983)

Rajiv Chowk
Parliament Street, New Delhi-110001,
Opp. Jantar Mantar

The original conception for the City Centre won a prestigious all-India competition held by the New Delhi Municipal Committee in 1965. The Centre was conceived as a monumental expression of the growth of New Delhi. Sited along a principal axis that links Parliament House to the old walled city, its forms were inspired by the old geometry of the 18th-century structures located across the road at Jantar Mantar, an astronomical observatory. The form of the eighteen-storey tower is integral to its structural concept. It is supported on a central core and four shear walls which curve outwards from a width of 28m at the top floor level to a width of 64m at the ground floor level. A large three-storey high opening between two shear walls provides a monumental entrance hall. Four large bells salvaged from the clock tower of the old town hall hang here, symbolizing historical continuity. The shear walls at the apex open into a vast sky gallery providing a panoramic view of New Delhi's verdant townscape. All facades have the impression of concrete in handcrafted shuttering. Internal public areas are clad in polished granite stone to minimize maintenance costs. In keeping with the building's public function and monumental character, each aspect of detailing has been motivated by functional efficiency and long-term economy. The building has two basements and 19 floors of office space. Basements contain parking, storage, plant and equipment. The third level, accessible by an independent direct lift, houses the Committee Room, President's office and offices for the members. Phase II of New Delhi City Centre, is conceived as a meeting place for citizens of New Delhi and their civic officials. Development of the site is in the form of a large elevated open plaza flanked by Palika Kendra, (City Centre Phase I) built earlier, on one side and the new office building on the other. The focus of the new office building is an atrium-like space, generous and monumental in proportion. The office building has a structure of eight shear walls, which curve inwards and upwards to create the atrium, broad at the base and narrow at the apex, with 10 floors of column-free space on either side of the atrium. Two sets of vertical cores, comprising 14 high-speed lifts and three staircases rise up from the centre to serve the upper floors. At the four corners, along with the shear walls are the four service cores comprising toilets, electrical rooms and an additional four staircases. A small separate block has been conceived as the focal point for the open plaza. This block was planned to house an auditorium seating 800 and a three-storeyed public library, however it is now constructed as a convention centre.

Engineers India House

Raj Rewal Associates (1983)

🚇 AIIMS

1, Bhikaji Cama Place, RK Puram

092 B

Engineers India House forms part of the commercial district centre at Bhikaji Cama Bazaar, New Delhi. The building is the first major office to be constructed within the Bhikaji Cama Bazaar area. It houses the administrative, design, financial and public relations offices of a public-sector organization dealing in design consultancy for industry and technology in India and elsewhere. The design has four cores on the corners, each containing lifts, staircases and services, resulting in a large hall in the middle for flexible office planning. These cores form major structural elements and, along with four central shear walls, support an average office floor of 54 × 24.6 metres. The long spans and cantilevers expressed on the facade create the appropriate image for an engineering organization. The office floors are stepped creating overhangs on the south side, protecting the building from sun, and creating space for roof terraces on the north side. The aim was to create an air-conditioned office space which would have the least possible initial outlay and subsequently minimum running expense. It was also decided that the larger parameter of the building should face north-south and use cores and floor overhangs to create a micro-climate. The form of the building is derived with the aim of saving energy. The cores are designed in such a manner that they also cut down harsh glare from the south-west, while three-quarters

of the slabs are in shadow during the day. The stepping of floors within the cores and extending different floors to the east and west ends of the building creates a zone of surface under shadow, thus reducing temperatures. The structural cores along with the extended floors form a giant sun breaker. Engineers India House is entered by car directly from the road and has two levels of parking underneath. Pedestrians enter the upper ground floor either by means of external steps or directly from the plaza. The central part of the entrance is ten metres high and gives access to the mezzanine at three levels, providing changing views of information and exhibition spaces. Lifts and staircases are provided at two ends of the hall, to allow for rush-hour traffic and provide two distinct fire exits.

The structure of the reinforced concrete diagrid is exposed internally, and the ribs on the roof slab form a ceiling pattern incorporating lighting panels and air-conditioning ducts. The sheear walls and structural cores are clad, externally and internally, with beige sandstone two and a half centimetres thick. The textural and tonal variations of stone create a rich surface. The internal stone cladding is polished to harmonize with the flooring and the teak paneling. The partitions within the halls are movable and can be varied according to functional requirements. The lower two floors are used as public relations offices, containing exhibition spaces and small conference rooms. The building is 52.5 metres high and has a total floor area of 18,200 square metres with a capacity of 1,800 people.

Belgian Embassy 093 A
Satish Gujral (1983)
Race Course
50-N Shantipath, Chanakyapuri

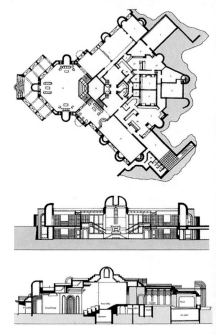

Satish Gujral was commissioned by the Belgian government to design and build the Chancery, the ambassador's residence and servants' quarters of its embassy in Delhi. Satish Gujral's (b. 1925) experiments with sculpture, paintings, murals, graphics, architecture and interior design had established him as a pivotal figure of Indian expressionism. His forays into architecture are few but he will be remembered for his striking design of the Belgian Embassy. Gujral based his design on the concept of organic architecture. This he defined as design which places an emphasis on the direct use of materials, the exposure of their surfaces, and an independence of all parts of the structure with one another, as well as the sum total of parts and its relationship to the environmental setting. 'Organic' therefore implies logical and natural growth, a harmony within the structure and a sense of belonging evident in the relationship of the building. The design was laid down along a central east-west axis; the Chancellor's residence and a sunken tennis court were added later. The design places each building in such a manner that they are all independent yet tied together by a series of passages and landscape, which becomes the binding force. The landscape was designed as a means to integrate the various buildings in the compound. To create private

and semiprivate areas in a way that did not impose on the built form, the landscape rises in parts forming upper-level gardens and gets cut out at parts forming tennis courts. It also helps to conceal the servants' quarters and at the same time protects them against the Delhi sun. The building is finished in exposed brickwork, an abundantly used local material, to create an organic aesthetic inherent in the material. The buildings are moulded in such a way that the structures look more like sculpture rather than a building. The facades are punctuated with well-crafted brick arches, domes and window openings of varied sizes that let in natural sunlight.

Indian Institute of Technology
J. K. Chowdhury (1984)
🚇 Hauz Khas
Hauz Khas

094 B

The Indian Institute of Technology is an autonomous educational complex situated in South Delhi on a site of 126 hectares. It was designed for an initial student population of 1,750, expected to rise to 3,000 eventually. The Academic complex is located roughly in the centre of a linear site between two natural storm-water channels. The residences are on the far side of these channels — faculty and staff members on the Southeast and students on the Northwest. The staff housing is designed to be a self-contained community with residences of several types planned around a primary school, staff club and shopping centre. The undulating topography of the site has been preserved and landscape elements are so planned as to merge with the natural environment. The Academic blocks consist of three-storeyed parallel buildings oriented north-south, housing the teaching and research facilities in specialized disciplines. A seven-storey block placed at right angles to these blocks houses the common basic disciplines. It connects the longest three-storey academic block with the administrative block. On the roof of this big block are two floors of common rooms, dramatising the skyline. Lecture theatres of various sizes and forms are placed along corridors which are the major spines of communication. The courtyards formed by these link-corridors provide a sequence of open spaces punctuated and embellished by different types of multi-storeyed open staircases. The lecture theatres are finished in rough stone aggregate in pleasant contrast to the exposed concrete surfaces of the blocks. A reinforced concrete hyperbolic paraboloid shell covers the 1,200-seat auditorium. Hostels for the students and research scholars are four-storey brick buildings with common sleeping terraces at the end of each wing. An activity centre with a club swimming pool, a multipurpose hall, an auditorium and an amphitheatre serves as a recreational and cultural focus for the students and faculty.

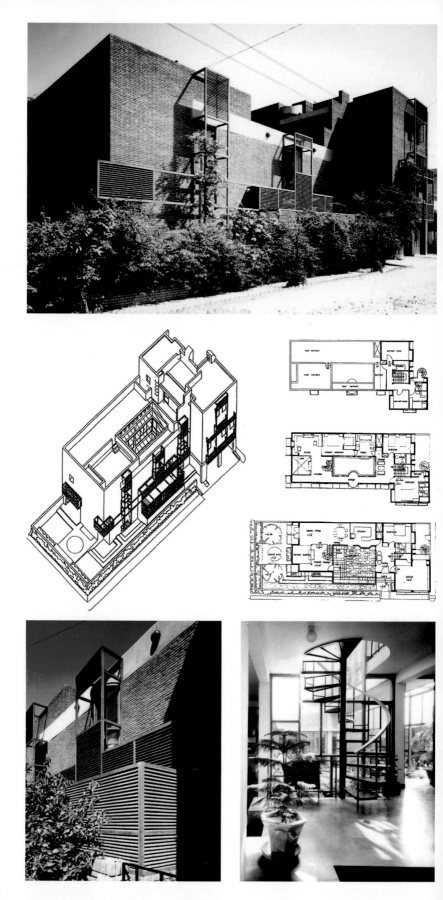

Kubba House «
Ashish Ganju (1984)
Paschim Vihar West
J-2, Reserve Bank Enclave,
Paschim Vihar

095 A

Located in a western suburb of New Delhi, this is the house of a couple of doctors and their aged parents. The site is a rectangular plot of 400 square yards with a long south-facing side and a short west-facing side fronting access roads, while the north side is a party wall and the east side fronts a service lane. The design was evolved around a central courtyard into which the major openings focus. The courtyard is screened from the street outside by a timber frame inset partly with louvers. The frame extends over all the external walls with the louvers set at different angles to provide visual privacy, to allow the winter sun to penetrate into the courtyard, and to protect the windows from the monsoon rains. The interior planning allows the house to function as two discrete but connected sections — an open plan series of spaces on two levels for the doctor and his wife, and a more conventional series of bedrooms around lounges for the parents and live-in guests. At first-floor level the courtyard is bridged across the south side by a gallery which connects the two sections and shades the courtyard in summer. The main building materials are brick and timber, with roof/intermediate floors of reinforced concrete, and flooring of stone.

Gyan Bharti School ⌃ ⌄
C.P. Kukreja Associates (1985)
Malviya Nagar
Saket, Near PVR Cinema

096 B

The school consists of 64 classrooms, laboratories, an assembly hall and ancillary buildings for a student body of 2,000. The complex consists of three blocks of buildings, one for the primary school, one for the middle school and the third for the senior school. These blocks were built one at a time in three phases. The large sports field of the school campus is located to the west end of the site. Subsequently, a large open-air theatre with a tensile roof has been added between the senior school and the middle school building. The underside of the seating areas contains reception offices and other smaller spaces in the lower ground floor level. The building is part of the earlier oeuvre of C. P. Kukreja's style where arched openings and exposed brickwork were provided over the windows on the facade to create an association with the region's historic architectural heritage, particularly that of the Islamic Era.

Regionalism

Baha'i Temple
Fariborz Sahba (1986)

🚇 Kalkaji Mandir
Bahapur, Kalkaji

097 C

The Baha'i faith originated in 19th century Iran when Mirza Husayn-Ali (1817 – 1892) declared that he was the Prophet of a new religion. Central to the teachings of this religion are the oneness of God, the oneness of religion and the oneness of mankind. Although there is a Baha'i World Centre located in Akka and in Haifa in Palestine, near where the faith's founder Mirza died, it has neither priesthood nor ritual. Local Spiritual Assemblies numbering over 27,000 exist throughout the world; members are encouraged to obey the laws of their respective states and the legally-constituted authorities, but they are forbidden to participate in any political parties or ideological movements. The teachings of the faith place emphasis upon the development of good character through prayer, meditation and work done in service to humanity — all considered expressions of worship of God. The Baha'i faith imposes only two constraints on the design of a house of worship: that it be nine-sided, with a central hall, and that it admit natural light. Iranian-born architect Fariborz Sahba conceived of the New Delhi House of Worship as a lotus flower, a completely symmetrical form. The lotus, a symbol of purity commonly associated with religion, is found throughout Indian art and architecture. The structure is composed of three ranks of nine petals each, springing from a podium upon which the building rises above the surrounding plain. The first two ranks curve inward, embracing the inner dome; the third layer curves outward to form canopies over the nine entrances. The petals, constructed of reinforced concrete cast in place, are clad in white Greek marble panels, pre-cut in Italy to the surface profiles and to patterns related to the geometry. White marble also covers all the interior floors, while the insides of the petals are bush-hammered concrete. The walkways and stairs in the podium are finished in local red sandstone. The double-layered interior dome, modelled on the innermost portion of the lotus, consists of 54 ribs with concrete shells inbetween. The central hall is ringed by nine arches, which provide the main support for the superstructure. The entire superstructure is designed to function as a series of skylights, with glazing at the apex of the inner petals, the internal vertical surfaces of the outer petals, and the external side of the entrance petals. Light is thus filtered into the central hall in the same way that it passes through the lotus flower. Nine reflecting pools surround the building, their form suggesting the leaves of the lotus. External illumination is arranged so that the lotus structure appears to float on water. Additional landscaping consists of earth berms surrounding the podium, laid brick pathways, and plantings.

Structure and Building
Unlike many other natural forms, the lotus proved structurally sound and buildable. The completed House of Worship is a full and unmodified realisation of the architect's original scheme. Owing to the enormous complexity of the concept, nearly 18 months of work with state-of-the-art computer techniques were needed to translate the lotus into structural designs and working drawings. It was necessary to evolve geometry for preparing the layout and determining structural dimensions. Using computer-generated diagrams and geometric information, it was decided that the entrance and outer leaves would have spherical surfaces and that the inner leaves would be formed from toroidal surfaces. Ventilation and cooling are based on techniques

traditional to the Indian subcontinent whereby the building itself functions as a chimney. Fresh air, cooled as it passes over the fountains and pools, is drawn in through openings in the basement, up into the central hall, and expelled through a vent at the top of the structure. During the three month humid season a set of exhaust fans in the basement recycles air from the main hall into the cool basement and back. The Baha'i House of Worship represents a striking marriage of architecture and engineering, of a natural form with state of the

art computer technology. As little as ten years ago, it would have been impossible to realise the design as faithfully and elegantly. Earlier methods would have required a far more simplistic approach to design and at least two years longer to complete. The building derives its form, not symbolically or in its ornamentation, but literally from the shape and symmetry of the lotus flower. No refinement of the architect's concept seems to have been lost in translating the flower form through the complex geometry to working drawings to the fully realised structure.

Embassy of Finland

Raili and Reima Pietilä (1986)
Race Course
E 3, NyayaMarg, Chanakyapuri

Architects Ms. Raili Pietilä and Mr. Reima Pietilä won a national competition for the Finnish Embassy in New Delhi in 1963. However, their plans were not implemented until the 1980s and the Embassy was completed in the summer of 1986. It was built by Indian contractors under Finnish supervision. Awarding the first prize to the Pietiläs' entry bearing the lyrical pseudonym 'Snow speaks on the mountains', the assessors complemented its aesthetic uniqueness against mere rational excellence. When building of the embassy finally got under way in 1980, it was found that the idea behind the project and the form of its message were still fresh. The competition brief stated that the purpose of the building was to be 'a portrait of Finland abroad'. The Embassy stands like a Finnish island adrift in the middle of India, permeated by an Indian spirit of place. Reima Pietilä was a highly individualistic architect in the era otherwise dominated by rationalist aspiration. He sought to develop an architecture adapted to the Finnish geographical and mental reality on the basis of his morphological studies of the Finnish landscape and analyses of the unique characteristics of the

Finnish language. The Finnish Embassy in New Delhi is an example of his expressive style. The embassy's design ideas focus on the roof shapes, which create a sculptural site layout seen from the air. The architects thought back to the shapes of Lake Kitkajärvi in Northern Finland, where the Ice Age combed the rock into parallel furrows and hills, and where glaciers created lakes, serpentine peninsulas and islands. The irregularly cut roof eaves resemble the snow sculptures that are formed in the winter ice around the Gulf of Finland. Being geographically and climatically estranged and thrown into the Embassy district's international exhibition of national building styles, it would seem impossible to practise the regional origin for a building. But the Pietiläs' felt that this doesn't have to apply to nature-architecture, for trees have the same crowns of foliage in India as they do in Finland. The building reaches upwards with its slender roof-forms and builds itself naturally into the place and landscape. Often said to be among the most beautiful buildings in New Delhi, the Embassy compound comprises the Ambassador's residence, the chancery, the staff apartments, and a Finnish sauna. The interior of the residence was planned by Antti Nurmesniemi, and the large ceramic bas-relief in its hall is by Rut Bryk. Maj-Lis Rosenbröijer was in charge of landscape and garden design.

Jeevan Bharti Building
Life Insurance Corporation
Charles Correa (1986)
Rajiv Chowk
Janpath, Outer Circle, Connaught Place

This office complex for the Life Insurance Corporation of India (LIC) is situated on the outer road of Connaught Circus, and acts as a pivot between the colonnades of Connaught Place and the new generation of high-rise towers that now surround it. Thus the building is both proscenium and backdrop: a twelve-storey stage-set whose faceted glass surfaces reflect the buildings and trees around Connaught Place, and beyond which the new high-rise imagery of Delhi can be glimpsed. The two lower levels of the complex consist of shopping decks

and restaurants, while the upper levels of offices are located in two separate wings, generating a total built-up area of 63,000 square metres. Connecting the two wings is a great pergola, 98 metres long, supported at either end by masonry piers and in the middle by a single column. A city proposal for an elevated pedestrian walkway (not constructed) was to pass between the two blocks, allowing pedestrians to traverse the building as a great *darwaza*, i.e. gateway, defined by the portico-form. The red sandstone of the piers wraps around the rear facade, culminating in the twin elevator towers which frame the slot for the pedestrian bridge. On this side of the building, the windows are deeply recessed into the masonry so as to protect them from the heat of the Delhi sun.

Regionalism

Central Institute of Educational Technology (CIET)

 100 B

Raj Rewal Associates (1986)
🜨 Hauz Khas
Aurobindo Marg

The transformations in the Central Institute for Education Technology (CIET) illustrate many of Raj Rewal's dual concerns. The courtyard as a space is based on an urban typology, while the walls, finished in sandstone, allude to the vernacular architecture of Jaisalmer and Fatehpur Sikri. The treatment of the exposed concrete structural system and infill stone panels also illustrate Raj Rewal's simultaneous concern for context and type. The use and treatment of the stone screens relate to a vernacular, while the monumental quality of the exposed structural system in a distinctly urban manner, represents the public nature of the building that presupposes distinct public and private realms. The courtyard typology has been used in a traditional *madrasa* character, with its multiple levels of terraces and shaded alcoves reminiscent of the screened balconies of Jaisalmer. The building is designed for the CIET and contains, besides classrooms and administrative offices, sophisticated studios for sound and film recordings. Courtyards at various levels and an amphitheatre in the main courtyard form a series of open spaces that collectively offer a unique opportunity for discussion groups, theatre and even educational film making. The essence of the courtyard typology is instituted in its morphology. The courtyard opens up into terraces at the upper levels; setbacks are introduced, rooms are pushed towards the edge and pavilion-like structures define the internal edge. The courtyard and the internal surfaces are treated as the public realm. With most of the classrooms along the outer edge of the building, the internal edge is formed of circulation spaces on all levels and modulated to create semi-open

spaces, sitting alcoves and terraces, thereby further reinforcing a public realm along the edge of the courtyard. The essence of the building appears in the modulation of its scale as interpreted at various levels. The monumental public scale is maintained by the rhythmic structural system with its characteristic exposed concrete circular columns and waffle slabs, and the human scale, conducive to small gatherings, is defined by the sandstone infill panels and a variety of fenestration treatments. While the facades allude to a vernacular scale and texture, the treatment is modern. The sizes of the sandstone panels are those that are easily available and the detailing provides the tolerance required for such work by unskilled labour. The patterns in their arrangement are based on a module derived from the size of the stone as well as by the variations in window openings, thereby allowing windows of different dimensions to be placed as per requirements. Rewal has also experimented with using sandstone as a means of concrete shuttering as well as using 2.5 centimetre sandstone slabs to construct partitions and even external walls referring to the vernacular systems derived from Jaisalmer and Fatehpur Sikri. The sandstone slab representing a basic building tool has been used with versatility and imagination, akin to its use in traditional architecture.

Janakpuri District Centre ⌃ 101 A

The Design Group (1986)
🚇 Janakpuri West
Near the B-1 periphery, Janakpuri

The District Centre at Janakpuri, developed on a 35-acre site, serves as an important shopping centre, catering to the needs of the area's large residential population. Simultaneously it provides for social, cultural and recreational requirements through the provision of cinemas, a meeting hall, library, cultural centre and a hotel. The graceful colonnaded arcade and the landscaped central garden of Connaught Place is an image of New Delhi that is easily identifiable. In the creation of a major new commercial centre in West Delhi this image represented an important point of reference. Thus the proposed shopping centre at Janakpuri has a handsome double-height colonnade, which defines and ties together all shopping spaces. This in turn extends visually and relates to the landscaped courts and gardens of the District Centre. Easy access has been ensured for retail shopping. The high colonnades were brought to the threshold of the main arterial roads and were carried through the entire District Centre, creating covered walkways and shopping courts for the dwellers. All car parking was to be put below ground.

National Dairy Development Board Staff Housing

102 C

The Design Group (1988)
NOIDA Sector 16
Near MAX Hospital, Sector 17, NOIDA, UP

This project has a hundred dwelling units on a two-acre site for the National Dairy Development Board (NDDB) staff at NOIDA. The site, which is almost triangular, faces a storm-water drain and embankment on the west. The residential units are distributed along the boundaries. All parking has been restricted to the northeastern edge of the site and partially extends along the southeastern boundary. The remaining land is landscaped. The scheme is composed around a large central garden and the design is based on multilevel streets connecting units of apartments. The residents' need to socialize in multilevel urban housing has been addressed by including a leisure club. The Type D (65 sq) units are located in a staggered row along the western boundary of the site. A pedestrian walkway serves the apartments and forms a bridge at upper levels, which is 0.52m lower than each apartment, thereby ensuring a certain degree of privacy. The bridge extends all along the length of the site and is served by four separate staircases. The club is designed on two levels in the centre of the development and provides recreational facilities for the residents. A small guesthouse is located above it on the second floor, whilst service facilities and apartments for personnel are proposed towards the northern corner of the site.

Kali Bari

Sumit Ghosh and Associates (1988)

🚇 Hauz Khas
Outer Ring Road,
Opposite Vasant Vihar

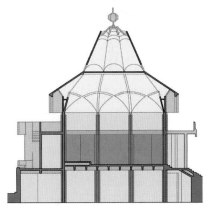

The design of a modern Kali temple is particularly challenging as there has been a radical change in the physical relationship of spaces traditionally assigned for the devotees (*sabhamandapa*) and the Deity (*garbagriha*). The new liturgy has thrown open the walls of the *garbagriha* to the worshipper. The amalgamation of the *sabhamandapa* and the *garbagriha* leads to a situation which may be described as the creation of a 'temple within a temple'. This is exactly what is attempted at the Dakshin Delhi Kali Bari. The bronze-clad *garbagriha*, designed in traditional architectural style using the 'Bengal roof', sits like a jewel within the *sabhamandapa*. The superstructure of the temple employs the conoid, whose form and shape help recall the curved forms of traditional Kali Baris. Its geometry not only gives the form a light, soaring feeling, but is manipulated to provide soft, indirect light and natural ventilation to the main congregational area which houses about 300 devotees. The *shikhara*, which has traditionally been the symbolic external expression of the Deity, is further enhanced by divorcing it from its function as a roof and treating it more like a crown to the temple. A copper *kalash*,

designed to hover delicately above it, further accentuates the *shikhara*, which itself is sculpted to give it a sense of lightness and transparency. Chandrakant Bhatt and his wife Manimala collaborated on the bronze cladding design for the *garbagriha* and the design of the *kalash*. In retrospect, it is interesting to note that from the quite contemporary expression of the *shikhara* and temple, the modernity gradually fades out as one approaches the Deity. The Kali Bari reflects a fairly traditional architectural form. Indeed, it must be noted that the architects, despite their modernist stance, were quite willing to accept traditional images and forms when they seemed to emanate a timeless power which contemporary expression would not be able to match. This acceptance, indeed defense, was highlighted dramatically in the climactic stages just before the dedication of the temple to the Deity.

Delhi Public School, NOIDA
Sikka Associates (1988)
🚇 Golf Course
Sector 30, NOIDA, UP

104 C

The Delhi Public School Society, whose schools have a distinguished reputation for maintaining a high standard of education, set up this branch in the new and developing township of the New Okhla Industrial Development Area (NOIDA), outside New Delhi. It was decided to develop the school gradually, starting from a four-section junior school consisting of 20 classrooms in 1982 and finishing with a four-storeyed building in 1988. School buildings were no longer looked upon as merely mundane shelters for the teacher and the taught. In planning the school, the designers endeavored to create an environment conducive to the children's learning and character building. At DPS this has been achieved by providing a playful environment for junior children and creating a sophisticated arrangement for the senior students, while at the same time meticulously maintaining a rigid formality in planning. A plot of land measuring 258 metres × 233 metres in Sector 30, NOIDA, was allotted as the site for constructing the school. This plot is situated at the intersection of a road 60 metres × 30 metres wide. Five acres of green space were earmarked by the masterplan at the rear, which of

the site have been usefully assimilated in the design and development of the school. Each classroom is oriented north-south to maximize comfort, and is open on at least two sides to ensure adequate light and ventilation. Thus, learning in the classrooms is not meant to be a closed-door affair but is very much a part of the surrounding environment and activities. The school is grouped into junior, middle and senior sections in order to retain the identity of the different age groups while at the same time allowing for considerable interaction. In addition to the usual regular spaces for academic activities, other spaces for sports facilities and a multi-purpose hall were also developed. Efforts have been made to keep the academic activity away from the noisy highway. By locating the entry points for the students on the side road, they are totally insulated from the highway traffic. Moreover, the students' movements are only restricted towards the play area while the front landscaped open space remains a pleasant foreground serving as an entrance space for visitors. The structure, which has been designed to ultimately become a four-storeyed building, is a composite load-bearing one with columns and beams where necessary. The entire exterior has a natural exposed brick finish, which has helped in maintaining visual uniformity and continuity.

State Trading Corporation Building

105 D

Raj Rewal Associates (1989)

⊖⊝ Rajiv Chowk

Jawahar Vyapar Bhavan, Janpath

This skyscraper for the State Trading Corporation (STC) in the heart of New Delhi's commercial centre exemplifies the very nature of contradiction that has become the focus of Raj Rewal's work—how best to adapt localized conditions of labour, technology, climate and context to a complicated brief from the client. The massing of the building is a direct outcome of the programme, which required the three tenants, the Central Cottage Industries Corporation, the Handloom and Handicrafts Export Corporation and the State Trading Corporation to have independent control of circulation and services over their sections of the building. This brief from the client and the location of the site at a critical junction on Jan Path provided Raj Rewal with the necessary context for design. It is an L-shaped building of staggered heights, enclosing a three storeyed retail podium that faces the road intersection. The massing is developed towards the centre of the site so that the various steps of the building, including the retail podium, maintain the street scale. These building setbacks, along with the podium are designed as rooftop gardens. While being of direct advantage to the offfices that overlook them, these gardens also soften the edges of an otherwise large building. Aside from the massing, the dominant feature of the building is the expression of its structure which, besides determining its floor plan, defines its aesthetic. The building is composed of a series of 'Vierendeel' trusses, cantilevered from the cores and stacked one over the other in a 'plug-on' fashion. An expression of advanced technology in the early 1970s, this system is brought to India in a manner that has 'Indianized' it: steel has been replaced by concrete, skilled work accomplished by unskilled labour, and finally, a technological answer to the Mughal trellis. It establishes the *rasa* of the building, that of signifying a vigorous and assertive urban intervention. In the late seventies, this was an appropriate expression not only of the architectural profession, but also of the aspirations of the Indian economy and in particular, of a monolith like the STC. With the structure removed to the edge, it offers uninterrupted office space and also maximizes the floor area ratio (FAR). Since the structure falls within the cantilever, which is free of the FAR, the usable office space is partially equal to the FAR, a fact which is appreciated by clients even more today. The trusses here define a composition that provides sun shade as well as an aesthetic. The variations in the facade, through modulations of the truss cantilevers and building steps, project an unmistakable outline in the skyline of modern New Delhi. This building, however, signifies the culmination of a period of Raj Rewal's works. It is also a departure from an architecture that is primarily dependent on structural innovation and programmatic requirements, to an architecture that is typological and regionally ingrained. The red sandstone bands on the facade appear to provide a clue to this transformation that signals a new sensitivity to scale and colour, to tradition and context; a clue to an architecture firmly rooted in the values of Modernism, but also one capable of extracting from within the traditional values that could help define a new vocabulary for Indian architecture.

SCOPE Complex

106 A

Raj Rewal Associates (1989)
⊖ Jangpura
7, Lodi Road

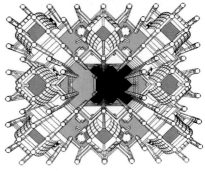

SCOPE is an office complex designed for large autonomous public-sector organizations and was built in 1983–1989 in New Delhi not far from Mughal Emperor Humayun's tomb. The facade is designed to shield the offices from the sun's direct rays so as to reduce the air conditioning costs. Eight polygonal interlocking blocks are grouped around a central courtyard to provide some 75,000 square metres of office space for diverse organizations. Planning regulations restricted the overall height of the building. The architect therefore opted to emphasize the strong, fortress-like mass through the repeated use of corner columns (containing ducts and services) and stone facing and has articulated the facades with deep recesses. Various social activities have been located on the roof terrace, so that the impression is more of a small city, accessible at many levels and in many ways, than of an ominous citadel. It has an architectural presence of its own which has already left an imprint on the cityscape. Although massive in form, the periphery of the complex has upper floors which extend further than those nearer ground level, creating deep shadows. At roof level, where terraces, restaurants and observation decks have been created among the cooling towers and hidden machine rooms, there is a rich articulation of forms and spaces; with boxes for hanging plants, concrete trellises for canvas covers over sun-decks and passageways where the employees can relax. There are splendid views across the New Delhi landscape from these hanging streets and gardens. Each of the eight interlocking pavilions has a central core, containing lifts, stairs, and lavatory facilities; from this core there is access to the offices and meeting rooms on each floor. Natural light reaches deep into the interior as a result of the recesses on the principal facade. The pavilions can be endowed with an individual identity if the diverse organizations they house so desire. The structural system consists of four columns supporting a square diagrid of structural slabs with 12-metre centres, or 16 metres at the two uppermost levels.

Indian National Science Academy

Raj Rewal Associates (1990)

107 A

⊜ Pragati Maidan

Bahadur Shah Zafar Marg

National Institute of Immunology

Raj Rewal Associates (1990)

108 B

⊜ Hauz Khas

Aruna Asaf Ali Marg

The Indian National Science Academy was established in January 1935 with the object of promoting science in India and harnessing scientific knowledge for the cause of national welfare and society. The *Rasa* or the character of the building is based on creating a bold and progressive image. A dynamic form, which fulfills the diverse functions of the academy, was evolved. The lower floors with large spans accommodate an auditorium; intermediate floors with smaller spans and roof terraces provide for guest rooms. The topmost rooms jutting out contain seminar areas and offices. An X-shaped structure of concrete shear walls provides for an economical solution to the complex problem of varying spans at different levels. The building is clad with sandstone. The horizontal bands of the stone are bolted with stainless steel to a substructure of concrete, which in turn support the vertical stone panels.

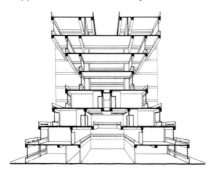

A biological research institute, incorporating laboratory and teaching facilities and living accommodation for both permanent and visiting scientists, was conceived for a hilltop site on the campus of Jawaharlal Nehru University in South Delhi. It has been endowed with a distinctive, almost urban identity on what is otherwise relatively open terrain. This has been achieved through a tight clustering of the numerous buildings by relating them to the contours of the site, through architectural massing and detailing, and by linking the blocks ingeniously together with footpaths, courtyards and passageways. The complex contains five residential blocks situated around two sides of a kind of central quadrangle, with a lecture hall on a third side and the fourth side left open. The ancient sites of Delhi and the Qutub Minar are visible on the distant horizon. Housing for senior scientists and their families was the first thing to be constructed. Twelve ample apartments, (120 square metres) stand in two-storey duplexes. The units have their own terraces and are disposed around a central courtyard which offers a focus for community interaction. Moreover, the upper duplex apartments are reached by diagonally-placed open staircases along facades, contributing to a sense of individual access but also to social visibility.

The central courtyard, in shadow most of the day, is also intended as a place for children to play, especially as it is easily supervised from roof terraces. Each of the succeeding housing clusters, for junior scientists, for research scholars and for essential staff, has been given its own identity. For example, the hostel for unmarried scholars comprises individual rooms around an octagonal court, envisaged as a small amphitheatre following the contours of the site. The plan is symmetrical on both axes and follows an orderly solution for providing roof terraces on successive upper storeys. Essential staff housing is arranged along a single axis, with a series of courtyards between opposite units that are stepped downwards from the hill-top quadrangle. A central auditorium building is multifunctional, and has numerous terraces on the roof where residents of the Institute can congregate, relax, and view performances. This building, which is neither residential nor a laboratory, forms a focal point in the institute's design. The whole effect is of a coherent, interrelated cluster of structures. Unity is achieved by the use of a grit finish consisting of red and beige sandstone pebbles on the exterior. The colours recall those of monumental buildings in the Delhi region from the Mogul and British colonial periods.

Matti Ghar, IGNCA

`109 F`

Sanjay Prakash,
DAAT: Design, Architecture &
Associated Technologies (1990)
Central Secretariat / Patel Chowk
Mansingh Road, Janpath

Capturing the concept of time in all aspects of design and construction, the *Matti Ghar* is directed, not by engineering, construction or aesthetic guidelines alone but is meant to instigate the harmonious design thought of an endless space and the 'cosmic dimension of a temporal reality'. It is composed as three concentric rings, their radii in the proportion of 1:2:3, and with the radial division of the outermost, middle and innermost ring into twelve, twenty-four and thirty-six equal divisions respectively. Adjacent to the structure is an open-air amphitheatre, an exact replica of the building footprint. The labour-intensive construction process encompasses innovations in material. It uses sundried stabilized earth blocks as frames and infill. In addition, cement was added to the soil mix for increased structural strength and water resistance in the construction process, avoiding plaster application. The largest brick dome of its time is constructed only by hand tools and a central guiding arm of aluminum in place of an extensive supporting framework. The structure was originally designed as a temporary exhibition space to last only a few years. The intent was to use it to house a special exhibition about time (*Kala*) as part of the activities of the IGNCA (Indira Gandhi National Centre for the Arts). However, the life of the structure was extended through some modifications and the structure has been retained for about two decades. It will stay at least until the main building of the IGNCA is completed. The building consists of a set of circumferential spaces. The spaces are kept dark and windowless in order to house the exhibition. The outer ring has gallery spaces including entries and exits. The middle ring contains a ramp leading up to an upper level in the Centre, but is wide enough to be used as an inclined exhibition space. The two-storey inner circle consists of a 'cave' below and a dome above. Two staircases outside the outer ring complete the connections that allow for various ways of entering and exiting. The volume was closed and required ventilation to cater for the large numbers of visitors expected. Therefore, an underground system for distributing air was devised. This is similar to the ancient Roman system of hypocausts (ducts within walls and floors). A fan room in a toilet block, 30 metres away from the main building, pumps air into an underground pipe 0.9 metres in diameter and at a depth of 1.5 metres below ground. The air is then distributed into the spaces through masonry ducts that lead to PVC pipes and mouths near the floor level of the gallery.

DLF Centre ↱

`110 D`

The Design Group (Building)
Hafeez Contractor (Facade)
(1990)
Rajiv Chowk
Sansad Marg

A showcase building for the DLF conglomerate, the building was designed by Ajoy Choudhary in association with Hafeez Contractor who was responsible for the design of the external facades and skin of the building. The 1.14 acre plot adjacent to the historic Jantar Mantar and

close to the colonnades of Connaught Place formerly housed Narendra Place, DLF's previous office building. It was demolished in 1988, and by 1991, the new building was up with ten floors clad in glass and granite. The DLF Centre follows the curved form of the erstwhile Narendra Place building on the same site and also reflects the curved form of the Park Hotel on the opposite side across Parliament Street. Conceived as a sophisticated office complex, the building was the most up-to-date structure of its kind in the capital with central air-conditioning,

a sprinkler system, fire detection system, reverse osmosis water system, and a full capacity stand-by generator. Parking and services are accommodated in three levels of basement below ground level and the offices are distributed in the ten floors above ground. Externally, the building is expressed in a simple curved curtain wall on the front and back with a granite colonnade defining the lower two floors. The two end walls have long uninterrupted curtain walls, which provide a spectacular panoramic view of the Jantar Mantar Complex to the south.

Garden Estate
ARCOP (1990)
🚇 Guru Dronacharya
Mehrauli Gurgaon Road,
Sector 24, Gurgaon, Haryana

111 J

Garden Estate is a premier condominium housing development in Gurgaon on the outskirts of Delhi. In a way it was a precursor to the later development that followed in Gurgaon. It is located on Mehrauli Gurgaon Road, which is one of the main roads connecting Delhi to Gurgaon. 373 units including 100 townhouses are sited in a rich 23-acre landscape incorporating gardens and common facilities. Garden Estate was the trendsetter and one of the finest condominium complexes in India. The mini-city has facilities like a leisure club with a swimming pool, squash courts, table tennis, a beauty parlour, gymnasium and other recreational facilities.

Crafts Museum

Charles Correa (1990)
🌐 Pragati Maidan
Pragati Maidan, Bhairon Road

112 A

The Crafts Museum, casual and accepting of the artisan's vernacular, is organized around a central pathway, reflecting the space as a metaphor for the Indian street — in fact, for India itself, where all kinds of crafts have always co-existed down the centuries.

Walking along this spine, one catches glimpses of the principal exhibits that lie on either side (the Village Court, Darbar Court, etc.). One can visit any particular exhibit, or alternately, progress through all the various sections in a continuous sequence. Towards the end of the sequence, the exhibits get larger and include fragments of actual buildings — since the crafts of India have always been an essential element of architecture. Finally, one exits via

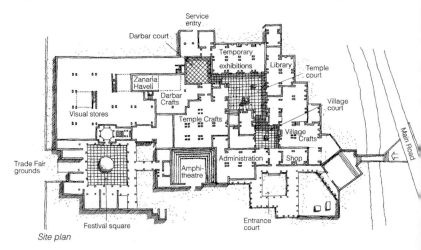

Site plan

the roof terraces — which form an amphitheatre for folk dances, as well as
an open-air display for large terracotta
horses and other handicrafts. There are
more than 25,000 items of folk and trib-
al arts, crafts and textiles in the permanent collection. Less than half of the total floor area of 5,500 square metres is
open to the public; the rest of the collection is stored in special areas for the
use of the very finest craftsmen who are
selected from all over India to come and
study these archives. As the Director of
the Museum, Jyotindra Jain, has stated:
'We call it a museum because it has been
dubbed so for a long time, but in reality it does not behave like one, and while
hesitating to assume a conventional nature and role, it asks many questions of
itself, eventually emerging as an institution that strives for identity, but in
no hurry to find a slotted definition of
itself. The core collection of the Crafts
Museum was put together to serve as
reference material for the craftsmen
who are increasingly losing touch with
their own traditions in terms of materials, techniques, designs and aesthetics
of their arts and crafts due to the sudden changes caused by modern indus-
trialization. Thus, it was primarily addressed to the craftsmen who have now
been brought into a close and integral
relationship with the Museum. Over the
last decade, this Museum has been altered time and again — it is being continuously improvised. It has an uncon-
cluded air about it in the sense that it
does not appear to be 'finished' so as to
make a pretty picture postcard. It is a
flexible building in the same sense as
an Indian village street would be flexible — affable, accommodative, informal
and active.'

1991–2000:
Liberalisation

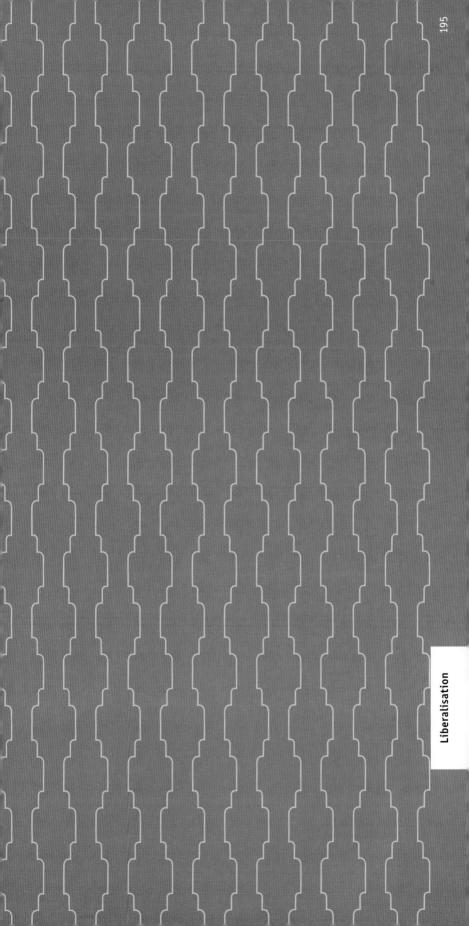

Liberalisation

Liberalisation and its effects on the Architecture of Delhi

Malini Kochupillai

After Independence in 1947, India adhered to socialist policies, following the Russian model of 5-year plans for its growth and development. These restrictive policies resulted in India having a low annual growth rate, with the GDP stagnated at around 3.5% from the 1950s to the 1980s. The huge public sector and state owned enterprise, responsible for everything from infrastructure, farming, communications etc, were running at huge losses. India started having balance of payments problems in 1985, and by the end of 1990, it was in a serious economic crisis. The assassination of Prime Minister Indira Gandhi in 1984, and later of her son Rajiv Gandhi in 1991, crushed international investor confidence in the economy that was eventually pushed to the brink by the early 1990s. Its central bank had refused new credit and foreign exchange reserves had reduced to the point that India could barely finance three weeks' worth of imports. Most of the reforms of the 1990s were forced upon India as a part of the IMF bailout, which required India to undertake a series of structural economic reforms. The then government of P. V. Narasimha Rao and his finance minister Manmohan Singh, the current Prime Minister of India, started breakthrough reforms to stabilize the downward spiralling economy. The new neo-liberal policies included opening of international trade and investment, deregulation,

initiation of privatization, tax reform, and inflation-controlling measures. The main objective of the government was to transform the economic system from socialism to capitalism so as to achieve high economic growth and industrialize the nation, increase job opportunities and propel production. Today India is mainly characterized as a market economy. The opening up of the Indian economy led to a large number of changes and opportunities appearing in cities almost overnight. Economic reforms resulted in total foreign investments in India growing from a minuscule US$ 132 million in 1991/1992 to US$ 5.3 billion in 1995/1996. Cities like NOIDA, Gurgaon, Gaziabad, Bangalore, Hyderabad, Pune, Chennai, Jaipur, Indore and Ahmedabad rose in prominence and economic importance, and became centres of rising industries and destinations for foreign investment and firms. A sudden increase in the demand for office space, to accommodate the growing number of multinational corporations setting up back offices in these cities, and the request for new housing for the rapidly growing middle class that followed brought massive, and sudden, transformations in the built environment. Prior to liberalization, a majority of the architectural practices in India focused on projects of a relatively modest scale, large scale public and infrastructure projects being the almost exclusive purview of

Housing in Greater NOIDA

the government or public sector entities which usually had their own in house design departments. Post liberalization, the government relegated its responsibility to build large scale housing and infrastructure projects to private investors keen to capitalise on a changing market structure. Post-liberalized India witnessed a gradual boom in the real estate market. With the development of the economy, the Indian real estate market, which was traditionally an unorganized sector, turned into one of the fastest growing industries in the country. NOIDA, Gurgaon, and lately, Gaziabad and Faridabad, all suburbs of Delhi in the neighbouring states of Haryana and Uttar Pradesh, saw immense growth as a result of India's emergence as an attractive off-shoring destination with vast reserves of highly qualified technicians and engineers. High demand generated by the IT industry, offering much healthier pay packages, led to a rapid growth of the middle class. The growing economy and a new corporate culture also resulted in a demand for plush residential and commercial projects of global standards. At the time there were only a handful of large design firms used to working with private developers on 'commercial' projects, who had the resources and ability to deliver the kind of large-scale projects that were being asked by private developers. This, combined with a new desire to project a more 'global' image, resulted in the outsourcing of design to foreign corporate practices used to delivering out-sized mixed use developments in a glass and steel aesthetic that appropriately reflected the aspirations of an emerging economy.

New Typologies

With liberalization, Delhi and its suburbs also saw the rise of new typologies of built form. New economic opportunities and a growing middle class, many of whose representatives were educated or had worked abroad, now expected a lifestyle and accompaniments previously unknown in India. The most prominent of these new typologies were large retail malls, suddenly more fashionable and desirable than the old neighbourhood markets common in cities across the country. One of the first malls to be erected in Delhi was the Ansal Plaza (1990) by Jasbir Sawhney architects. Designed in a donut shape, the built form encloses a circular public amphitheatre. The double height colonnaded building, clad with brick and glass, is typical of the Post-Modern style of architecture practised at the time. Offering a whole new shopping experience for the city, the completely air conditioned mall was immediately popular with the masses, and led the way for the profusion of malls that have been built in the NCR since. Ansal Plaza was quickly followed by a series of malls erected in a short time span in Gurgaon. The Metropolitan Mall, with over 250,000 square feet of retail space, was one of the first of the new generation of mega malls clad in glass and alucobond that are now peppered around Gurgaon and NOIDA.

Private enterprise also started to play a major role in developing large-scale high-rise housing solutions for the fast growing middle class, a task previously undertaken by government agencies. With fewer regulations, high-rise condominium towers started to spring up

Gurgaon Housing

Ansal Plaza, Jasbir Sawhey (1990)

Beverly Park, Hafeez Contractor (2005)

in what was farmland until a few years before. Hafeez Contractor, one of the most prolific architects to have had an impact on the skyline of Gurgaon, popularized the practice of adopting visual imagery and elements from different locales, regions and histories in order to evoke a sense of nostalgia of a better past, to seduce, fascinate and excite the prospective buyers in an era of speculative building. His projects Beverly Park I & II located on the Mehrauli Gurgaon Road in Gurgaon typify this notion. The Spanish-style details give its own identity to the whole complex within the already fragmented and disparate texture of the Mehrauli Gurgaon Road. The use of sloping roofs with tiles, terraced form and balconies contained within this apartment complex are perceived as images of another, more desirable culture and space. These highly secure, hermetic colonies are designed with a variety of visual elements from Palladian villas, Spanish castles, Florida art nuevo or Roman arches, anything that evokes a sense of 'otherness', effectively rejecting local building traditions and tectonics in favour of an applied, pastiche aesthetic. Institutional projects like hospitals and universities, previously the monopoly of state governments, also saw private investors capitalising on the privatisation of these services. The Apollo Hospital (1996) designed by Hafeez Contractor, one of the first private hospitals to be built in post-liberal India, uses the Post-Modern vernacular of the mall atrium to liven an otherwise dreary and intimidating environment into an inviting and comforting space for the patients' relatives.

Global Identity

The large plots of land required for the demands of this changing economy were either unavailable or unaffordable in the existing cities across the country.

Janakpuri Business Centre,
The Design Group (1986)

DLF Corporate Park,
Hafeez Contractor (1991)

Gurgaon, Commercial Hub

Enterprising developers, like DLF in Gurgaon, foreseeing the upcoming boom in the demand for commercial and residential properties, acquired vast acreages in the immediate vicinity of larger cities with the intention to develop global suburbs replete with freeways, shopping malls, new corporate centres and gated residential complexes for the new middle class. The architectural response of these new mega projects focused on creating a 'global' image completely detached from the local vernacular and context, often not even dependant on otherwise state-provided infrastructure like power and water, and creating self-contained islands of prosperity. Gurgaon and NOIDA quickly developed into IT hubs, playing host to a large number of multinational companies looking to set up back offices to outsource their operations. The DLF Corporate Park in Gurgaon, designed by Hafeez Contractor, was one of the first such office parks to

appear in the mid nineties, surrounded by landscaped greenery and comprising seven glass and steel towers and over 250,000 square feet of office space. The high-performance glass and alucobond cladding system used in these structures is state of the art and particularly suited to achieving the 'global' image recognized all over the world for it's acontextual sameness. The 'global' image aspires to establish a dialogue with the international clients that these spaces cater to. Signature Towers (1998), First India Place (1999), Indian Oil Building (2005) are all prime examples of the desire of large corporations interested in projecting a certain image that is associated with large glass facades, atrium spaces, modular offices and plush interiors.

Over the past 10–15 years, with fast depleting natural resources, developed countries across the world saw a newfound concern for the environment and actively worked towards becoming more

Signature Towers,
C.P.Kukreja Associates, (1998)

Institute for Rural Research and
Development, Ashok B Lall (2008)

Commonwealth Games Village, Sikka Associates (2010)

conscious of energy consumption in built areas. The construction industry in the United States developed a rating system based on mechanical technologies and advanced building and fenestration systems to minimize the amount of energy a new building would consume while in operation. This internationally recognized LEED rating system quickly became another USP for builders and developers in India to sell valuable real estate. A majority of these LEED rated buildings rely on mechanical systems instead of developing innovative typologies and materials. A few architects have gone beyond the expected and developed new systems to limit energy consumption based on traditional vernacular building practices and by the contemporary use of time-tested construction elements used in hot South Asian climates. Ashok Lall's IRRAD building (2008) is an excellent example of a sensitively designed structure which uses both mechanical and passive sustainable systems to create an energy efficient office environment. Relying more on innovative design practices, and adapting local materials and architectural elements like screens and sun-shades, the building manages to create the global image so desired by clients without resorting to the tired aesthetic of curtain walls and steel cladding.

Over the years, the scale of corporate parks, special economic zones, gated housing colonies, private institutions of education and health care and industrial developments has only grown, with Gurgaon and NOIDA becoming the leading markers for growth and development patterns.

Stylistically, institutional and cultural projects, while interested in projecting a progressive global aesthetic, tend to show more sensitivity to location, site and vernacular tectonics. Architects concerned with developing a unique aesthetic informed by local tradition and materials while using new technologies and methods of construction, are successfully shaping a new architectural narrative for our cities. Romi Khosla Design Studio's Castro Cafeteria at the Jamia Millia Islamia University (JMI) has skillfully taken the now standard technology of the cantilevered canopy and crafted its application into an elegant semi-open canteen facility for students. Similarly, in their gallery at JMI, screens are employed in a contemporary and fresh configuration to filter light while subtly suggesting a universal language that straddles both the locale (the Islamic university in which it is located) and its aspiration to relate to a global style. Museums and Art Galleries, privately commissioned and funded by architecturally informed and interested clients are some of the most engaging projects in the new urban landscape. The Devi Art Foundation, or Sirpur Mills Building, in Gurgaon uses brick and corten steel in its facade to create an unusual and striking addition to the otherwise uniform glass and alucobond finishes that surround it. The South Asian Human Rights Documentation Centre (2005) by Anagram Architects is another example of a small-scale institutional project that, despite its tight budget and site constraints, uses the local material and traditional building element of brick *jaalis* to create a beautiful pattern that engages playfully with the street while minimizing heat gain on the wide west facade and maximizing air flow with its porosity.

The rapid development of the Metro over the past 15 years has spurred growth to an ever-increasing area in and around Delhi. New commercial complexes have been built adjacent to some metro stations, like the Saket District centre (2009) by Kuldeep Singh combines malls, office space and hotels spread over 220,000 square metres, all clad in the expected glass and steel gloss of 'global' architecture.

The Commonwealth Games, held in 2010, led to the construction and renovation of many large infrastructures, cultural and residential projects. The Commonwealth Games Village, a large gated development built to house the athletes travelling to the city for the games, developed by Emaar MGF, is a prime indicator of the change in the way architecture is commissioned, designed and built in the new global age of India. Similar athletic housing commissioned for the Asian Games of 1984 was designed by Raj Rewal, a well known and regarded architect of the time, and paid for by the government. In contrast, the design and completion of the Commonwealth Games Village was handed over to a private developer, as a private-public partnership. The government handed over large plots of land at heavily subsidized rates to the developer, who then got to keep a portion of the profits made after the apartments are sold at market rates to private

Castro Cafe, Romi Khosla Design Studio (2010)

individuals. The focus being not so much on architectural design and experience, but the delivery of 'world class' interiors and services, packaged in a generic high-rise housing aesthetic.

While there has been a boom in the architecture and design industry in post liberalized Delhi, not all the developments have been heartening. A majority of buildings have been designed and built thoughtlessly, sacrificing form, function and beauty at the alters of time and profit. The result has been growing suburbs with a cacophony of glass, steel and pastiche where every building seems to be screaming louder than its neighbour for the attention of the buyer. A lack of planning and foresight on the part of government agencies has only added to the noise. A small but growing number of architects, refusing to give in to market forces, continue to design sensitive and innovative buildings that are able to reconcile India's rich heritage and traditional building practices with its need to project a global, modern image. As more such projects are acknowledged for their design among an informed global and local clientele, one hopes that the Indian building industry matures into an innovative and thoughtful practice befitting our rich cultural heritage.

References

1. Khanna, Rahul & Parhawk, Manav the. *Modern Architecture of New Delhi*, 1928–2007

2. Lang, Jon. Desai, Madhavi & Desai, Miki. *Architecture & Independence — The Search for Identity — India 1880 to 1980*, Oxford University Press, 1997

3. Mehrotra, Rahul. *Architecture in India since 1990*, Pictor, Germany, 2011

August Kranti Bhavan

The Design Group (1991)
⊝ AIIMS
Africa Avenue,
Bhikaji Cama Place

113 B

August Kranti Bhavan developed by Housing and Urban Development Corporation Limited is also known as the HUDCO Bazaar. It is an exclusive and multi-user commercial complex developed by HUDCO at a major intersection of the ring road in South Delhi. It is built on a plot of land measuring 18,830 square metres. with a built-up area of 18,823 square metres. The building has been developed to suit the requirement of variety of commercial space users. While the ground floor primarily accommodates a large number

of shops, the upper three floors are designed mainly to accommodate independent office units. It was built for accommodating commercial and office spaces varying in size from about 5 square metres to 136 square metres. Located in the heart of South Delhi, it is eminently accessible from various locations in Delhi. Along a linear site sandwiched between two entirely different architectural conditions, the architecture of the complex tries to mediate the scale and activity between Bhikaji Cama Place on one side and the Mohamadpur Village on the other. While the side facing the Bhikaji Cama Place contains large shops and offices in three-storey stepped buildings, the building edge joining Mohamadpur village, with its lower height and shaded pergola areas for informal and other service activities, is more sensitive to the character of the village. The space between these two distinct layers was opened up to provide a grand piazza, a shopping street and a small office square. This central space forms the hub of activity and also the main linkage to the Bhikaji Cama Place. The building is finished in permanent materials, using a combination of Red Agra Stone and Beige Dholpur Stone identical to the rest of the Bhikaji Cama Place complex. One can particularly observe the stone craftsmanship of the *jaali* facade on the south side of the building.

Parag Dairy

The Design Group (1992)
🚇 NOIDA City Centre
B-219, Phase-2, NOIDA, UP

114 C

As part of an ongoing exercise by the Government of Delhi to boost its milk production, a dairy with a production capacity of 400,000 litres per day was proposed in NOIDA, a township in the periphery of the National Capital Region of Delhi. The site of 11.5 acres was found to be inadequate for a normal, horizontally planned dairy, and after consultations with National Dairy Development Board dairy experts, a decision was taken to design an automated vertical structure. A suitable structure was required to house the production block and establish efficient linkages with the worker's amenities, administration and the service block. Thus, the bridge connecting the service area and the bucket elevator to the main body of the production block was conceived. The ramps to the basement emerged to provide access to the workers' amenities and the service area. The administrative block was perched over a grand independent access canopy and connected closely to the production block at all levels. The central core of services, freight lifts, ramps and bridges brought every part under a vertical atrium at the centre of the composition as if they were limbs of an efficient production body.

National Science Centre

Achyut Kanvinde (1992)

🚇 Indraprastha

Near Gate No.1, Bhairon Road,
Pragati Maidan

115 A

For the National Science Centre in New Delhi, Kanvinde was presented with a constrained urban site in the shape of a trapezoid. A high ratio of floor area to site size was needed to accommodate the extensive program. Acknowledging the importance of circulation for the resulting five-storey building, Kanvinde developed a clear path for the visitor: the main entry is on the second floor, where an atrium offers an escalator to the fourth-floor level. There the visitor proceeds through a tropical forest to the top floor and across an open air court to the starting point of the exhibition spaces. The itinerary involves a descent through the building. Terraces with gardens cascading to the ground level break down the mass of the building, and allow staff and visitors to step outside in many locations. These outdoor gardens provide a break to museum-goers and create possibilities for the exhibitions to extend to the outdoors. The building comprises an auditorium, conference rooms, lecture hall, library, training centre,

exhibition areas, and a cafeteria, total-
ing 14,000 square metres of built-up area. An entrance concourse on the first
floor leads to the multi-level display;
and terraces provide additional outdoor
exhibition areas. The building is finished
with aggregate plaster using local Delhi
blue quartzite stone chips with bands in
Dholpur stone chips, and polished Kota
stone with Jaisalmer stone (ochre) bands
are used for the flooring. The design of
the National Science Centre relies on a
powerful geometry to give it architectural clarity and strength. Although the
forms are forceful, the architecture is
not monumental. Instead, the building
assumes a human scale inspite of its
large size. The National Science Museum
asserts itself as a strong and confident
modern building with a distinctive profile that confidently co-exists with the
powerful architecture of the past.

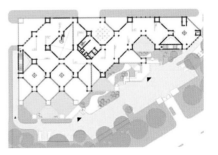

British Council

Charles Correa (1992)

🚇 Barakhamba Road

17 Kasturba Gandhi Marg

116 D

The Indian architect and RIBA gold medalist, Charles Correa, was commissioned to design a new building for the British Council on Kasturba Gandhi Marg. The building was formally opened in October 1992 and houses the British Council's largest overseas operation. The five-storey building, with interior and exterior spaces flowing into one another through the use of courtyards, pillars and fountains, was designed to reflect a conceptual progression of the history of India. The building houses a number of diverse rooms, including a library, an auditorium, an art gallery and the headquarters of their offices in India. These elements are arranged in a series of layers, recalling the historic interfaces that have existed between India and Britain over the past several centuries. From the main entrance gate, one moves down the main axis which extends right up to the rear garden wall. The three nodal points along this axis are structured around three axes *mundi*, each recalling one of the principle belief systems that exist in the Indian sub-continent. At the farthest end is the axis *mundi* of Hinduism, a spiral symbolising *Bindu* — the energy centre of the cosmos. The next nodal point, located in the main courtyard, is centred around another image: the traditional Islamic *Char Bagh*, i.e. Garden of Paradise. The third nodal point along this axis is a European icon, inlaid in marble and granite, used to represent the Age of Reason, including the values of Science and Progress. The walls around the *Char Bagh* are clad in red Agra sandstone. The head of Shiva and the *Bindu* at the farthest end of the axis are sculpted in the black rock quarried near the sacred site of Mahabalipuram. On the entrance facade, encompassing all these many layers, is a mural by Howard Hodgkin. Commissioned by the Visual Arts Department, Hodgkin collaborated closely with the architect in the production of the mural symbolising the shadow of a tree, a metaphorical image as sheltering and pluralistic as India herself. The mural is constructed of small, rectangular, hand-cut tiles of white Makrana marble, and black, locally quarried Cuddappah stone — a technique often employed on Mughal buildings. Hodgkin wrote that his first concern 'was to make a design which would change dramatically when seen from different points of view and thus display the complexity of internal spaces on the facade of Charles Correa's splendid building'. The moving shadow cast by a large tree, a symbol that embraces both life and knowledge, seemed an appropriate image for the library and meeting place.

Buddha Memorial

Ashish Ganju (1993)

🚇 Dhaula Kuan

Upper Ridge Road

117 A

As a symbol of gratitude His Holiness the Dalai Lama presented a statue of Buddha to the people and government of India. The statue was installed under a canopy set in a garden designed to be a public monument. The location chosen was a public park situated on the Delhi Ridge, a spur of the ancient Aravali mountain range, which once formed the western edge of New Delhi. The canopy design embodies a cluster of Buddhist symbols. The iconography was carefully chosen by the Tibetan Lamas including the Dalai Lama. The construction of the canopy was entrusted to a team of Rajasthani stone masons who belong to a community of traditional temple builders. The architect's role became one of mediating between the esoteric knowledge of the Lamas and the constructional expertise of the stone masons as practiced for many centuries. The statue and canopy are set on a large rock which forms an

island within a system of water channels running through the park. The island is treated as the sacred enclosure while the garden around the waterway is landscaped for the day-to-day recreation of the general public. After the statue had been consecrated it was necessary to indicate its location on a map on New Delhi. On that occasion it was discovered that the statue coincidentally extends the ceremonial axis planned by Lutyens between the Viceroys House and the War Memorial. Today the house (now the residence of the president of India) sits on this axis with the War Memorial at one end and at the other end Buddha Memorial with its message of universal peace.

Sanskriti Kendra (Anandgram)

Upal Ghosh Associates (1993)

🚇 Arjangarh

Mehrauli Gurgaon Road, Near Aya Nagar

118 B

The Sanskriti Kendra, set up by the Sanskriti Pratishthan and inaugurated on 31 January 1993, is the culmination of the Pratishthan's activities in the fields of art, craft, literature and social work. Located in Qutub-Mehrauli on the outskirts of Delhi enroute to Gurgaon, the Kendra was expected to accommodate a varied range of activities connected with art and culture both in the traditional and the contemporary sense. This broad objective was the only guideline to the design process. As a result, the two main natural features on site—the rainwater drainage channel that ran down the centre, and existing clumps of trees—became the major structuring elements of the layout plan.

A basic movement pattern together with the entry points was defined with activity zoning to regulate the location of buildings and other structures according to function. This explains the absence of an articulated complex. The buildings are 'objects in space' separated by a variety of spaces. All developments on site were largely organic with the architect as guide. A living, creative complex, the Kendra is intended to provide temporary residential and working space to both traditional and contemporary artists and craftsperson, and in doing so, it aims to promote interaction between the two. Thus, the complex includes in addition to two museums, an open-air auditorium, conference hall, and studio apartments. The apartments consist of four single and four double residences, each with a living room, a bathroom and a studio. For rural craftspersons, a separate cluster of huts with individual cooking facilities is provided. The Kendra is

spread over three hectares on the foothills of the Aravali range. With the landscape recognized as focal to the scheme, a minimalist approach was adopted. No activity that would disturb the basic character of the land was undertaken. A few fundamental design parameters were established for all construction and these were thereafter adhered to. The typology of the buildings is modernist; simple, but made interesting with varied levels, heights and spaces. Construction materials used are RCC, brick, stone, steel, etc. However, in the finishes and textures, some innovations have been attempted. For example, straw reinforced plaster has been used in many places. In others, ordinary cement plaster has been textured with a steel comb to give it a rough look. The low-profile buildings are all painted in shades of brown, which gives them an earthy look. Landscaping, carefully supervised by landscape architect Mohammed Shaheer,

is the most critical aspect of the Kendra. The rainwater channel has been converted into a linear water body, the *nahar*. This starts from a semicircular pool fed by a water retention pond, passes under a couple of foot bridges, washes up the steps of the ghats on either side, and ends at the *manch*. Excess water is run off through a bypass drain. Every open space has been defined and has a character of its own. A judicious mix of formality and informality both in plant and hard landscape characterizes the Kendra. Geometric forms, pavements, paths, and

hedges intersperse the lawns, *vans*, the *nahar* and meandering paths. Eventually, it was envisaged that the approximately 2,000 trees planted on site will predominate the complex which came true in the years to come. The *Baithak* is the 'common room' of the Kendra, housing facilities such as the dining room, conference room, library, computer room and office. A two-storey structure, it is internally connected, both visually and physically, by a double-height covered court with steps so configured that they can be used as tiered seating during conferences, etc. The building can be entered from various levels. Except the office and library, all other spaces flow into each other, giving the interior a very open feeling. In keeping with its supervisory role, the office has been strategically placed at a higher level overlooking the entire complex. The *Haveli* is the residence of the director, the moving force behind the organization. Single-storeyed, the plan is based on six and a half overlapping squares with intersecting pyramidal roofs. The living, dining, bedroom and kitchen are arranged around an *aangan* (courtyard). The most

striking feature is the meticulously restored old entrance door from Rajasthan from where one gets the first glimpse of the *aangan* — a perfect square patch of green with an equally geometric rectangle of water along one side. There are eight studios in two blocks placed along the *nahar* where participants with an urban background can live and work. The units are small and simple but provide a variety of spaces, both indoor and outdoor. Each studio is self-sufficient with private enclosed courtyards, verandas, balconies, counters, and aisle spaces to work in. The living/dining/work space is on the lower level, while the sleeping area is located above. The Kendra incorporates two museums — the Sanskriti Museum of Indian Terracotta and the Sanskriti Museum of Everyday Art. These, the most 'public' of all the spaces, needed special attention for clarity of movement. A series of modular units have been carefully arranged around landscaped courtyards. The module, square in plan, has been used in various forms, sometimes as just a platform, a room without a roof, a room with roof but no walls, and sometimes totally enclosed with regular doors and windows. The roof is always pyramidal as it suits the square plan and blends well with the scale and rural setting. The layout of spaces is such that a visitor moves from one exhibit to the next without repeating any. The Museum of Everyday Art is housed in a building sunk partly below ground, and its roof is effectively used as outdoor exhibition terraces for the terracotta museum.

Ambadeep Building

C. P. Kukreja Associates (1993)
Rajiv Chowk
14, Kasturba Gandhi Marg,
Connaught Place

119 D

The Ambadeep is an iconic building, amongst the tallest in Delhi and prominently located in the central Connaught Place when it was built in 1993. Designed for the Ansal Group of Companies, Ambadeep is a blend of the traditional and modern high-tech. Located on a 1.3 acre corner plot in Connaught Place, the building has the advantage of a segregated car park with vehicular entry from the side road a major plus in the busy area it is situated in. The building is an interesting massing of three vertical tower blocks, basically square in plan, of varying heights arranged around an atrium, which represents the cohesive design element. The tallest tower is 21 storeys (84 metres) high and overlooks the arcaded terraces of the smaller towers (14 storeys and nine storeys high respectively). The two smaller blocks as well as the glass encased lifts overlook the landscaped atrium. Storage areas, the air conditioning and mechanical plant along with an electric sub-station and the mandatory car parking requirements are all housed in the three basements of the building. Essentially commercial in nature, the structure is carefully designed to allow for maximum floor area coverage. Landscaping is an integral part of the design and strong elements that penetrate into the interior of the

building include the atrium with its terraced waterfall and planters, the periphery of the roof of the basement with continuous built-in planters, and a court at the back of the buildings which is overlooked by the staff canteen and the ground floor. The bold facade treatment in long continuous bands is broken at the corners by square pilasters and uses geometric patterned glass tiles in shades of white, yellow and blue. This is perhaps the first example of such strong colours in a modern building of this scale. The aesthetic evolved as a result of the architects' conviction that art compensates for the deprivation of a natural uplifting environment — the blocking of the sky, the sun, plants and trees — and that even a dense commercial area should be able to incorporate beauty and art and display it on a street facade.

ICGEB ⌃
(International Centre for
Genetic Engineering and
Biotechnology)
Raj Rewal Associates (1993)
Chhattarpur
Aruna Asf Ali Marg, Vasant Kunj

120 B

The International Centre for Genetic Engineering and Biotechnology is situated alongside the Jawaharlal Nehru University and the Sanjay Van in a bush forest area. The Laboratories comprise a main building, a guest house facility, bio-experimentation unit, BSL-3 facility, and a number of greenhouses for agriculture related research. The ICGEB is engaged with research in agriculture, human and animal health. The centre also provides training facilities to scholars from developing countries. Within the site, a road is proposed which connects all the diverse building blocks at the rear. This ensures segregation between the pedestrian and vehicular movement and allows all the major blocks to have uninterrupted views of the landscape. The concept is based on providing distinct areas comprising of the laboratory, the administrative block and the animal house, all linked in front with a water pool facing the sweeping park land. The design aims to merge the distinct functional elements with the landscape. The Architectural expression aims to create an ambience in harmony with the surroundings where scientists can explore in a serene environment, nature's secrets. The buildings in the campus are built in characteristic Raj Rewal style where the structural elements are expressed clearly with Red Sandstone cladding while

the infill walls have been clad with light coloured Dholpur Stone. The skyline is marked by the expression of traditional element of *chattris* and single flight staircases expressed on facades much inspired by the architecture of Indian desert in Rajasthan.

India Habitat Centre »
J. A. Stein (1994)
Jor Bagh Khan Market
Lodi Road, Max Mueller Marg

121 G

The India Habitat Centre (IHC), located on a 9.6 acre site off Lodi Road on the fringes of Lutyens' Delhi, is one of the largest projects designed by Joseph Allen Stein in India. It is very different both in character and scale from the entire complex of buildings designed by him at Lodi Estate. The IHC was conceived as a complex of institutions dealing with a wide variety of issues related to habitat and was intended to house a variety of functions to stimulate and facilitate many levels of interaction. The ground was perceived as a vehicle-free environment, and a fairly elaborate system worked out to deny entrance to all motorized traffic except for repair and fire. All cars and scooters are directed into two levels of basements. The conference block is the only one that allows entry to vehicles, which, however, can only pause and have to park elsewhere. The complex is, nontheless, accessed from all sides, the major pedestrian entrance being from Lodi Road on the north. Building volumes are articulated to form interconnected internal courtyards that are the major public spaces. The other factor that governed design was the

effort to modify the climate as much as possible by non mechanical means. Thus, the top two floors of the building have been projected twice. This results in a building shadow that is larger than its footprint. It also creates a classical order of the pediment. The introduction of the sun-screen pergola, a highly dramatic feature of the IHC, ingeniously protects the courtyards from the summer glare while letting on the winter sun, and is a very successful innovation that greatly enhances the enclosure qualities of the courts. The external finish was originally visualized in brushed aggregate (grit), carefully controlled to result in a dark base that became progressively lighter as the building was viewed against the sky. This could not be implemented. Also the promoters, HUDCO felt that brick symbolized habitat better. Custom-made ceramic tiles add colour, variety and give identity to the vertical circulation. The landscaping here, as in all of Stein's buildings, is integral to the design. Each internal courtyard has been designed to impart a distinct identity to the spaces and is conducive to the type of functions or activities that can be anticipated. This has been achieved by paving patterns in different materials, the use of water, a play of levels and plants. The external spaces have a more formal quality, to act as a foreground for the building. The IHC contains a variety of functions that cater to almost all types of requirements. Major office spaces are located in the blocks adjacent to the main streets, the associated functions such as guest rooms, staff quarters and the auditorium are adjacent to the Lodi Colony Housing. The blocks housing the offices are articulated to form the three courtyards, the ground levels of which contain public functions such as exhibition spaces, fast-food restaurants, banks, etc. and access to the vertical cores. The blocks adjacent to the housing area have been progressively reduced in volume and the auditorium is set back substantially from the plot line to create a distinct entry. The campus like character and facilities of the IHC are intended to provide not only an oasis of quiet and greenery in the midst of the traffic of the city, but to stimulate and facilitate many levels of interaction and make the centre a demonstration of the rich potential of urban form in contrast to the chaos and ugliness that ordinarily characterizes institutional areas divided into relatively small individual plots with unresolved parking.

Dilli Haat

Pradeep Sachdeva (1994)
⊜ INA
Opposite INA market,
Aurobindo Marg

122 B

The Haat is modelled as a traditional Indian weekly market where craftsmen, artisans and farmers from across the country sell their wares directly to their consumers. Conceptually, the space tries to merge two diverse but highly successful shopping types: first, the ethnic bazaars which are tourist attractions in most Third World cities today (the souk of Marrakesh, the Hauz Khas Village of Delhi); secondly, the extremely potent concept of the shopping mall (especially in North America) where consumers are expected to 'shop till they drop' in a relatively controlled, secure and undisturbed environment. The overall area available was approximately 100 metres by 300 metres. The site was in disuse and its central part consisted of a concrete slab spanning a storm water drain which could not be built upon. Beyond 'the slab', the two side ribbons were land-filled pieces. In addition, there were quite a number of trees lining both sides of the erstwhile drain. Therefore, the planning of the entire complex was done by composing a large number of small building blocks into a coherent whole. The designers have used the edges of the slab, since there are retaining walls just below and these are the only places where foundations could be made

easily. The strong linear axis was determined by site constraints that necessitated the placing of buildings on the edges of the slab covering the *nallah*. The entry from the Sri Aurobindo Marg side is well set back to avoid the noise and dust of the busy main artery. One walks past the sandstone columns of varying height which represent the entrance, to reach an entirely pedestrian space, containing a landscaped mall with shops and hawker platforms for short-term lease, cafes with open-air dining tables and benches, and stores for merchandise. A small performing arts theatre ends the vista. Near the same end is the central multi-cuisine food court of the complex. The shops, arranged in a veranda-like arcade, have different kinds of built-in shelves to provide a variety of selling styles: off-counter, on the floor, stepped display, and so on. A set of bamboo matted verandas form the usable walks. The shops and pavilions in the front are higher, roofed in grey slate with a fair slope, or flat with red sandstone. The cafes at the back, due to requirements of hygiene and dust proofing, are finished in Kota stone flooring and RC roofs. The sweep of the roof emphasized by exposed beams is used here as a decorative element as well as to convey structural clarity. The buildings are crafted in detail and display a consistent character due to the use of plain exposed brick wall, with segmental and soldier arches and *jaali* parapet walls. On the inside of the shops, the rough sides of the walls are simply painted over. Slate on timber battens, pre-cast concrete rafters, and sandstone slabs form the vocabulary of the complex. The shutters are made of bamboo plywood, while the windows are all framed in sandstone from Karauli. A fair amount of attention is paid to detail, such as the use of the stainless steel slating nails, brass brackets to firm up the sandstone frame edges or the steel gargoyle extension pieces that form such an important architectural feature. The variation in interior design is also carried through in the design of individual ceramic tile murals for the front dado of each cafe. Quartz flagstones with ordinary and *Lakheri* bricks are liberally employed in extensive paved areas. Dilli Haat is one of Delhi's most popular public spaces and is visited by over 1.5 million people every year. In 2003 Diili Haat was renovated to be made one of the first completely barrier-free public spaces in India. The project also points the way towards creative use of marginal inner city areas such as drains and service lines which can be treated as a positive resource.

Housing for British High Commission

123 A

Raj Rewal Associates (1994)
INA/Race Course
British Embassy Compound, Chanakyapuri

Housing for the British diplomats is located in the High Commission Compound in the Diplomatic Enclave, an exclusive zone for foreign missions in New Delhi. The site had existing chancellery buildings, residential bungalows and a series of six-storey-high flats. It was full of mature trees of tropical grandeur giving the compound a flavour of elegance, dignity and unity. The programme called for 12 new quarters of three-bedroom

units of two sizes. The design is based on low rise compact development around a central communal enclosure, respecting the location of existing trees and plants. The two-storey houses are arranged around a square, which contains a circular pathway giving access to all units. The demarcation of central enclosures is clearly established by framed gateways with pedestrian passages connecting the site to garages on two ends adjoining peripheral roads. Each dwelling unit has a private enclosed garden at the rear which reflects the traditional British terrace housing. The ground floor comprises living, dining, kitchen and utility areas and the first floor contains three bed rooms and a terrace. It is the second floor roof of the house which makes a specific concession to diplomatic living and provides a gracious terrace for parties along with roof top umbrellas (*chattris*). The architectural language of the housing complex is based on energy saving devices, e. g. deep set windows, shaded balconies, verandahs, roof umbrellas and overhangs which keep the walls, roof and glazing protected from the harsh glare of the sun. The buildings are constructed with a composite wall of brick and stone with an external cladding of sandstone. The texture of stone and its changing colour forms an important feature of the design, complimenting the natural foliage on the site.

World Bank Regional Mission 124 G
Raj Rewal Associates (1994)

Khan Market ⊜ Jor Bagh
70, Lodi Estate

The World Bank's regional mission in New Delhi is located in a prestigious and sensitive location, surrounded by the Lodi Garden and with a thick foliage of mature trees up to 12 to 16 metres high. On the opposite end, the plot faces a large open space that was intended to be a plaza with underground parking for this area; now it is being used as an open parking space. The aim of the architect was to create an elegant building using stone and concrete. The intent of the design was to situate the mission within the context of an Indo-Islamic past while maintaining a modern vocabulary. The design is based on a central courtyard ensuring natural light and ventilation to all the rooms. All the offices including secretary workstations have external views or look inward into the courtyard. The reference to the classic symmetry of Lodi monuments enveloping a forecourt finds an echo in the design of the World Bank building enclosing a sunken garden. The building mass encloses the central court, providing diffused light and ventilation. The scale of the court creates a zone under shade, thereby reducing the air conditioning load. It acts as an open area with a controlled microclimate and

provides relief to the building users. It also functions as an open spill out of the lobby and exhibition areas and has multi-purpose use. At the upper levels the rooms overview the courtyard. The area between the Lodi Gardens and the building periphery has been scooped out to create a sunken court, which functions as a stage for multipurpose public activity. It is an extension of the public area on the lower ground floor. The court and exhibition spaces are linked to the sunken garden at the lower ground level and lobby. A series of steps enclose it on three sides, connecting the court at the lower level to the garden at the upper natural ground level. The beige sandstone cladding of the building offset with red sandstone at floor levels reflects in a different manner the cladding and surface treatment of Delhi's great monuments. The boundary wall and the steps of the sunken court are made of Delhi quartzite stone with brown hues. The World Bank, is seen through a very thick foliage of trees and textures of Delhi quartzite and Agra sandstone are complimentary materials to the garden. The barrel vaults on the roof accentuate the conference rooms underneath, emphasize the axis and complement the curves of the nearby domes. The beige sandstone cladding is offset with pink sandstone. Abstract patterns are important features of the design.

Sitaram Bhartia Institute of Science and Research

125 B

Sumit Ghosh and Associates
(1994)

Malviya Nagar
B-16, Qutab Institutional Area

Situated on about 1.5 acres of land in the institutional area of Mehrauli in the vicinity of the Qutub Hotel, the Sitaram Bhartia Institute of Science and Research (SBISR) is dedicated to the study of both medical and lesser known 'emerging sciences'. For the architects the challenging task of providing an appropriate architectural solution derived from the commitment to identify an environment conducive to research of the type being pursued by the Institute. While requirements of the medical research wing could reasonably be identified and quantified, those of the 'emerging sciences' could not so easily be established. The evolving programme led to the transformation of a cluster of meeting rooms into a place for congregation — an art gallery or a large conference hall. The amphitheatre, which initially emerged as a result of tucking the services away, grew into an entity on its own right. What evolved was a building wrapped around and focused on a central landscaped court. The court itself presents three levels, with the amphitheatre, which can be considered the first level, tiering downward to the water-fountain before stepping down again to allow light to enter the basement and open up vistas and views outward from the basement. Though the Institute gives the appearance of a small building, it covers a large area, which has been massed and articulated to give it a sense of intimacy and human scale. A careful spatial sequence begins with the sensation of experiencing the soaring airy pergola. Rather than a car-oriented entrance portico, there is a pleasant landscaped pedestrian approach as the driveway unobtrusively moves away from the entrance pergola to lead to the parking space at the rear. The lofty two-storeyed entrance lobby and reception offers a sense of arrival and acts as a space to pause before one is directed into the building. Movement is through a series of gentle transitions and visual surprises, as when the layered landscape of the garden court, hidden behind the reception area, unfolds and delights with its fountain, flowers and changing vistas. Particular attention was paid to the medical wing. The courts provide a sense of scale and intimacy and help give a specific identity to the various departments. Architectural elements such as columns, parapets, stone-cladwalls and windows were orchestrated to create a serene and restful atmosphere conducive to a research environment. The Kotah stone cladding was allowed to retain its rough texture, and two shades were employed with the blue-green forming the backdrop and the greenish-grey stone punctuating and accentuating windows, lintels and sills. Yellow Jaisalmer stone was used as bands to articulate walls from circular columns. The stone cladding, projecting slightly beyond the exposed concrete beams, creates a sharp shadowline as division. The variety in texture imparts a sense of movement, allowing the eye to wander over the surface. The multi-purpose hall and the spacious foyer have been so designed as to accommodate exhibitions and displays. The multi-purpose hall and open-air theatre were seen as valuable assets in helping to bridge the gap between the people of a city and its Institutions.

National Institute of Fashion Technology

126 B

Vastu Shilpa Consultants (1994)
🚇 Green Park
Near Gulmohar Park, Hauz Khas

The National Institute of Fashion Technology at New Delhi recreates an inwardly bazaar, livened up by designed displays and movements of students as well as visitors through the entire space. Catering for academic, administrative and residential activities, the campus reinterprets the traditional town square through its inward looking building with interactive corridors, bridges and terraces, *kund*-like steps and communicative facades. The front court, surrounded by the terraced academic block and glazed administrative wing becomes a culturally appropriate and climatically comfortable outdoor space. Animated by a series of high and low platforms, soft and hard landscaping, a water channel and a mirror-like wall backdrop, the space multiplies as entrance court, central green, display platform, informal theatre and a visual focus. Open as well as glass screened bridges separating *kund*-like court from amphitheatre court, not only remain as movement path, but also double up as the catwalk for the fashion shows which can be viewed over from the class rooms, corridors, library as well as the administrative block. Fragmentation of the built mass and facade articulation illustrate a tenuous yet experientially rich inter-relationship between various parts of the ensemble. Formlessness and fragmentation of buildings at NIFT renders it flexible to adapt and express various form and elements of different edges, an effective response to their specific functions and context. While the common set of elements — namely court, steps and corridors-integrate these parts into a unified whole. Heightening the drama is a juxtaposed co-existence of the random stone masonry wall fragments mimicking ancient ruins along with stone grit plastered walls of yester years, and steel frame screen, clad with reflective glazing, of the present times. Serving as visual reminders of the 'time and space', they evoke a sense of belonging with their inherent contradictions and metamorphosed manifestations.

School for Spastic Children

Romi Khosla Design Studio (1995)

Green Park

2-Balbir Saxena Marg, Hauz Khas

The School for Spastic Children was the first custom-designed school for physically challenged children, and was initiated by funds made available from the British government to support a local NGO. The school was designed for 500 handicapped children and provides not only specialized facilities and training, but also courses for parents of children with special needs. The school also acts as a centre for fieldwork to be carried out in rural areas in North India. Romi Khosla's design of the building with its use of abstract forms is regarded as a foremost example of post-modern architecture in India. The building uses exaggerated iconic forms and reflects a psychological concept so that there is also a narrative to it. The idea was to create a protective womb, almost as an abstraction of the rock-cut cave temples at places such as Ajanta. The architect deliberately did not set aside any spaces for a specific function and sought a building where movement was easy and space expansive. The building provides a sheltered environment with a courtyard open to the sky. To ease movement for the pupils, ramps and wide openings have been provided and there are no high plinths. Attention was also paid to the students' conveniences with every two classrooms having an adjacent toilet. With specially designed ramps and natural light penetrating into the building, the architect not only provided for a comfort zone for the children but also expressed his love of iconography in a poetic manner. Tall and deep recesses evenly spaced along the facade run from ground to roof. They include balconies that alternate in shape — squares and semi-circles. The forms of the tiers of windows with their sloped profiles are echoed in the low outer wall. This building is an outstanding example of the Post-Modernist style popular in the 1990s.

Corporate Office and Production Facility for CREW B.O.S. PVT. LTD.

128 **B**

Neeraj Manchanda Associates
(1996)

🚇 Guru Dronacharya

199 Phase I, Udyog vihar, Gurgaon, Haryana

The commission for this project included a clear brief from the client at the outset which asked for the building to communicate what the company stood for. As a leading leather-goods design and production company, which has since gone public, CREW B.O.S. has been known for

its Indian design sensibilities, its intensive use of handicraft in its products and high quality. In recognition of this brief and the fact that this building, in its role as the corporate office and showroom for the company's products, could contribute to the company's image and communicate its core focus, NMA designed it as a series of brick panels on the exterior, similar in size but, drawing from the tradition of high Indian craftsmanship such as in the carved *havelis* of Rajasthan, always different in detail. The contractors for the project, M/S Gurbukhsh Singh B. A. Builders Pvt. Ltd., put in exemplary effort in order to ensure high quality in the brickwork. Though the overall cuboidal volume of the building is circumstantial to the site and regulations that govern it, these brick panels have succeeded in both tempering the overall building volume and creating a unique method of communicating the idea of quality and Indian hand-craft through a rich fabric of brick patterns and textures.

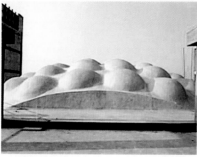

Gas Training Institute   129 C
Raj Rewal Associates (1996)
⊜ NOIDA Sector 18
Plot No. 24, sector 16 NOIDA, UP

The Institute is located in the satellite city of NOIDA near Delhi on an area of 17,300 square metres. The function of the building is to impart technical education to those working in the gas and petroleum sector. The client's brief includes classrooms, research laboratories, a small auditorium, canteen and an administration wing. There is also an industrial workshop for petroleum and plastic products along with a hostel for visiting students. These diverse functions are grouped around a series of interlinked courtyards. The central enclosure is interspersed with an open air teaching theatre, which forms the focal centre. It is linked to the auditorium with a seating capacity for 200 persons. The open spaces are surrounded by verandahs congenial for learning and informal discussions. The ground floor is dedicated to various activities like workshops, display, cafeteria and auditorium, integrated into a well-knit complex by covered corridors facing the courtyards. The first floor includes a conference room, audio-video and publication, demonstration and recreation facilities, and the second floor houses the library, seminar room and classrooms. All the floors including the third floor have offices for the administrative staff. The structure of the complex is based on RCC frame with coffered ceilings. The infill walls are of sand lime white bricks. The sunscreens around verandahs and balconies are of Delhi-Agra red sand stone. The lattice *jaalis* with intricate patterns exhibit a display of light and shade in the corridors at different times of the day, and lend an ingenious quality to the facades of the institute. The primary structure of the auditorium consists of steel pipes supporting ferro-cement 'bubble domes'. The meeting rooms on the top most floors are overlaid with stone ribs supporting ferro-cement domes, as an experimental structure. All the materials are expressed frankly on the facade. The vocabulary of design is based on the extensive use of red sandstone *jaalis* and their changing relationship with white bricks and concrete columns.

National Media Centre
Housing (NMC) »   130 J
Space Design Consultants (1996)
⊜ Guru Dronacharya
Shankar Chowk, NH-8, DLF, Phase III, Gurgaon, Haryana

Most housing schemes are designed as typical units being repeated to create a housing block or cluster. The requirements of an individual user are ignored and he has to fit his requirements in what is offered. Also, in most cases the unit design is inflexible and doesn't allow

or changing requirements of a growing family. To create user centric expandable units within the larger framework of community housing was the design goal for NMC housing. The scheme consists of 190 houses. The users were members of a co-operative society with considerably varied requirements and finances. To accommodate they different needs, a flexible framework was required. Once the colony was laid out and the plots allotted, a large number of house types with variations in layouts, number of units on the plot and number of floors built were designed from which the users chose their preferred house plan. This resulted in a visually rich urban fabric. The site was planned with vehicular movement and parking restricted to the peripheral ring road. Houses are approached from cul-de-sacs, an arrangement that discourages residents from driving all the way to their houses and creates ample opportunities for chance encounters as people walk to their house. Children can also use the streets to play. A central green space with a pedestrian path ties the different streets together and gives pedestrians an advantage over cars. The walks serve as pedestrian shortcuts between different parts of the community. All colonies in new Gurgaon area depended upon tube wells for water supply as there was no municipal supply. It was realized that the ground water table

would eventually get depleted because of over extraction. A combined system of rainwater drainage and ground water recharge was developed. The normal drainage pipes were connected to a system of infiltration pits located in the green areas. This scheme was designed and executed long before rainwater harvesting was talked about. The houses are designed to be thermally comfortable and energy efficient. The buildings are oriented to face the favourable north-south axis but with sufficient variation so as to avoid monotony. The windows are protected with appropriately designed sunshades and west facing walls are shaded by plantation. Each house has a sunny side for winter use and a shaded side for summer use. For additional cooling, each house was equipped with a chimney where an evaporative cooler could be fitted. An arrangement for installing solar water heaters is provided in all the houses. The whole scheme is a constantly evolving housing where residents can extend/modify their houses as per their requirement. Due to appropriate elevation controls and a system of involving the architect in design decisions taken by individual members, the Housing Co-operative Society has been able to maintain a coherent character ever after 15 years of its existence. The additional construction has added to the richness of the urban character.

Apollo Indraprastha Hospital 131 C
Hafeez Contractor (1996)
🚇 Jasola-Apollo
Sarita Vihar, Mathura road

The Apollo Indraprastha Hospital was a collaborative project of the renowned Apollo hospitals and the Delhi Development Authority. It spreads over 15 acres of prime land in South Delhi. Prior to the initial conceptualisation, the architects conducted research into various facets of hospitals and the primary design deliberations and gave a careful attention towards the Indian social milieu. In the Indian scenario, the families are close knit and most patients are often accompanied by their relatives. This social context was usually ignored by most of the previous hospital designs in the subcontinent. Responding to this background, the architects arrived at the core idea of creating a central spine atrium plaza from which the entire design sets off. The design made a conscious attempt to prioritise the needs of the users and establish an environment that is more humane, pleasant and most of all conducive to rejuvenation and relaxation. The is especially reflected in the central atrium, which has several landscape elements. It is a vast sky-lit area, dotted with wrought iron tables and chairs evocative of garden furniture. This pedestrian atrium enlivens the hospital with an almost street-like atmosphere. The flexible setting allows ample space for patients and visitors to relax, eat their lunch, take a breather or catch a quick nap. The plan is also an early example of the central circulation spine used as an organisational device in Indian hospital designs. The two major blocks of the hospital are connected by this atrium of huge volume which acts as the large waiting area. The outpatient departments and diagnostic flank the atrium on both sides. The less complex outpatient department is separated by the pedestrian atrium from the complex acute care, diagnostic and inpatient areas. The design was also primarily conceived as a tower on a podium structure with all its services in the basement; clinical and treatment zones on the ground and immediate upper floors while keeping all the nursing zones on upper floors. Segregating the outpatient department from the rest of the hospital has eased the pressure on the hospital machinery while making the whole hospital experience simpler, faster and more convenient for the outpatient. The in-patient wards have cross-ventilation and every bed has a visual connection to the outdoors. The wards are reassuringly grouped around a central nurse station and are placed above the clinical zone in the podium. The clinical zone consisting of the diagnostic and acute care areas, is located with the operation theatres and set within a deep-spanned podium floor, on top of a double basement housing the complex support zone consisting of the various services.

INTACH
132 G

Vastu Shilpa Consultants (1997)
Khan Market — Jor Bagh
Plot no. 71, Lodi Estate

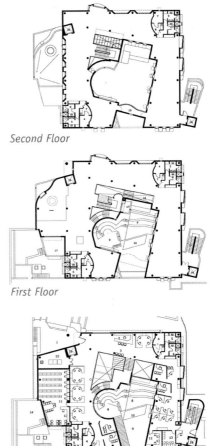

Second Floor

First Floor

Ground Floor

INTACH is an autonomous, non-government organization. The trust was established in 1984 to promote the cause of natural, cultural and architectural heritage of India. The proposed building for the trust was required not only to provide for its administrative offices but also to become a resource centre and an open house for the dissemination of information, spreading awareness and promoting issues pertaining to heritage and conservation. The INTACH Headquarters is located in the Lodi Estate, an area set aside for some of the premier national and international organizations in the country. The architects conceived a nearly cubical block with a built perimeter and central void thus providing a contiguous built mass, which helps in defining the street edge. This void or atrium forms the focus for movement, light, ventilation and view besides providing a spill over space for the institutions large number of public activities. The scheme of centre and periphery, of core and edges, is mutually reinforced with a diagonal movement link aligning further with the historic monuments beyond, on the same axis. The diagonal axis acknowledges the presence of the Lodi monuments beyond and helps to orient and connect the core to these historic references framed in vignettes. The void also reinstates the spatial organization of a traditional built form in a hot dry climate. With a pool at its base, the outdoor space conceived as a courtyard transforms into a space akin to the void within a *baoli*, a stepped water well. The court helps to create a favourable microclimate through the overshadowing of the court walls. With a cooling pond at its base, the form of the court induces thermal movement of air, which cools the interior of the building. The roof terrace at INTACH with its high parapet walls coupled with pergolas and built in seats within terrace gardens commands views over the court, plaza and the monuments across. The building has a flat slab RCC structure on a regular column grid. This renders the space flexible yet gives freedom for future space subdivisions and combinations, thus providing for change and growth in the institutions program over time. The diversity of functions such as administration, library, exhibition space, seminar areas due to their intense interactive value are accommodated in a range of spaces with varying shape, size and volume. The material palette of the project consists of reinforced concrete flat slab and circular column construction with brick masonry filler walls, aggregate stone plaster with granite bands on external walls and Kotah stone flooring.

225

Liberalisation

Delhi College of Engineering   133

Ajoy Choudhury (1998)
🚇 Rithala
Shahbad Daulatpur,
Main Bawana Road

The Delhi Technological University (DTU), formerly known as Delhi College of Engineering, is a premier government university, established in 1941 under the control of Government of India. DCE was converted to a state university in 2009 and has been rechristened Delhi Technological University. The new campus is a lush green compound well connected by roads. Facilities include a library, a computer centre, a sports complex, eight boys' hostels, three girls' hostels, and a married couples' hostel. The campus has residential facilities for faculty and staff. The campus also has an auditorium and an open air theatre. The campus has been planned on a flat piece of land measuring 164 acres beyond the urban

limits of West Delhi on Bawana Road, Badli as a micro-city within the city, composed of diverse fragments assembled according to functional and spatial requirements. The academic zone has been built around a central multilevel plaza embracing the sweep of the existing circular road with faculty housing and students hostel at close proximity on either side. The department of engineering and the workshops extend radially from the plaza while the other group of buildings consisting of the administration, computer centre and the library is composed around a cluster of existing trees and a proposed podium, interconnected through elevated walkways and a semi covered space frame structure. These two radically different geometrical compositions are held together in a compatible relationship by the multilevel central plaza. The various departments are planned around internal courts, interlinked by stilted areas. The laboratories span across these courts radially. The lecture theatres are placed towards the concourse adjoining the central plaza where a cycle track runs along the outer edge of the plaza, connecting all departments and extending to the students hostel. Future expansion is limited towards the outer circular road only, leaving the Central Plaza undisturbed.

International Society for Krishna Consciousness (ISKCON)

Achyut Kanvinde (1998)

134 C

Kailash Colony
Dhirshain Marg, Sant Nagar
Near East of Kailash

Along with Jeet Lal Malhotra and Habib Rahman, Kanvinde introduced the modern movement into India much before Le Corbusier's and Kahn's arrival on the scene. Kanvinde's experimentation with new forms took another leap in his design for the ISKCON Temple that also includes a multimedia centre and an institutional block. Although made to look like an ancient temple, the ISKCON Temple is a modern building and, like all Kanvinde's previous works, the design takes into account the topography and climate of the site. The plot was made of undulating rock whose contours the architect deliberately maintained. He also planned the site in a manner of a pilgrimage where one has to ascend to the top to get their darshan, a feature central to ancient temples across India, especially in the north. Kanvinde has used

the eleventh century temples of Orissa, such as the Jagannath Temple as his model, but abstracted traditional forms in an almost Post-Modern manner to indicate the building's place in time and space. The complex incorporates the historical curvilinear towers (*shikhara*) that are typical of temples in Orissa. However, while historically *shikharas* were heavy, austere structures symbolising mountain peaks, Kanvinde inventively used an RCC framed structure that duplicates the traditional form of the shikhara, but is hollow on the inside, making it a much lighter structure. Kanvinde employed Dholpur stone as his chosen material for the facade of the temple.

Institute of Social Science

Christopher Charles Benninger Architects (1998)

Chhattarpur

8 Nelson Mandela Road, Vasant Kunj

The Institute of Social Sciences near the Jawahar Lal Nehru University in South Delhi is constructed on a narrow and deep plot, requiring a shared party-wall on one side and a mere three metre set-back on the other. A C-shaped plan was evolved using the area along the 'party wall' for services, stairs, elevator, vertical shafts and circulation. Two working wings extend between three garden courts, providing shade and ventilation. The composition employs a variety of special types: the public street front; a lower basement garden connected straight through to the rear of the site; interior areas, and a central atria. The three atria are to be covered with sunshades to cool the courtyards, which buffer the institute from the severe heat of summer. The building is finished in tooled Jaisalmer stone, sand stone *jaalis* and a variety of polished flooring stones set into intricate designs. As in Moghul compositions the building attempts to create a separation from the chaotic 'exterior' and pristine controlled spaces, through the integration of gardens within the built form.

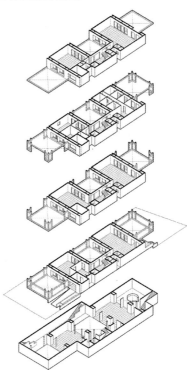

Signature Towers ⌃

136 J

C.P. Kukreja Associates (1998)

🌐 IFFCO Chowk
Sector 46, Gurgaon

This landmark office complex was promoted as a joint venture project between Unitech of New Delhi and Singapore Consortium. The complex, located in Gurgaon along the Delhi-Jaipur highway NH8, has an area of 600,000 square feet. The central air-conditioning, 100 % back-up power, high-speed lifts and comprehensive Building Management System are some of the facilities available. At the time it was built it was one of the first curtain glass facade buildings in Northern India. The Towers have a distinct architectural form with a large 15 storey 'puncture' which is an 'urban window' through which the skyline of Gurgaon is visible as one drives along the express way.

Corporate Office for TCI »

137 J

Ashok B Lall Architects (1998)

🌐 HUDA City Centre
69 Institutional Area, Sector 32
Gurgaon, Haryana

The office building provides high standards of environmental comfort, integrated systems to support information technology and arrangements for flexible office layouts at low capital, operational and environmental costs. The design uses the principle of bio-climatic design coupled with the traditional *Haveli* form, to establish its regional and cultural identity. The building was built in 12 months. The structure is in-situ RCC and most finishing material are prefabricated. The street facade is conceived as a simple continuous order produced by the construction vocabulary of the skin. The landscaped entrance forecourt and the terrace garden above are active participants in the street. The fountain court is an environmental device that seeks to combine the principles of physics, perception and cultural psychology to produce an aesthetic language in which nature is reinstated as a beneficent force in architecture. The gentle play of water as it trickles down the column and over the cascade together with the changing light, caught by the sculpture and water, conveys the passage of time and seasons. The aesthetic of water, the precious tended garden, gentle light, with the tracery of patterned shadows and colour remembers a beautiful architectural tradition. The central fountain court is the generator of the office environment. The primary orientation of the workspaces is towards the court. The basement too participates in the court. The external skin is solid with windows for view and day lighting clerestories above. All workplaces are daylit. Dryhung, rough split sandstone, coloured terrazzo and concrete precast window surrounds and bands provide the aesthetic vocabulary of the building skin. The building is more open towards the inner court, the terrace garden and the entrance forecourt, spaces that have structural frames for stretching shading screens according to season.

Corporate Office for Jindal Industries ⌃

Sumit Ghosh and Associates (1998)

🚇 AIIMS

12, Jindal Centre, Bhikaji Cama Place

138 B

This office building is part of the Bhikaji Cama Place District Centre that had a set of urban controls guiding material use and elevation lines. An existing structure, originally planned as a cinema hall, was retrofitted to suit the functions of an office building for a leading producer of stainless steel and mild steel in the country. The office spaces are organised around two landscaped courtyards while the exterior envelope is terraced to form gardens at upper levels. Clad with sandstone as per the urban controls, the building exemplifies the use of stone masonry in its use of monoliths in railings, sills, lintels, jambs and balusters beyond the 'veneering' practices common with such stone. Stones weighing up to a ton were hand-crafted at site by masons from the neighbouring western state of Rajasthan. The building is detailed to a high level of sophistication and attempts a marrying of the high-technology of stainless steel glazing with the dying traditions of stone craft. Rounded edges and delicate lines add sensuality to the notion of weight: reminiscent of a 'Hindu' tradition of building.

Birla Office Building «

ARCOP (1999)

🚇 Barakhamba Road

Barakhamba Road

139 D

Birla Corp Office by ARCOP is located on Barakhamba road near Connaught Place. It is one of the numerous offices of one of India's largest business house: the Birlas. The 12-storey building has a symmetrical plan with two cores located in the centre. The building has a total area of 120,000 square feet with three levels of underground parking entered from the rear. The external facade consists of primarily two materials: granite stone cladding and structural glazing. The front facade is recessed at the top with a large steel pergola over the terrace.

The American Institute of Indian Studies

Space Design Consultants (1998)

🚇 HUDA City Centre

22, Sector 32, Institutional Area

Gurgaon, Haryana

140 J

The American Institute of Indian Studies provides scholars with facilities for research in Indian art, architecture and music. The building houses administrative offices, research facilities, archives and libraries. Since AIIS was set up to conserve Indian art, architecture and music, the building design refers to the traditional Indian way of building without trying to be traditional or monumental. From outside, the building appears to be a small single-storeyed structure while actually it is a basement and ground floor organized around two sunken courtyards. The passages around the courtyards form a thermal transition zone between the uncontrolled outdoors and the controlled indoors. The building form emulates the peaceful internal environment of a traditional courtyard building while maintaining modern standards for lighting and ventilation.The sunken courtyards provide an element of surprise to the visitor and bring adequate daylight into all areas of the building including the basement. The archives (tapes and negatives) have to be maintained at a temperature of 18 degree and need to be air-conditioned. To reduce the cooling load, these areas are located in the earth-sheltered basement. The work areas located at the ground floor are protected by specially insulated external walls and cooled by a terrace garden. The north-south orientation of the building and the external sunshades over windows reduce heat gain. Light shelves and glass brick panels improve quality of day lighting and minimize the need for artificial lighting during the daytime. For additional thermal comfort in the work areas, a two-stage evaporative cooling system has been provided. The first stage provides normal direct evaporative cooling in which air is cooled by addition of moisture. In the second stage, air is cooled indirectly without adding any humidity to it. By controlling the operation of the two stages, it is possible to achieve cooling with some degree of humidity control. With changing standards of comfort, this system of evaporative cooling had to be replaced with air conditioning for individual rooms. As in traditional Indian buildings, diversity of functional spaces in the form of gardens, courts, verandahs, pavilions and passages are provided in addition to the normal enclosed rooms. These allow people to be comfortable at those times when the fully enclosed rooms feel uncomfortable. The courtyard is designed for holding small meetings in summer while the terrace garden with its modern pavilions is suitable for larger gatherings, which usually take place in winter. The breezy central verandah is ideally suited for the monsoon period.

Laburnum

ARCOP (1999)
IFFCO Chowk
Dlf City Phase IV, Gurgaon

141 J

Laburnum is a condominium complex, developed by Landbase and is located in a fast growing residential area of Gurgaon. Spread over thirteen acres of land, it comprises a mix of low, mid and high rise buildings. The design brief given to the architect was to create a lifestyle product and not simply a run-of-the mill housing development, and to achieve a living environment that would give exclusivity and comfort to its residents. Accordingly, large apartments were designed, which helped in achieving the permissible FAR (which is presently 175 in Gurgaon) with a low population density. To create substantial open spaces, only twenty six per cent ground coverage has been utilised, as against the permissible thirty five per cent. The design that emerged has 261 dwelling units in a configuration of three-level town houses, seven-storey apartment blocks and three 18-storey towers. The design approach has been inward looking with the three-level town houses on three sides of the plot, which then give way to the seven-storey apartment blocks, leaving the central portion of the plot for the three 18-storey towers. The town houses have been designed with sunken gardens and dedicated covered car parking. Accessed from the internal road, each town house faces inwards. The mid-rise seven-storey apartment blocks are located opposite these town houses and these have been laid out around internal courts that have been landscaped extensively. Each apartment on these blocks gets a view of the court and also the external surrounds which highlight the available openness and provide cross ventilation. The three 18-storey towers, with two apartments to a floor, have a square profile in plan, which is accentuated in the vertical scale by shear walls on all four sides. Structurally, these shear walls provide greater stiffness to the entire structure and have been a factor in keeping the cost of the structure relatively low. Double basements have been provided below the towers. Use of aerated cement concrete blocks with fly ash as the main constituent, for all masonry works also contributed to structural cost control. A proprietary form-work system (MIVAN) was used to reduce, considerably, the cycle time for RCC work of the superstructure and this contributed to appreciable time savings in raising the structures. Architecturally, these shear walls form a significant component of the towers and stand out as dramatic elements in the facade. The COURT GREENS apartments have been designed with a diagonal access corridor with the main staircase at one end along with the elevator bank and servants' rooms and the fire escape staircase at the other end. The external treatment of the facades is in white sandstone, with accents of red sandstone used as parapet railings and copings. Textured paint has been used above the second floor level. Though the stone cladding has been limited up to the second floor, its use has been continued for balcony and terrace parapets on all floors. All blocks have stilted areas on the ground floor. These areas can also be used for gatherings and social functions and have been finished accordingly. Landscaping has been given great importance and facilities like jogging tracks, children's play areas, swimming pool, tennis court and even a dog walking area have been integrated into the landscape.

The Manor `142` `C`
Studio U+A (1999)
🚇 Moolchand
77, Off Mathura Road,
Friends Colony West

Studio U+A were the Design Consultants for this project. The Manor, located in the long established Friends' Colony neighbourhood, has only 18 rooms, each with a distinct character and layout. Studio U+A converted the 1950s two star guesthouse into a deluxe hotel of understated elegance. The contemporary design is complemented by rich local materials including silks, hand knotted carpets and inlaid mosaic flooring. The Manor was one of the first to be listed in the Condé Nast publication *Top Hotels in India*.

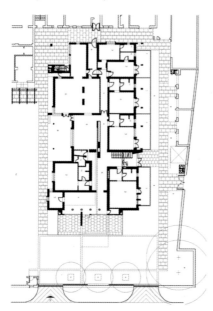

Residence at Civil Lines » `143` `A`
Ashok B Lall Architects (1999)
🚇 Civil Lines
2B Ramkishore Marg, Civil Lines

Civil Lines had large open lots of land with bungalows. They are now been sub-divided and re-developed to provide more upper-middle-income housings. The resultant urban structure has the nature of a close-grained texture with low-rise, high-density housing. It can be seen as a mutation of the traditional North Indian City form. This project incorporates the traditional built-to-edge buildings with internal spaces to establish the intimate city scale that produces a habitable and lively streetscape. In addition, the designs takes in consideration passive strategies for climatic comfort. Salvaged beautiful pieces from the bungalows that were dismantled are re-deployed to recall the traces of past history. The craft of coloured terrazzo flooring inlayed with patterns has been utilised extensively. The buildings express a continuity of the delegate sensibility of Delhi's pre-colonial architecture. The architect's own house is a part of a residential redevelopment in Civil Lines, New Delhi, which develops a prototype for compact housing design suited for the wide seasonal range of north Indian plains — hot-dry summer, hot-humid monsoon, cold winter and gentle climate around the festivals of Holi, Deepawali in Spring and Fall. The project consists of four residential units built-to-edge on a street. The houses on the north face

of the street are courtyard houses leading towards gardens on the south side. Whereas the houses on the south side of the street have their gardens on the north side and are linear. These are all large single family houses two- to three-storey high. This enables the sections of the buildings to be designed integrally for enjoying the winter sun. The passive devices that interact with the external elements are given a central place in the architectural language of the buildings. The general orientation of the buildings is aligned east-west making most of the windows on the north and south faces. The courtyard houses, because of their squarish proportions in plan, have faces towards the east and west as well. The windows on these faces look into narrow protected alleys or the small courtyard between the two houses. The alley space on the west side is shaded by retaining the wall of the original double-storey building which had lined the side street. For the linear houses on the north side, the width of the driveway that separates the two rows of houses is just about enough to enable winter sunshine to enter the first floor windows. The sections of these houses are designed with a cut-out such that the winter sun is brought into the living/dining space, the heart of the house on the ground floor. Terraces on the second floor have skylights that again admit winter sun into the first floor rooms on the north side of the house. The roofs are finished with broken marble, laid on 30 millimetre thick polyurethane board insulation above the

RCC slab. The marble is a reused material which has high reflectivity that helps in reducing heat gain in the summer. The roofed courtyard of the house is intended to be the main climate responsive device. The hipped steel frame roof has frosted glass with a panel of clear glass on the south slope. This is underslung by a pair of *razais* (quilts) which can be pulled across for insulation or let hang down vertically for heat transfer. On the outer surface of the roofed courtyard is another frame where chicks are placed which can similarly be stretched to shade the roof or rolled away when the sun is desired. All rooms communicate directly with this central space. This passive cooling method is supplemented with a conventional mosquito-proof evaporative cooler housed on the roof, blowing through the side wall of the courtyard roof. This is an ideal system for the hot-dry season and for night flushing during the humid season as well as during autumn and spring.

French Resource Centre

144 A

*SPA Design & ABRD Architects
(1999)*

🚊 Khan Market ⊖ Race Course
2, Aurangzeb Road

The site for the centre was a typical plot of Lutyens' Delhi, with a colonial bungalow in the middle and servant quarters on the rear boundary wall. In 1966, the staff quarters were built by Raj Rewal in remarkable modern brutalist style with exposed brick and concrete structure. The French school, the auditorium and offices were constructed in 1986 on both sides of the bungalow. These buildings form a courtyard around a huge Neem tree. The Information Centre came into this context made of different types of buildings. An attitude was defined to respect the past but claiming autonomy for the project, the building is erected on the periphery of the plot. The first consideration was to make the project the crossing point of Indian and French culture. In many aspects, the building borrows from histories of architecture, technologies and building, material, of the both cultures. The project forms a 'public strip' on the western side of the plot. The status of each area is clearly established by the new building, which reveals the nature of the surroundings: the space between the buildings becomes a square paved area in red Agra stone which can be used for cinema screenings or for meetings. While the cafeteria opened out into a garden with stone benches and tables, the library had a lawn in front of it. The exposed steel structure is composed of a main frame, with the beam resting on a brick wall and a pillar. All the building materials used are from India.

TERI RETREAT

145 J

Sanjay Prakash,
DAAT: Design, Architecture &
Associated Technologies (2000)
Gual Pahari Complex, Haryana

RETREAT (Resource Efficient TERI Retreat for Environmental Awareness and Training) is TERI's vision of building a sustainable habitat. The 36-hectare TERI campus constructed in 2000 at Gual Pahari, Gurgaon, is a lush green habitat, 30 kilometres south of Delhi, in the state of Haryana. Built as a model-training complex, RETREAT is energy efficient and demonstrates sustainable and integrated use of both natural resources and clean, renewable energy technologies, and efficient waste management. With a built-up area of 3,000 square metres, this 30-room training hostel is designed with a conference facility for 100 people, dining space and kitchen, recreational area, computer room and a library. What makes it unique is the total independence it enjoys from the city's grid system, and near-complete freedom from city services and infrastructure. The RETREAT projects sustainable solutions in energy, environment and related areas. Realising path breaking building concepts in provision of training facilities and hostel, the design focuses on energy-conscious features so as to practice near-total energy autonomy and minimal resource depletion, while providing a comfortable lifestyle. The layout and orientation of the blocks maximize daylight year round and winter sun for natural heating. Summer gains are reduced by deciduous trees and devices like *jaalis*. Insulated walls and roof (the latter finished with broken tiles) further reduce heating/cooling demand. An atrium with imported transparent solar photovoltaic (SPV) panels and skylights with regular SPV panels (total 10.7 kW SPV) provide electricity in combination with a 50kW wood waste based gasifier. An intelligent building management system guides a power control unit to manage the large battery bank. The residential block utilizes the 'earth-air tunnel system'; an underground network of tunnels terminating in openings in each space. It takes advantage of the relative constancy of the earth's temperature to provide rooms with airflow to keep them between 22°–30°C throughout the year. Solar chimneys assist ventilation while chillers supplement the earth cooling. The administrative block depends on an ammonia-based CFC-free system for better humidity control. The flat plate solar collector hot water system is mounted at an incline matching the facade and provided with a catwalk for easier maintenance. A reed bed that thrives on sewage while cleaning it manages wastewater. The load bearing structure reduces steel use and lowers the embodied energy. The project breaks myths about the 'straight' forms of solar architecture, aspiring to achieve a sense of the 'campus of the future'.

Since 2001:
Post-Liberalisation

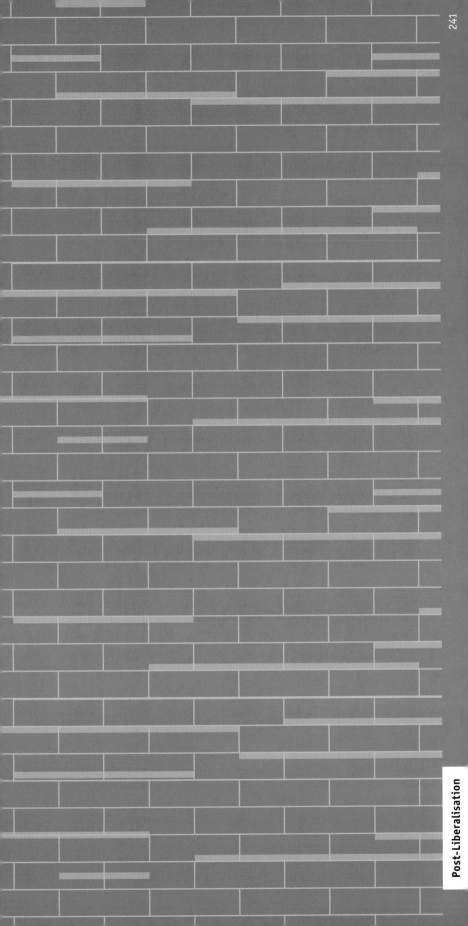

Andrews Ganj Housing

S. K. Das & Associates (2001)

⊖ Moolchand ⊖ Green Park
Siri Fort Road, Behind Ansal
Plaza, Andrews Ganj

146 B

The Andrews Ganj housing is located in Delhi, about four kilometres to the south of Lutyens' colonial capital, in a predominantly residential zone, between two major city arteries. This was the first attempt since 1947 on the part of the Indian Government to engage private architects to supersede the 'type designs' they had followed for nearly half a century. It is part of a larger development and urban design proposal to provide a zonal-level commercial facility, guest houses, and approximately 850 rental dwellings for civil servants in five different quarters. This project pertains to one such quarter, of 100 dwelling units, spread over approximately one hectare and meant for senior civil servants. The project was promoted by the Ministry of Urban Development and the Government of India. HUDCO, the Housing and Urban Development Corporation, was named

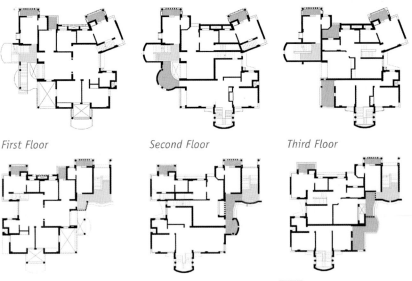

First Floor　　　*Second Floor*　　　*Third Floor*

▨ *Balcony and terraces*

the nodal agency on behalf of the Ministry to handle the design and execution. The size and internal composition of the dwellings were predetermined. Each dwelling covers 2,200 square feet including a parking garage. In addition to the usual living and dining spaces, each dwelling has three bedrooms and a study, as well as a room for domestic help. The 1960s and 1970s saw philosophies of housing that emphasised autonomy and dwellers' freedom, heterogeneity, a strong link between the personal and the social, and housing as a process and not a product. Globalization had undermined this. The architects have tried to reclaim it in practice. Projects like this usually involve gated neighbourhoods, set back from the surrounding streets and parks, with an ill-maintained intervening open space and isolated building blocks as showpieces. Rather than shying away from the surroundings, the architects tried to dissolve the boundaries and let them in. The design compels inhabitants to interact with the open spaces and with one another. The footprint of this project is spread over the entire site, containing within it a network of courtyards, streets and alleyways. These internal streets link up with the streets of the city, encouraging people to cross through. The primary structure consists of a central pedestrian spine juxtaposed with an elevated podium perpendicular to it. These are supported by streets, squares and alleys

that offer a variety of routes responding to extreme climatic variation. A block typology consisting of eight apartments is altered with each repetition, based on immediate specific contexts, to ensure privacy, encourage sociability, and circumvent the standard geometric progression. The streets, alleys, courtyards, parking spaces and pedestrian plaza are carefully layered to produce a functional open space with a familiar density reminiscent of the mediaeval Indian city. The streets are arranged in broken grids, emulating the informal streets of traditional cities. Semi-public interiors and covered spaces of varying height within and outside buildings orchestrate the creation of a new urban landscape that encourages proximity and socialization, dissolving boundaries. Each home has balconies and terraces that respond to different needs, in which people can wash and dry clothes, or sit outdoors and be part of the street, or look out onto the street and not be seen. Each home comes with a semi-private space for landscaping, encouraging dwellers to express their individuality and collectively shape their environment. Landscape thus becomes a seamless flow between structured design and people's actions. Tenant status notwithstanding, it was preferred to treat inhabitants as participants in, rather than consumers of, their space. Legal ownership is subordinated to the fact that dwellers have a right to shape their environment.

Residence at Aya Nagar

Ashish Ganju (2001)
🚇 Arjangarh
Mandir Marg, Aya Nagar Phase V

The residence is to house a couple, an architect and his wife, with visiting children, relations and friends; as well as serve as the architect's studio. The site was part of a cooperative subdivision of a one-hectare farm in a rapidly urbanizing village, originally settled by *gujjars* and *adivasis*. There was minimum urban infrastructure; the building, therefore, had to rely largely on natural resources for its life-support system. The house is a low-rise building with sloping roofs to regulate solar heat gain, and to provide shelter from the rain, using a low embodied-energy material like clay tiles for roofing. The plan form is ordered by a series of service spaces, like staircases, bathrooms, closets, and utility spaces grouped around the internal courtyard which forms the centre of the built environment. The internal courtyard brings natural light and ventilation into the studio which is built against the northern compound wall of the property, thereby increasing the area of the south-side garden for the residence. All habitable spaces are oriented to have major openings on south-facing walls. This allows the winter sun, low in the southern sky in Delhi, to penetrate indoors and maximize solar heat gain; while the summer sun, high in the sky, does not enter any of the rooms thereby minimizing adverse heat gain. The external walls are load-bearing brickwork laid in rat-trap bond to improve insulation, both thermal and acoustic. Embodied energy in the building fabric is kept low by minimizing the use of reinforced concrete, using RC filler slabs for the intermediate floors of bedrooms, with compressed earth blocks, made on site, for the filler material. The mezzanine floors are sawn hardwood (*shisham*) planks supported on mild steel structural hollow section framework. This kind of mild steel framework is also used for supporting the roof, taking advantage of its beneficial weight-to-span ratio for structural efficiency and energy-saving.

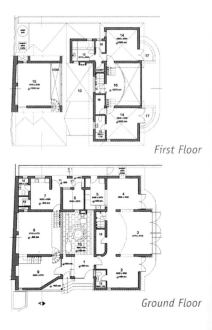

First Floor

Ground Floor

Global Business Park
Sikka Associates (2002)
⊜ Guru Dronacharya
Mehrauli Gurgaon Road,
Gurgaon, Haryana

148 J

The Global Business Park attempts to combine Indian materials in conjunction with contemporary global aesthetics and technologies in a cost-efficient manner. The location and scale of the project warranted that the project be a landmark, unique in architectural style, material specifications, technical features and the quality of workscape environment in the complex. The layout plan created four medium-rise and large floor-plate buildings around landscaped piazzas. Since the project was to be executed in two phases, the four towers were grouped into two, each around the piazzas, which are used as entrances to the tower. These two piazzas are connected by a dual carriageway spine with surface parking and intensive landscaping. To keep parking off ground and to maximize the natural landscape, two

large-sized and continuous basements were created to house close to a thousand cars. The geometry of the floor plans was devised with a view to providing single or multiple tenant occupancy on each floor. The positioning of service cores at the ends consolidated the office space within open views on both sides of each tower. The geometry also heightened the visual impact along the corners and entrances so that they vary as one moves around the complex. It also makes the building block seem lighter. The buildings themselves use a combination of double glass insulated glazing, aluminium composite panels and solid surfaces with granite and Dholpur stone cladding. This combination was knitted into the geometry of the plan to give maximum aesthetic beauty where required, while minimizing the cost of the facade elsewhere. The piazza landscape is made of low-cost and low-maintenance materials in tandem with bands of richer stones to create a fascinating pattern, which holds the eye from all floors.

Tata Consultancy Services Office

Mario Botta (2002)
NOIDA Sector 15/16
C-56, Phase-II, NOIDA

149 C

The administrative offices of software firm TCS (Tata Consultancy Services) are headquartered in NOIDA. Located about thirty kilometres from New Delhi, the site was remote at the time it was built and approached by semi-deserted roadways. The emptiness of the surrounding countryside and the first few settlements sparsely dotted an environment that had yet to express its geometric layout and had struggled to establish itself as a post-industrial district. As part of the quest for a sense of urbanity that had yet to be created, this work seeks to interpret the potential of a territory that is completely flat, with the exception of a straight barricade to protect the area from flooding caused by the heavy rains of the monsoon season. In the plans for the new urban district, this

barrier becomes the border between the constructed area and the countryside. On a territorial scale, the new building is set perpendicular to this border, expressed as a 150-metre-long beam suspended over the terrain. Since construction of the TCS headquarters, NOIDA has become very much a part of the development story of India. Thus the area has not remained either semi-deserted or empty as experienced by the architect initially.The ground floor is completely clear, providing shelter from the elements and effectively becoming a stopping place and privileged vantage point for the users housed inside the structure. The plans originated by developing the initial insight of a brise-soleil to be constructed in red Agra stone, with the workspace to be organized inside in India's scorching summers. This simple idea became the driving force for a complex story. The construction features two main volumes, the straight one housing the programmers, and the cylindrical one for the administrative and educational offices. A third lower structure houses recreational areas and encloses the new courtyard-garden within a private space. The outside walls of the buildings are presented as a filter 'embroidered' with stone motifs. These walls are set more than two metres away from the glass walls — the last physical barrier between the interior and the outdoors — which are thus protected from the harsh weather typical of the region.

Pathways World School

150 J

C. P. Kukreja Associates (2003)
HUDA City Centre
Aravali Retreat, Sohna Road,
Gurgaon, Haryana

This school is designed as a state-of-the-art residential school on a sprawling 30-acre campus situated on the picturesque Aravali Hills in Gurgaon. The centrally air-conditioned school includes academic facilities for 1,000 students along with international-level sports facilities, a media centre, hostels and housing for the staff. The school is affiliated to the International Baccalaureate Organization. The design uses local stone and brick. Lush landscaping and a magnificent lake on campus have earned Pathways the distinction of being one of Delhi's most coveted schools. There are abundant shaded outside areas for conversation and tranquil reflection. Residential facilities are based on the model of a British independent boarding school with professional staff and comfortable study-bedrooms.

Garden of Five Senses
Pradeep Sachdeva (2003)
Saket
Said-ul-Ajaib Village,
Mehrauli Badarpur Road

151 I

The Garden of Five Senses was designed as a leisure space and offers a wide variety of spaces for its visitors — food courts, speciality shops, a solar energy park, an amphitheatre and themed gardens, all inviting public interaction and exploration. It is an ideal ground to realize the twin objectives of the need for a public leisure space as well as the awakening of human sensitivity to the environment. Developed by Delhi Tourism Transportation Development Corporation, the Garden is located near the Mehrauli Archaeological Park at the village of Said-ul-Ajaib in South Delhi. Spread over a rocky ridge, the site commands a spectacular view of the 800-year-old Qutub Minar and the surrounding city. Majestic rocks stand silhouetted against the sky, others lie strewn upon the ground in a casual yet alluring display of nature's sculptural genius. It was the ideal ground on

which to realize the concept of a public leisure space that would awaken a sensory response and thereby a sensitivity to the environment. Soaring stainless-steel birds mounted on slate-clad pillars welcome you into the park. An expansive plaza, set on the natural slope of the site, invites you up the spiral walkway. Across, a troop of elephants, cut in stone, luxuriating in a water bath, tempts exploration. The ridge has been left in its natural wild state and planting restricted to the lower areas. Over 200 species of plants create a rich collage of form, colour and texture. The architecture may be described as quirky and fun, where quixotic concrete columns and animal capitals, mosaics and dramatic planting effects play off the straight forwardness of traditional brickwork and stonework. The project is one of India's largest commissions of public art, featuring works of over 25 artists. The Garden has been designed to the imagery suggested by the name 'Garden of Five Senses'. Colour, fragrances, texture and form all come together in an evocative bouquet that awakens the mind. Visitors are encouraged to touch the rocks and displays; to smell the flowers. Fragrant flower beds stimulate the olfactory senses, while landscaping appeals to the eyes. Ceramic bells and waterfalls create a soothing sound pleasing to the ear and the food courts serve a variety of cuisines to please the tongue. Thus the five senses of sight, sound, smell, taste and touch are all stimulated by this garden.

French Trade Commissioner's Residence

 152 A

SPA Design & ABRD Architects (2003)

Ⓔ Khan Market
68 Sunder Nagar

Sunder Nagar is one of the most remarkable colonies of the post independence period. It borrows its particular identity from British colonial planning of symmetrical twin houses facing parks, high ceilings, and verandas on one side and an international modern style with long sunshade slabs, simple straight lines on the other side. The project of this new house aims to keep a typological analogy with the neighbour in order to preserve the character of the colony. Square proportions, floor heights, verandas and terraces are directly inspired by this inherent quality of Sunder Nagar. On the other hand, the project focused on giving a very contemporary image of an old typology. This was achieved by creating large open spaces at the ground floor, transparent between the front and the back garden, in order to improve the space and light quality and provide large reception areas. A central courtyard brings light and ventilation to all bathrooms, which are kept away from the facades. A new type of structural glazing integrating a perforated aluminium sheet was especially developed in order to provide transparency and heat rejection at the same time. This keeps the soft light of a traditional *jaali* wall with a low-maintenance material, ever changing with the sun course.

Parliament Library Building
Raj Rewal Associates (2003)
🚇 Ⓔ Central Secretariat
Sansad Marg

153 E

The Parliament Library was conceptualized as a house of knowledge, symbolically a place of enlightenment. The design concept, with its connotations of an inward-looking building, reflects a specific preference for subtle spatial enclosures rather than forms of grandeur. The design is based on the context of the site and the nature of the proposed building. The aim was to seek a low-key architectural expression signifying sagacity, even spiritual elegance, rather than compete with the power of the parliament. Both visually and symbolically, the central hall of the existing Parliament, denoting peoples' power, consensus and democracy, is linked to the central core of the new complex, symbolizing knowledge on a central axis, through a sequence of spaces culminating in a new auditorium for 1,100 people. The height of the proposed building has been restricted to the podium level of the Parliament building in terms of the urban context of the site. Only architectural features of glazed crystalline forms or domes protrude above it.

The Parliament Library complex broadly consists of the following facilities:

· Library and Research Reference Documentation Information Services (LARRDIS)
· Bureau of Parliament Studies and Training (BPST)
· Parliamentary audio-visual library/ museum
· MPs' reading area
· Auditorium with a capacity of 1,100
· Parking
· Service block

The complex is demarcated in three zones for easy accessibility and utility for the VIPs, scholars and general public. This zoning ensures privacy and security for the VIPs and segregates the scholars' area of BPST from public activity areas of the museum and the auditorium. This focal centre housing library activities is covered with a glass brick roof and around it are located an MPs' reading room, banquet hall, archives and LARRDIS. Further radiating from this space are the main arteries to the library stacks, museums and auditorium. Inner circulation for the MPs is extremely simple and direct and relates them to all activities of the complex,

without conflicting with public circulation or service facilities. Open spaces within the library complex complement the enclosures within the Parliament building, but are more subtle and complex. Courtyards form an important feature of the design vocabulary because they are suitable for the Delhi climate. They create a dust-free atmosphere and reduce the temperature during summer months.There are three courtyards symmetrically placed around the central built form complementing the distinct functions. The first court is built adjoining the MPs' reading room and BPST committee room. It has an atmosphere of tranquillity around a 'sunken garden' which is symbolic of liberty of thought, expression, belief, faith and worship. The MPs' dining hall, club-room and the auditorium enclose the second court. This courtyard features a tall tree symbolising social, economic and political justice. The third court is surrounded by the museum and auditorium. Its space can be utilized for outdoor exhibitions around the water-pool, which represents equality of status and opportunity. The Parliament Library has two distinct structural systems. The structural arrangement for the lower floors is based on a diagrid of prefabricated concrete coffers 1.2 metres apart, supported by circular columns of concrete, encased in sandstone. However, the major public areas of the building like the library reading rooms, museum and entrance hall, which have larger spans, are covered with shallow domes of light-weight concrete, supported by a primary structure of varied tubular steel lattices. The design of primary steel lattices vary according to the functional requirement but they are all supported by steel ring beams, which are connected to steel plates embedded in the columns. The circular steel ring beams are lifted above general roof level on point load of columns. This allows for a vertical area to be filled with glass bricks to light the interior spaces. The aim is to provide a light and elegant structural system. The structural diagrid of steel tubes and tensile rods supports light-weight fibre cement domes of five metres, diameter. For the central focal point of library activities, there is a dynamic glass dome framed with stainless steel structural members in the form of four petals. The focal domes provide the natural light for the two basements at the centre of the building.

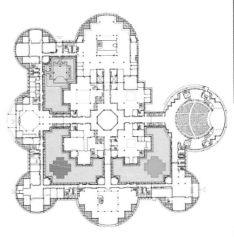

NATCO Head Office and Showroom

Design Plus (2004)

⊜ NOIDA Sector 15

A-106, Sector 5 NOIDA, UP

154 C

During the early 2000s, NOIDA's sectors 4 and 5 were undergoing a transition from completely industrial to a pastiche of industrial and commercial. With a number of offices sprouting, Natraj Trading Company commissioned Design Plus to create substantial extensions to the current factory building and to create a Head Office that would represent the brand and the product. NATCO Head Office reflects the trade of the company onto its interior detail, building skin and the immediate context. The clients are one of the largest exporters of varied stone types in India. In 2002, when the building was beginning construction, the company's major export material was slate. Design Plus decided to break the facade from a rigid plan and create varying volumes for the exterior and resulting internal spaces. These volumes were treated with slate cut in as many sizes as possible for external cladding. The building itself educates the owner's potential clients of the variations possible with the material. The interiors follow a similar narration, the only difference being that slate was swapped for granite.

Grape City

155 C

Raj Rewal Associates (2004)
NOIDA City Centre / Vaishali
Sector 62, Greater NOIDA, UP

Grape City is a Japanese multinational company with worldwide operations
stretching from Shanghai to Seattle. It
had been working from three distinct
premises in Delhi for a decade and decided to build a major centre in the satellite city of NOIDA, close to Delhi. It
was felt that the new premises should
offer a friendly ambience with the maximum of natural light, and spaces that
can be divided or enlarged according to
flexible working requirements. The design is based on a central atrium three
storeys high. Offices of varying scale, to
house ten to fifteen people, are arranged
around this central space on three levels.
The progression of spaces from the cafeteria is carried further to an enclosed
garden with flanking open-air seats
around a curved fountain. The inner edge
of the cafeteria opens onto another water cascade on slatted white marble. The

roof of the atrium is designed as a space
frame lattice pattern, reminiscent of
beehives, and covered with glass bricks
and reflective glass. The glass brick surfaces are translucent and keep the atrium glowing with natural light, creating a friendly and lively office, which
fosters creativity. The fluid space built
around the atrium links offices, cafeteria
and the open-air seating enclosure. The
fountain at the centre of the atrium sym-
bolizes the creative aspect of the software technology. Externally the building
form with protruding balconies obstructs
the harsh sunlight and keeps the building in shadow, reducing the energy load.

Post-Liberalisation

Mirambika Institute for Free Progress, Education and Integral Human Values

156 H

Sanjay Prakash,
DAAT: Design, Architecture &
Associated Technologies (2004)
Hauz Khas
Mirambika Free Progress School
Sri Aurobindo Ashram, Aurobindo Marg

Mirambika, Research Centre for Integral Education and Human Values, is a centre focusing on Integral Education, which is based on the Integral Philosophy of Sri Aurobindo and The Mother. It is situated at the Sri Aurobindo Ashram campus in New Delhi. From its inception, Mirambika has had a different approach towards learning. Here learning is based on the view that each individual comes into life with an evolutionary purpose and corresponding potentialities: educating means drawing out this potential. The building was conceived as a place to hold an innovative programme of education, research, training and scholarship. Mirambika is a 'free progress' school where the stress is on child-centric value-oriented education. There is a very light curriculum that is customized to each child, no strong subject divides, and no mainstream examination or testing—instead, there is continuous and ongoing feedback and

evaluation. The spaces were designed to be organic, amorphous, and such that the boundary between inside and outside space would vanish. This reflected the spirit of the organization—breaking of all barriers, actualizing the self and achieving excellence through consulting the inner consciousness. The building is planned as a space-filling modular grid on a basic structural dimension of 7.2 metres, with concrete ribs subdividing the slab into eight or four equal panels. Though there are very few, they can be shifted to any of these locations on the ribs. The electrical services in the ceiling are randomly arranged so that they can just drop down according to flexible arrangements of the spaces below. Water-based services (sinks, toilets, water play areas) are placed in defined, relatively inflexible, locations. Even the planning was done in parts by a participatory process so that after the basic modular structure the infill walls and windows were indeterminate. The building is finished with white terrazzo and china mosaic roofs, extensive courtyards and vegetation for cooling and ventilation, and integrated solar hot water. The design team was apprehensive that the type of building—almost like a verandah, with few walls, therefore open to dust—might prove a liability due to heat and dust, but as it turned out, the dust-free environment of the Ashram around has allowed this building to actually be comfortable in all seasons. This project is considered a pioneering interpretation of learning space representing an evolution towards openness and acceptance of the natural environment.

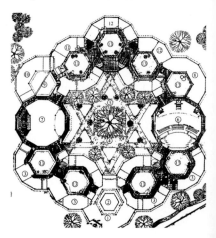

Asian Roots Spa

157 B

Morphogenesis (2004)
🚇 Green Park
B-5/15 Safdarganj Enclave,
Opp. Deer Park

Taking its inspiration from the birth of holistic treatments in Asian traditions, the Asian Roots Spa is designed as a tranquil sanctuary. The spaces, designed in a minimalist palette, provide a sense of serenity and wellbeing. The entry to the spa is through a Zen garden with a Japanese dry landscape garden or *karesansui* forming the focus of the entry. A bottle palm forms an asymmetrical natural accent to the space. Wooden seats placed on a floating stone bench provide a place for contemplation in this tranquil setting. This tranquillity is aimed at detaching the mind from its condition of urban congestion. Entering through the wooden floored reception one comes to the heart of the spa, a large triple-height atrium space. Light floods into the atrium, diffused through billowing fabric through a skylight three floors above. The space, overseen by a large wall painting of the Buddha, links the spa at various levels through internal windows and courts. This is the fusion lounge, a confluence of Asian traditions. The treatment rooms on the ground floor overlook the Zen garden, providing a connection with the natural even in this small urban site. The interior details extend the space of the garden inwards. Free-floating circular mirrors deconstruct the walls, reflecting fragments of the inner spaces. A glass floor recreates the dry-landscape Zen garden within the spa. These are more public zones of the spa. The treatment rooms on the upper floors are reached via a dramatic cantilevered staircase rising through the atrium. The treatment rooms are highly individualistic and minimalistic while retaining the functional aspects of Thai, Balinese and Malaysian treatments. Creation of a calm and soothing ambience is extended through a restrained palette of materials chosen for their sensory and tactile qualities, with texture and colour used to provide luxurious accents. Lighting controls synchronized with treatments heighten the experience.

Alliance Française de Delhi

158 G

SPA Design & ABRD Architects
(2004)

🚇 Jor Bagh 🚇 Khan Market
72, Lodi Estate

Alliance Française de Delhi (AFD), an Indo-French cultural centre, was founded in 1956 and is today acknowledged as one of the main cultural spots in the Indian capital. It became evident that the 'building' housing the centre had to be a conjunction of Indian and French culture, reflected in the brief which read 'creation of an institution reflecting the image of France and India together'. After winning the competition in 2001, Indo-French collaboration SPA Design & ABRD Architects spearheaded a complex that exemplifies perceptions of 'Indian crafts' and 'French technology'. The site of the project, the famed Lodi estate, was developed as an institutional area by architect Joseph Allen Stein in the late 1950s. It already housed some of the city's best-known buildings, like the India International Centre, the Ford Foundation, INTACH and the Chinmaya Mission. The AFD, with a built-up area of 3,000 square metres, was the last of the buildings to go up in the vicinity of Lodi Gardens. The building was conceptualized as a 'natural extension of the Lodi Gardens'. Towards this end, a concerted effort was made to protect the 17 trees that existed on site by integrating them into the landscape design, which included terraced gardens. The building stands as a strong geometric mass, being conceptually divided into three layers — the 3' raised plinth in Mandana Stone, the built form and a high-tech massive pergola sheltering the entire building. 15 metres hight, it functions as an umbrella for its visitors as well as for the grown foliage. Four star-shaped tapering columns bear the weight of the metal pergola. While on the one hand the pergola recalls or illustrates the architecture of *Shamianas* that Indian culture is much associated with, its high technology in the form of solar glass panels and fabric louvers is reminiscent of French technology. The solar panels are integrated into the mild steel frame and generate energy. Meanwhile, the fabric louvers fixed on the MS frames and made of synthetic fabric regulate the direct sunlight. The pergola in turn also permits a lot of cool outdoor spaces conducive to Delhi's subtropical climate. These outdoor spaces also double up as hubs for interaction amongst students and visitors. The functions are divided through the seeming 'pavilions' lounging in the garden. While the cultural court / front courtyard around the Pilkhon tree is restricted for cultural events, a central block houses the auditorium topped by the

library whilst another wing takes in the classrooms, offices and cafeteria. The art gallery holds a prominent space in the basement with an open-to-sky sunken court. The front courtyard leads into an auditorium for 100 people on one side; on the other side is a reception area, a bookshop, services and a cafeteria with an adjoining terrace. The first floor houses administrative offices plus six classrooms while the second floor has the remaining six classrooms, a meeting room, a translator room and the library. A huge office space spans the third floor. Terrace gardens opening from the library and the office spaces on these two floors yield unique opportunities for breaks. The structural system of RCC columns, shallow peripheral beams and precast RCC waffles 500 × 500 millimetres in size limit the structural depths to 300 millimetres, thereby admitting more internal height. These waffles also lend a pattern and texture to the roof slabs.

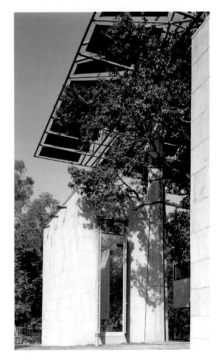

Osho Dham

Team Snehanshu (2004)

⊜ Dwarka Mor

44, Jhatikra Road,

Pandwala Khurd, Near Najafgarh

159

Osho Dham was designed for a commune of followers of the spiritual leader Osho. It is spread over 20 acres of land and provides space for meditation, listening to discourses and seeking the inner self. The land, before it was acquired by the Osho Commune, was used for farming by the nearby villagers of Jhatikara. At the start of the project there were very few trees on site and the soil had been denuded by over-use of chemical fertilizers and pesticides. After Osho passed away, the prime visionaries of this project, Swami Om Prakash Saraswati and Swami Atul Anand—two of Osho's close disciples—decided to start an autonomous commune, distinct from the older one located in Pune. The project were added, along with built in several phases. The very last phase that remains to be built comprises the public interaction areas and Reception Centre. The intention stated was to create a 'place' that would be conducive to meditation, a utopian condition for daily living. The only guideline provided by Swami Atul Anand was to build a complex that would enhance one's experience of nature, with buildings that sit in harmony with their surroundings. Apart from site landscaping and infrastructure planning, the first few structures to be designed and built were the Meditation Hall for 600 *sanyasis*, the Kabir Dormitories, and Swamiji's residence. The site planning, as can be seen even today, consciously preserved most of the land for natural farming which feeds the inmates of the commune round the year. The functional part of the complex is grouped around the Meditation Hall as the focus. The ceremonial path to the Hall is a spiral—symbolically related to the quest for one's inner self. The path also works in a practical manner by which the route to the Hall meanders through the landscaped 'forest', which does not allow the Hall to become visible till one is close to it. The design of the Hall too is like a huge Banyan tree—a steel and ferro-concrete shell roof supported on four columns spaced 80 feet apart. There are

no side walls enclosing the space, so from within the connection to the surrounding 'forest' is not lost. There is also a direct shorter route from the Kabir Dormitories to the Hall for day-to-day use. In subsequent years, the Kitchen with interlinked Staff Quarters and the Dining Hall was added adjacent to the direct route between Kabir and the Hall. Of these structures the staff quarters, like the Kabir Dorms, was dug into the earth to benefit from passive cooling action. The Kitchen was designed to let the *sanyasis* use its roof as an extension of the public spaces around the Kabir Dorms and the Hall. The Dining Hall was designed, like the Meditation Hall, as a pavilion. Each of the structures is unique in design, using different structural and construction techniques, often using local contractors. In the subsequent phases, the Meditation Hall was expanded on three sides with low flat roofs. Underground air-cooling ducts were added, along with and mist curtains from surrounding trees to make the Hall usable in the peak dry summer months. Additional living quarters were built that included the two-storeyed expansion adjacent

to Kabir with private sunken gardens. This addition completed the 'crescent' shape of the Kabir Dorms at the foot of the straight path to the Meditation Hall. Similarly a new Dorm named Farid was built on the other side of the Meditation Hall, amidst some of the agricultural fields. The generator rooms and additional staff quarters were planned at the furthest corners of the overall site to populate them, increasing the security of the campus. In each of the structures, innovative experiments were carried out with construction techniques and the form of the buildings, which were guided by principles of energy efficiency, economy of construction and conservation of resources. The buildings were mostly constructed on the basis of local skills available. *Sanyasis* today who stay at Osho Dham in groups that range from 20 to 750 (depending upon the nature of the programmes held) have found the environment of the commune conducive to their spiritual well-being. This has led to a steady increase in the population of Osho Dham over the years and has allowed the Commune to function all 365 days of the year.

South Asian Human Rights Documentation Centre (SAHRDC)

160 B

Anagram Architects (2005)
🌐 Green Park
B-6/6, Safdarjung Enclave Extension

South Asian Human Rights Documentation Centre (SAHRDC) is a non-governmental organization, which seeks to investigate, document and disseminate information about human rights. A small office with limited resources, the SAHRDC also runs an internship program attracting scholars from universities in India and abroad. It required an office to be made on a plot of 50 square metres emphasizing spatial efficiency and cost-effective construction. The site was located at a busy street corner with essentially pedestrian traffic. As the site is not very large, the acoustic and visual intrusion of the street activity into workspaces was a key concern. The method of construction adopted had to optimize the space available on site and a modest budget. The orientation of the site is such that the longer 10-metre sides are exposed to direct sun throughout the day. Reducing the resulting solar thermal gain was an important design generator. Although some fortification against the street was required, it was crucial for the facade to 'converse' with the external activity. The external wall is conceived as an animated, dynamic skin reflecting the bustle of the street and activating what would otherwise have been a mundane facade with minimal fenestration. The porosity of the wall maintains a degree of privacy while playfully engaging with the street corner. Efficient space utilization is achieved by creating a single consolidated volume on each floor to be flexibly partitioned as per the client's requirements. This volume is serviced by a flanking buffer bay of a single-flight cantilevered staircase and a toilet stack. Costs were minimized by using exposed brick construction and by creating a beamless soffit at every floor. To create a beamless soffit without increasing the thickness of the slab, a gently vaulting roof was designed. Lateral inverted beams were introduced and flooring laid onto an infill so that each floor plate insulation eliminated the need for a false ceiling. The buffer bay along the street forms a breathing thermal barrier along the sun-facing side. By situating the staircase and toilet stack in this bay, the internal workspaces are protected. The porosity of the wall ensures that the buffer bay is well ventilated and yet shaded so as to reduce the amount of heat transmitted to the workspaces. A single repeating brick module creates a visually complex pattern in the manner of traditional South Asian brise-soleils.

Jaypee Institute of Information Technology

161 C

ARCOP (2005)

NOIDA City Centre, Vaishali
Sector 62, NOIDA, UP

Jaypee Institute of Information Technology, located in NOIDA, is a private institute which accommodates around 2,200 students. It was initiated by the large industrial and property company, Jaypee. It is internationally recognized and offers multi-disciplinary courses. The campus design criteria emerged from three potent progenies of the inordinate development trends, namely scarce land, expensive energy and low finances. The approach is to question the development trends, rethink the answers and demonstrate to the campus community how the built environment can elevate our lives. The simple and compact campus is constituted of the Academic block, Library, Auditorium, Staff housing, Hostels, Sports block and dining hall. The built mass is woven around a central movement spine which transubstantiates from a four-storey volume atrium space to a tree-lined boulevard. On either side the built mass defines the edges of the spine as modules; each reflective of the use the module embraces. This central spine is perforated with a variety of indoor-outdoor gathering spaces for students. This manifestation of 'place making' is spurred through architectural features like terracotta *jaali* (screens), vertical and horizontal movement systems like bridges and staircases, concurrently enhancing collegiality, friendship and collaborations in studies. The campus has a compact plan with each building having its own personality. Bricks and terracotta provide the continuum. Traffic and parking is confined to the periphery, making the campus pedestrian-friendly. The plan and vocabulary is not just a visual delight but also has strong connections with the surroundings. It is sympathetic to climate in the way that spaces are shaped, buildings are oriented and linked. Native materials like locally-made bricks are used, as are crafted terracotta *jaalis* and traditional techniques for cooling. The buildings area simple RCC frame structure with brick walls, complemented by terracotta perforated screens to induce air currents and provide shade from the intensely hot sun. The outer walls of the buildings are an Indian version of the rain-screen principle two feet away from the inner wall. Inner walls have windows of varying sizes while the outer wall has more disciplined and organized openings, sometimes filled with terracotta screens. Thanks to the double-skin facade, the building is full of natural ventilation and is energy-efficient. The roof is a large parasol providing shade, protecting the outer wall from heat and moisture. As a detail, it is a passive cooling method, which allows the hot air between the cavity walls to rise above them and escape, making way for fresh cool air. The central non-air-conditioned atrium remains comfortable both in India's intensely hot summers and cool winters. It is covered with a shading device made out of corrugated galvanized metal sheet, which takes advantage of north and south light.

DLF Beverly Park

Hafeez Contractor (2005)

MG Road
Mehrauli Gurgaon Road,
Gurgaon, Haryana

162 J

DLF Beverly Park is a residential complex located on a site of 5.82 acres in the suburb of Gurgaon. Its red pitched roofs, projecting balconies, ornate balustrades, arched doorways, landscaped courtyards with fountains and patterned mosaic tiles are reminiscent of Mediterranian architecture. The initial design was done by DLF's in-house architectural team. The developer invited architect Hafeez Contractor to add value and enhance the design. The architect retrofitted certain elements and subtracted some to arrive at its present form. The Spanish aesthetic was adopted on the insistence of the client after a great deal of deliberation. It was favoured over the prevalent classical architecture because of its novelty value and a belief that the new consumer aspired to the artistry and prosperity associated with the style. The development was touted as the first multi-storeyed towers in India to resonate with Mediterranean architectural features. It later turned into a trend and emerged as a preferred aesthetic in a number of residential property developments across the country. Beverly Park includes two luxury residential complexes with amenities like clubhouses, swimming pools and extensive parking. These complexes consist of 3- and 4-bedroom luxury apartments which offer delightful views of the lush gardens. Geometry of parallels and diagonals marks the site layout. Rectangular building blocks with varying heights run along the length of the site. These blocks have two flats per floor, which include terraces, ample foyer space, lifts and servants' accommodation. Diagonal building blocks ranging from 7 to 10 storeys connect the rows of rectangular buildings at the corners. These buildings follow a similar floor plan to the rectangular ones, except that these flats have an occasional square or semi-circular balcony. Both the complexes feature 3-bedroom apartments, 4-bedroom apartments and penthouses on the higher floors. These complexes were early examples of the postmodern trend in residential architecture. Hafeez Contractor pioneered this vision and implemented it in his various projects all across the country.

Sushant Lok Office Building ⌄ 163 J

Raj Rewal Associates (2007)
Ⓢ HUDA City Centre
Sushant Lok, Gurgaon

While most of Raj Rewal's works are located in Delhi, this office building in Sushant Lok, Gurgaon is one of his very few works in the southern suburb. This building is characterized by Raj Rewal's architectural vocabulary of sandstone. In the midst of various steel, glass and aluminium multi-storeyed office buildings in Gurgaon, the building offers a calm and pleasant surprise by its sober expression and simplicity. It is a rare example of a contemporary office typology designed in a modest and sensitive manner.

Dilli Haat, Pitampura ⌃ » 164 A

Pradeep Sachdeva (2007)
Ⓢ Netaji Subhash Place
Pitampura (near TV Tower)

The success of the first Dilli Haat near INA market in south Delhi led to the commissioning of a second Dilli Haat at Pitampura in West Delhi. The site was located near the Netaji Subhash Place Metro station and has arterial roads on two sides. Construction on the front side of the site was not allowed due to the presence of the Metro line above. The space below the Metro line was developed as a plaza for hawkers, vendors and street performers. The entrance plaza and craft shops have been raised to accommodate a large parking area. The layout of the craft bazaar was inspired by traditional Middle Eastern market places — the *souks* and the buildings have vaulted 'green' roofs. Food courts are located at ground level at the rear of the site. An amphitheatre has been used to maintain continuity between both levels. The project was open to the public by the end of 2007.

Singaporean High Commission 165 A
SCDA Architects (2007)
🚇 Race Course
E-6 Chandragupta Marg,
Chanakyapuri

The design of the new Singaporean High Commission in New Delhi stems from the need to shed the conventional iconography of governmental structures and create one which, while still remaining monumental and figural, is accessible on a human scale. Four main strategies drive the design for the new Chancery and official residences. The first is the need to create a coordinated physical plan relating the existing buildings on the site to the new Chancery. This is done by constructing a sequence of interior/exterior spaces linked together by external landscape features that will harness the site into a harmonious whole. The play between mass (solid buildings) and transparent spaces (glass elements, open water/forecourts) allows spaces to oscillate between inside and outside as they fold into and onto each other.

Secondly, there is a need to carve out a series of clearly defined but related spatial components, which will house all the necessary bureaucratic programmes for efficient day-to-day functioning of the High Commission. Internal spaces are carefully defined into three distinctive zones: an open public zone, an office zone and a secure zone. Thirdly, the new High Commission is intended to serve and represent Singapore both physically and symbolically. While the vaulted quality of the pavilion gateway and solidity of the building foster an image of strength, security and diplomacy, it is balanced by open gardens, water features and external event spaces, which create an open and welcoming environment. Finally, Indian resources in the form of building materials and local crafts are used in a modern way. Details such as the lanterns above the gateways to Agra, which are fashioned in red stone and ornamented with carved *jaali* motifs, are a source of inspiration, showing an understanding of the building's local context.

Bhartiya Vidya Bhavan

Team Snehanshu (2007)

166 F

Mandi House
Kasturba Gandhi Marg

The Delhi Centre of the Bharatiya Vidya Bhavan extended its education programme in 2006 through the inauguration of a separate Management Studies building. The Bhavan is located on a 4.7-acre site near the India Gate Hexagon. The Management Studies building was the third building to be built adjacent to Prof. Himanshu D. Chayya's classic Modernist school building of exposed brick. The first building fronting the Kasturba Gandhi Marg circle is the oldest. This curvilinear building has a simple plan and is embellished with motifs derived from traditional Indian architecture. The Management Studies building was designed in exposed brickwork to sit comfortably with Prof. Chayya's building next door. The building design incorporates the older access to the main playing fields on the other end of the site from the school. Therefore at ground level, schoolchildren can go past and through the building to the fields without disturbing the management students. Entry to the Management building is possible from the two parallel roads, with basement parking entry from Copernicus Lane. The building is planned around covered courtyards that provide light and ventilation to the corridors, bridges and other public spaces that link the classrooms around the courts. The facade of the building incorporates a rhythm of tall exposed brick and cement concrete screens (*jaalis*) on the edge of the cantilevered service ledges that skirt each floor on the outer face. These screens help to derive an elevation that breaks down the separation of each floor into a continuous facade up to the full height of the building; this device in composing the elevations has helped to set apart the Management Institute in appearance from the adjacent school building. At a practical level, the screens provide space behind which to install utilities such as HVAC compressors unobtrusively. The utility ledges also allow for ease of maintenance such as regular window cleaning and attending to any other problems on the exterior face of the building. In an overall reading of the different buildings on site, the Management building, while respecting the adjacent school building, successfully creates a distinct identity for itself as a higher studies institute.

C & C Construction Office 167 J

Morphogenesis (2007)

◎ HUDA City Centre

Plot No. 70, Sector 32, Gurgaon

The office for C&C Construction was designed with the intent of creating a clean and minimalist, no-fuss office space that would be representative of the work ethos of the construction firm. The site was extremely tight and the main objective was to bring green into the working space. A linear core was created along the western facade, to act as a thermal buffer and protect the working spaces from the extreme environmental conditions. The building was conceived as a solid from which internal volumes were carved out. Spatial sculpting was the predominant theme; the floor plate shifted as one went up, to create voids and terraces on every floor and an atrium at the front wrapped around the shell. This also enabled interconnected sectional fluidity, which provides a sense of openness with daylight flowing into every floor plate. An innovative use of structure allowed the floor plates to be column-free to increase the flexibility of the office interiors. The interior of the office moves from being static to being more networked and tentacled. A contrasting palette of warm and cold materials is used to reflect the robust nature of the company's work profile. Resilient, no-fuss interiors are reflected with the use of stone and wood. For the interiors of a space to completely blend in with the architecture that contains it, glass helps to add transparency and connects the inside to the outside. This is also achieved by the provision of terraces, with every floor plate looking into double/triple height spaces.

House 1 » 168 B

Morphogenesis (2007)

◎ Dhaula Kuan ◎ Hauz Khas

Vasant Vihar

House 1 is located in an affluent neighbourhood of New Delhi. Though starkly modern, the design takes cues from Indian sanctuaries: the *haveli* or mansion organized around private courts, the step-well with an enfilade of semi-enclosed shaded spaces, and the temple sanctum, serene despite the chaos outside. The fortress-like entrance wall is punctuated by a large opening which allows a glimpse of the entry courtyard. This forecourt, shaded by a tree in a bed of white pebbles, establishes the minimalist mood of the residence. An orchestrated series of courts divide and sculpt the space of the house. Rooms respond to the programme, while boundaries are continuously defined by light and material. Even the major doors, which rise up to the full height of the rooms, add to the sense of unhindered space. The interior is animated through skylit courts where filtered sunlight continuously changes the feel of the space through the day and the seasons. Each court is an opportunity to stage a composition of materials, light, and foliage. Large picture windows and glass walls allow space to flow uninterrupted from the inside to the outside without the mediation of frames. Concealed cove lighting behind the floating ceiling in the living room washes the walls in a gentle glow. Polished concrete, glass, polished ebony and stainless steel surfaces play off each other, bringing texture and lightness to the spaces. They provide a tactile and sensual counterpoint to the white architectural surfaces. A pleated ebony staircase is contained within sheets of glass that separate it from the living room. The curving wood-clad canopy in the living room

captures the soft reflected light from the courtyard. The residence reflects the emergence of the home as a private retreat, away from the chaos of the bustling metropolis. The presence of rich details delineates the meditative spaces.

First floor

Ground floor

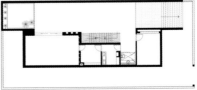

Basement

N85 Residence

169 H

Morphogenesis (2007)
Hauz Khas
N-85, Panchsheel Park

The house as a platform has been used to investigate two issues central to design today: the family as a social unit and the environment. The lifestyle of the Indian family has changed in the age of global travel and internet media, with new spatial needs and notions of comfort. Often, local resources are at odds with shifts in lifestyle. The designers demonstrate that it is possible to meet challenges of lifestyle and the environment with creative panache. The house sets out to create its own terrain, a veritable oasis, within its inscribed territory. The forecourt is landscaped with graceful steps and pools. Minimal planes are articulated with stone, wood and concrete, which are simply striated or set in interlocking patterns. Transparency is achieved with glass and a combination of water, reflection, and modulated lighting. At night the house appears like a lantern, allowing glimpses of activity within. The complex programme of the house is laid out in a series of spatial volumes that are revealed slowly. Steps cascade to subterranean offices or rooms and furniture framed by large picture windows. The central space is the fulcrum of the whole house and ties it together. The ceiling is dotted by circular skylights above an interior garden. A lap pool fed by harvested rain water runs the length of the terrace on the second floor.

Ground floor

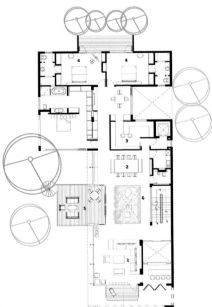

First floor

Second floor

Indian Oil Corporation Ltd. (IOCL) 170 B

STUP Consultants (2008)
📍 Moolchand
Corporate Office, 3079/3
Joseph Broz Tito Marg, Siddiqui Marg

The Indian Oil Corporation built itself a new corporate office that would exhibit state-of-the-art building technology, with sophisticated optimum automation and management systems, consciously integrating green building concepts to emerge amongst the leading and most intelligent corporate offices in the country. The IOCL Headquarters building, located in the heart of South Delhi, is designed as one of the country's first green and sustainable buildings, incorporating unique active and passive strategies for energy conservation and generation. The complex comprises two blocks connected by sky bridges: a facilities block with auditorium, canteen and conference rooms and an executive block with offices. The buildings are oriented north-south for minimum heat gain and maximum light. Sun breakers on the south face reduce heat gain, while service cores on the east and west shade the interior and provide for air conditioning optimization. A pergola-covered atrium provides summer shade and admits winter sun. Lighting is supplemented by photovoltaics integrated into the facade of the building. Floor plates are sized to allow for maximum penetration of indirect light. The building positions itself on the site to maximize visibility and also to take full advantage of the public garden on the adjacent site. The complex was designed to reinforce the corporate image of IOCL, by strategically designing the building to constitute a landmark facility with a contemporary outlook that promotes energy efficient architecture. Equally, it promotes the saving of precious natural resources like water and power by using passive and active design strategies.

Gautam Buddha University ⩘ ⩔ 171

C.P. Kukreja Associates (2008)
Gautam Budh Nagar,
Yamuna Expressway,
Greater NOIDA

This prestigious university was developed by Greater NOIDA Industrial Development Authority on an area of over 500 acres. The different disciplines include undergraduate and postgraduate courses in Information Technology, Bio-Technology, Law, Management and Buddhist Studies. Other facilities include an academic complex, a library, a meditation centre, an International centre, a utility block and sports facilities. Accommodation comprises hostels for 5,000 students and 500 faculty members. The university is a fine example of Buddhist architecture interpreted in the 21st Century. This inspiring campus design has earned it the distinction of being one of the finest university designs in India.

Spectral Building

ABRD Architects (2008)
⊜ NOIDA City Centre, Vaishali
A-197 Sector 63, NOIDA, UP

172 C

Spectral Services Consultants Private Limited was founded in 1980 with a vision of providing innovative engineering solutions and energy-efficient design. The company is now one of the foremost building services consultancy organizations in the country. In 2007 the company decided to construct its head office building in NOIDA. As the organization had always played an important role in the advocacy of Green Buildings in India, their brief for the project called for the creation of a Green Office Building. The objective was thus primarily to create a naturally pleasant and daylit workplace. While the building appears solid and monolithic from the outside, the experience within is completely the opposite. The impression is openness and continuous office space flushed with daylight and replete with potential for collaboration and dialogue. The site was located in an industrial area characterized by dense plotted developments, and lack of outdoor or recreational spaces. Because of the general banality of its context, the building is conceived as an inward-looking office space. The most prominent feature of the building is the toplit semi-cylindrical atrium which pierces the rectangular box of the building to create an 'interiorized public space'. All the office spaces and meeting areas are arranged symmetrical along the atrium, without any physical partitions, to enhance

interaction and visibility amongst various engineering teams working in the office. The atrium not only lights up the indoor spaces but at the same time provides a sense of grandeur to the building. It contains all public and interaction spaces for the occupants of the building. The atrium ensures that almost 85% of the interior spaces are day lit. The roof of the atrium is composed of a mild steel truss. Inclined louvres made of aluminium composite panels and laminated glass are a particularly well-crafted feature of the design. The incline of the louvers in the atrium roof is so designed to block summer sun but allow winter sun to penetrate in the building. The programme was distributed symmetrically about the atrium or void. While one enters through the reception and lobby located on ground

floor adjoined with meeting rooms, all the design teams are symmetrically dispensed around the atrium. The top floor contains the offices of the executives, thereby giving them maximum privacy and the adjacent terrace gardens. The narrow strip parallel to the diameter of the semi-circular atrium contains all services, circulation, staircases and elevators thus also making a clear distinction between the 'served' and the 'servant' spaces. In order to create a comfortable workspace in the basement, one side of the site is excavated all the way to the basement level. This provides a sunken landscaped garden and also the essential daylight required for the offices located in the basement. The cafeteria located at the bottom of the atrium overlooks and spills in to this sunken garden. The fenestration on the front facade of

the building facing the harsh sun from the west has been kept to a minimum. The vertical red sandstone fins further protect the windows on the west facade. These however allow the passage of diffused light in summer and direct sunlight during winter. The treatment on the facade is innovative as well. Although primarily expressed with the characteristic material of the region, red Agra stone and beige Gwalior stone, the cladding has varied textures. Wide-ranging features of site sustainability, indoor air quality, energy efficient air-conditioning, water conservation and recycling, alternative energy sources and use of local or regional materials were incorporated into the architectural and systems design of the building. This led to accreditation by the US Green Building Council as a platinum-rated LEED Green Building.

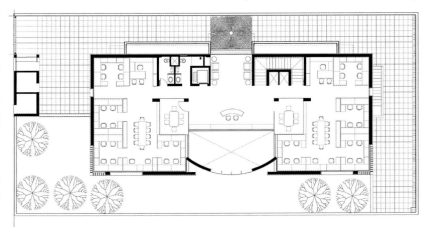

Ground floor

Institute for Rural Research and Development

173 J

Ashok B Lall Architects (2008)
🚇 HUDA City Centre
Plot No. 34, Sector 44,
Institutional Area, Gurgaon, Haryana

The owner, S. M. Sehgal Foundation, is an NGO working on development projects in rural Haryana. The Institute for Rural Research and Development (IRRAD) houses the Foundation's headquarters. It was designed to accommodate offices for staff and volunteers as well as training facilities: classrooms, a library and online training for villagers. The building was designed and constructed to be a model of sustainable development. The building is a platinum-rated Green Building under the LEED rating system. The appearance and aesthetic quality of the building is derived from the principles of sustainable design. The use of natural materials, little glass and interesting shading devices, plus the integration of sheltered courtyard spaces makes for its unique aesthetic and a comforting and graceful feel, wherever you may be in and around the building. In fact a special feature of the building is deriving beauty from waste. The entrance lobby, boardroom and central atrium use waste plywood crating planks, broken tiles and glass to demonstrate how waste can be converted into a beautiful resource. The 35 kw solar photovoltaic installation on the roof of the building

proves an important point. 100 per cent of basic electricity needs — computers, lighting, fans, and mechanical ventilation — are met directly from solar energy. This is a significant contribution to the state electricity supply system, and if this installation were to be integrated into the state electricity supply grid it could generate up to 35 kw of electricity to the grid on non-working days too. This office building is designed to minimize its own ecological footprint and carbon dioxide emissions due to the type of material used. For instance wood is used instead of aluminium for doors and windows, while the use of burnt brick is minimized. The building uses a combination of passive and active strategies to reduce consumption and then provide for the reduced demand with renewable and energy-efficient systems. This principle has been applied to building design and construction wherever possible. Internal courts are introduced in the built mass to let daylight into the interiors during working hours — reducing the energy used for lighting. Windows are designed to minimize glare and let in light for effective use. The building is insulated from the external environment, helping reduce the cooling demands in the peak of summer. The windows are shaded from the outside. The shading devices are designed to allow daylight into the space and views out of the building, but do not allow solar heat gain through the glazed area.

McKinsey Headquarters 174 J

Currimbhoy & Co. (2008)
HUDA City Centre
Plot No. 4, Echelon Institutional
Area, Sector 32, Gurgaon

The Indian headquarters of the multinational consultancy firm of McKinsey & Co. is located in Gurgaon. For the firm's offices, architect Tarik Currimbhoy has used an 'oasis' approach. The design, which marries the sophistication of the global to the romance of the local, is based on an abstraction of the Mughal garden and is created around a hierarchy of water bodies. One enters the offices through a pavilion that floats upon a lotus pond (lotus being the flower symbol of India) and continues through to the central courtyard, where a canal flows from a 'bubbler' into a still pond enlivened by handcrafted lotus fountains. The 60,000-square-foot structure is composed of four interconnected pavilions placed around a central courtyard garden, as is traditional in the hot arid regions of India. 'I wanted to make the offices inward facing in order to create a bubble of serenity amongst the ad hoc urban development in this fast-growing suburb of New Delhi,' says the architect. In the exterior, the sleekness of the steel and glass is juxtaposed with marble. The building is clad in hand-chiselled local white marble slabs, which serves to give the steel and glass building a rich, 'high touch' crafted look. The stone wraps into the interior of the building, bringing the outside in. Horizontal grooves echo the rhythm of steel bands set in the exterior glass.

Additionally, the texture of the hand-chiselled stone and indents of the polished grove create an interesting interplay of light and shadow. Fin-like metal sunshades block the harsh sunlight from entering the building while allowing a connection to the interior garden. 'The romance of this design is that every desk and office has a garden view,' says the architect. For the landscape designer, the essence of the building is that it floats upon the landscape.

Aman Hotel 175 A

Kerry Hill (2008)
JLN Stadium
Lodi Road

Located in the heart of New Delhi, just south of the Delhi Golf Course and adjacent to the medieval Nizamuddin complex, lies this beautiful city-based resort. From its prime location where the modern and historic are juxtaposed in perfect harmony, it is possible to enjoy many of the cultural wonders that New Delhi has to offer from the spectacular architecture of the Mughal Era to the grand monuments of the British Raj. Aman New Delhi is a contemporary oasis of sophisticated calm providing extensive recreation, meeting and leisure facilities. The resort has a North Indian aesthetic with regional architectural motifs like *jaalis*, materials and design. Aman New Delhi is wrapped around a peaceful internal courtyard pool lined with monumental grey stone columns. Inside, Khareda stone floors, *jaali* screens and handmade rugs bring a local touch to the 60 rooms and suites.

Trehan Residence ⚹

Design Plus (2008)
🚇 Botanical Garden
B-15, Sector 44, NOIDA, UP

176 C

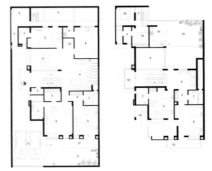

The Trehan Residence is a typical urban house that accommodates three generations of occupants. Daily operations, pragmatic social and professional requirements together with the proverbial budget constraints dominated the planning of the house. The residence was consciously not built to the full available Floor Area Ratio and was optimum for the residents, needs. The basement

operates as the public face, accommodating all business and socio-cultural gatherings. The ground floor was required to provide for three bedrooms and a large common space for the family to get together for meals or chats over a newspaper. The first floor is a private abode for the lawyer son, with a large party terrace. The receding plan not only provides an outdoor extension in terms of terraces to each room but also breaks the volume to provide self-shading from the harsh south-west sun. To further assist comfortable internal temperatures, double glazing was used on the south-west facades. The warmth of the residence is maintained with the materiality, and it features naturally treated wooden exteriors and teak in the interiors. Subtle shades of cotton with occasional bright highlights add life to the living spaces. The custom 'design and build' furniture fits perfectly in the created alcoves. With the numerous light shafts and clerestories, natural light is a predominant feature for the interiors along with the play of ceiling heights.

B-99 Residence

DADA (2008)

🚇 HUDA City Centre

B-99, Sushant Lok, Gurgaon

177 J

This new family house with three independent floors is spread over a 350 square metre plot of land. While the upper floors are living areas for architect couples, the basement houses their studio. Designed around a courtyard, the house incorporates a hierarchy of zones with formal living spaces in front and private areas at the back. The bedrooms and toilets are at the rear along the north–south axis, while the drawing, living and kitchen areas are grouped together at the front arranged along a linear east–west axis forming the spine of the house. The courtyard that forms the centre of the house faces south and is overlooked by living and bedroom areas on the ground and first floors. Adjacent to the courtyard is a steel staircase connecting the upper floors. On the ground and first floors, rooms at the front and rear are connected by 'bridge-like' spaces that run along the courtyard. Also running in parallel is a wall two feet deep

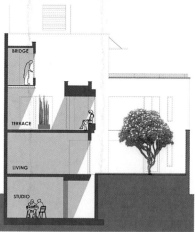

that at places acts as a shading device for large windows or incorporates built-in timber benches overlooking the open courts. The double-height entrance area is connected with a precariously placed staircase that forms the focus of the house. This three-storey high stair zone forms a connection between the basement void, ground floor entrance and the first floor. Another unique architectural move was to highlight the south-west corner of the house that forms the carport and the main entrance. This

corner houses a study-cum-library on the first floor. Also adding to the drama is the V-shaped steel column that supports this corner, reinforcing the impression of weightlessness. Ground and first floors are predominantly masonry while the second storey is lighter, mainly clad in timber. The composition of the architectural form required timber cladding on the second level. The west-facing area on this floor is protected with the use of an extended steel and aluminium parasol. The use of clean lines and white expanses enhance the contemporary aspect of the house. It is a visual and architectural delight that appropriately caters to the needs of a younger generation looking to break away from conventional house designs without losing the essence of their traditions.

Ground floor

Bartholomew Farmhouse

178 **J**

Neeraj Manchanda Architects
(2008)

🚇 HUDA City Centre
Junoon, Village Bidwas, Tavuru,
Sohna Gurgaon, Haryana

Located roughly 65 kilometres from central Delhi, the Bartholomew Farmhouse is conceived as a retreat for a busy globe-trotting professional. Keeping in view the requirements of its single occupant, the house uses the outdoors in two ways. While the house is planned so as to allow unhindered visual and physical connectivity with the well landscaped external spaces, the internal courtyard allows it to have an 'outdoor' space inside. A central courtyard separates the private and public wings of the house. The private wing contains two distinct areas. The master space uses the geometry of nine squares in order to organize its sleeping, study and relaxation facilities around its central square, which is a small ornamental

court that provides visual reference and relief to spaces in all other squares. In this manner, the master space becomes a complete unit, with its own piece of sky, and offers a high level of privacy and self-sufficiency to its occupant. The second area of the private wing is a circular bedroom suite with a dome above and framed planters all around. A circular living and lounge space and a dining area, both domed above, along with a kitchen-cum-pantry, a bar area and facilities together comprise the public wing of the house. The entire house employs the vocabulary of compressive structure both in order to reflect its location and to conserve cost. Arches, corbels and domes of different types, together with brick walls, provide the farmhouse with a unique visual and experiential character that refers to history but has a contemporary spatial character. Rugged rough plasters used in the house complement the design vocabulary and reinforce an Indian countryside experience.

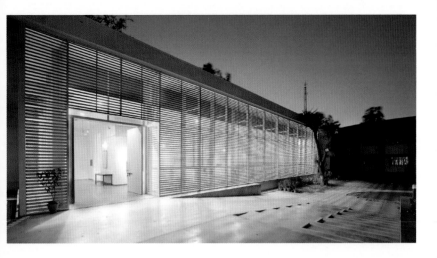

M.F. Husain Art Gallery

Romi Khosla Design Studio
(2008)

🚇 Jasola-Apollo
Jamia Millia Islamia,
Jamia Nagar

The university of Jamia was established in the 1930s. As the university evolved, it introduced a wide range of contemporary academic disciplines such as media studies and central Asian studies. Jamia University is popularly regarded as a progressive avant-garde campus. In 2008, the Vice-Chancellor proposed a new cultural hub for the university that would have as its core a contemporary students' canteen, a unique art gallery and landscaped lawns. The architects chose white marble in the canteen and white metal louvers in the art gallery to express this contemporary identity. The art gallery has become a community space for gathering alternative expressions of culture and identity. This role signalled the canteen and the art gallery as iconic models of architectural expression in contemporary Indian academic institutions. The art gallery has three main parts to it. The first space is the front gallery. It is naturally lit and primarily designed for the display of popular art and student exhibitions. The second space is the main internal gallery, which is lit by controlled light and can be divided into two smaller galleries with the help of a centrally pivoted wall. This gallery is designed for the universitiy's art collection, as well as for external artists who want to exhibit their work here. The third exhibition space is the open-air sculpture court at the rear of the building. The art gallery also has two artist's studios adjacent to the sculpture court, which are designed for visiting artists to use over short periods.

Vatika Tower ⌃
Studio U+A (2008)
🚇 Sikandarpur
Golf Course Road,
Gurgaon, Haryana

Studio U+A were the Design Consultants for this project. A unified composition of folded plates, this dynamic group of buildings begins with a single-storey wing-like restaurant, develops to a low-rise office block with an inclined roof plane and culminates in the office tower, its outward canted face inflected in response to the neighbouring structure and joined to it by a glazed atrium.

DMRC Head Office »
Raj Rewal Associates (2008)
🚇🚇 Rajiv Chowk
Metro Bhavan,
Barkhambha Road

The operational head office of Delhi Metro Rail Corporation (DMRC) was established in 2008. The nine-storey high building has a total covered area of 16,306 square metres and two basements of 5,000 square metres each. Architectural expression reflects the dynamic and progressive values of the organisation. The functional requirements of the DMRC Operational Centre's work spaces are grouped around distinct areas. The concept is based on three wings for offices, which enclose an atrium filled with light. The back-up operation monitoring zone is located in a separate enclosure at the rear. The top two floors are cantilevered to protect the lower floors from the south-west sun. The entrance allows dual access to the offices at the upper levels. The rear of the site has a service entrance. The building has a logical and economical structural system based on four vertical cores and external peripheral shear walls of reinforced cement concrete, supporting floor slabs. The core walls contain lifts/staircase and toilet/service facilities. The perimeter of the structure is in the form of a Vierendeel Girder spanning between vertical concrete walls. The extra sunshade of lightweight stainless

steel (with sun-reflecting surface) forms a protective girth around the north and south perimeter of the office complex. In other words there is an 'eyebrow' of lightweight metal on every floor providing sun protection. The external lattice, which echoes the structural system, also cuts down the glare. The architects have designed stainless steel cladding for the building, involving stainless steel tubular trusses with SS panels interspersed with toughened glass panels. The entire system is modular to take care of various aspects like structural stability, oil canning effect, precision, ease of installation and finally the aesthetics.

Tahiliani Design Headquarters 182 J

SPA Design (2008)

HUDA City Centre
708, Pace City-Ii, Sector 37,
Gurgaon

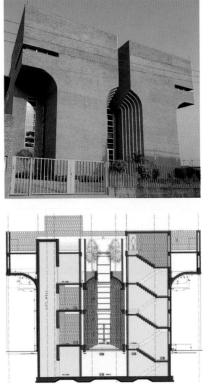

Tahiliani Design Pvt Ltd. is one of the leading apparel design companies in India. The new building for the Tahiliani Design headquarters is a three-storeyed structure in exposed brick, with spaces organized around a large courtyard. It houses space for apparel production, administration, studios for designers and a showroom. Gurgaon Sector 37 is an industrial area characterized by dense plotted developments, and a lack of outdoor or recreational spaces. Because of the general banality of its context, the building is almost forced to behave as an introverted box. The project aims at creating inward-looking spaces around a garden, like a traditional cloister, a calm environment ideal for long hours of work. The studios and offices are suspended above the buzz of production located on the lower floors, getting zenith light most suited for precision work. The construction is rectangular in shape with numerous skylights giving subdued light to the working spaces, adapted to the harsh climate of Delhi. Assembly production and embroidery are located in the basement and on the ground floor. The first floor is assigned to the design studios and the sampling rooms. The trial rooms, showroom, personal design studio and offices for the executives are located on the top floor. The production area on the ground floor is the heart of the building with its vaulted skylight and magnificent double height. The building is a reinforced cement concrete structure supported on large mushroom columns and flat slabs, allowing beam-free office spaces with generous height. The central grid of mushroom columns in the production hall transforms the flat ceiling into a vault with a skylight in between. The vault forms the planters for the upper floors. The main design studio areas get a double-height space with one side of the hall looking, at the hanging gardens on either side of the courtyard from below. On the upper floor, there is a terrace garden above the skylight—enclosed in

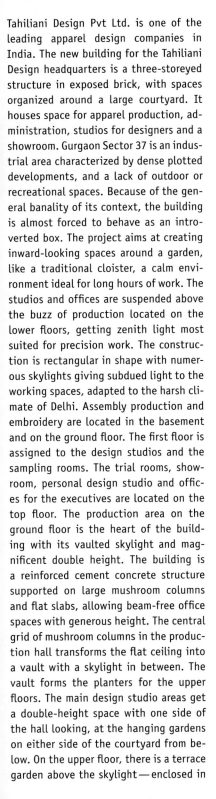

a noisy and dusty area of this industrial area. The main atelier of the fashion designer is placed in another vaulted space on the second floor looking onto the garden. The project has used exposed ordinary bricks for the external facade giving the precinct a warm character. In the interiors, a dialogue is apparent between the warmth of exposed brick and the solidity of exposed concrete. Influenced by the ruins of the Jamali Kamali complex in Mehrauli, the constructional idiom tends to be monumental and monolithic. The bare concrete of the interiors enables the building to expose the heavy weight of the structure and materials and also exposes the process in which they are assembled together. The experience of the spaces involves interplay of natural light and volumes. Delhi's Islamic monuments, reinterpreted into a contemporary design, inspire the arched shape of the structure. The entrance is an entre-deux created out of a vault open in the centre between two T-shaped pillars, the logo of the company. The entrance faces east, and it is almost surreal when people enter the factory in the morning with the morning sun beaming through the building in the foreground.

Dental College

Romi Khosla Design Studio (2009)

🚇 Jasola-Apollo

Jamia Milia Islamia University,
Jamia Nagar

183 C

Teaching hospitals are particularly complex buildings compared to other institutions. The Dental College of Jamia had these characteristics. It serves to provide dental care to the people in surrounding areas and is also one of the primary teaching centres of dentistry in India. So at one end the users are the general public and at the other end the users are the dental students. The College was therefore a place where three users interacted with each other: the general public, the dentists who treated and taught and thirdly the students who learned and practised. The programme was therefore conceived as a series of capsules which were designed to act as nodes for the three users. The site

given for the building was a neglected and overgrown part of the campus. It had two levels , both of which provided access to the building for the public and students. To fulfil the requirements of its varied users, the building was to house a substantial reference library, staff facilities, seminar facilities, wards, operation theatres, pathology laboratories and a mortuary as well as X-ray rooms and a museum. These facilities have been arranged in a rectilinear plan form that encloses two large courtyards and has a certain formality to it. It was a design judgement to simplify the formal layout of the building in order to contain the enormous volumes of spaces in a simple form that would be easily readable by all three categories of users. A dental college is a very complex institution in which the users have to keep moving from one part to another. In order to reduce energy consumption, the treatment clinics have been provided

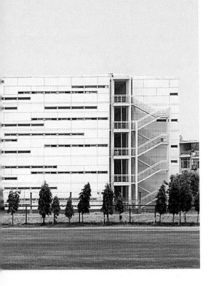

with full 80% north-side glazing that allows ample daylight to flood the clinics. This helps treatment during power cuts and naturally well lit spaces ensure a higher level of cleanliness. The materials used for the structure of the building are reinforced concrete frames, structural steel staircases, corridors and brick walls. Stone is used for cladding wall surfaces, structural glass for the north light window facades, and aluminium sheeting for cladding the brick walls. Each facade of the building is treated as a canvas for artistic composition. The fenestration has been designed to have twin functions. On the north faces of the building, where the clinics have been located, the structural curtain wall glazing provides abundant daylight for dental treatment. On the south side, the glazing has been confined to narrow slits which run horizontally and protect the south of the building in the clinic areas from heat gain. These staggered fenestrations also break the scale and the thin strips of windows help in exaggerating the horizontality of the structure. The building was conceived by the architects to be a contemporary building without references to the historical burden of architecture from which much of the buildings on the Jamia campus suffer. Like their Castro Cafeteria and M. F. Husain Art Gallery on the Jamia University Campus, the architects have sought to provide the campus with modern, state-of-the-art buildings.

Bharti Airtel

184 J

Hafeez Contractor (2009)
🚇 Guru Dronacharya
Airtel Centre, Plot no 16,
Udyog Vihar, Phase IV, Gurgaon

Located on NH8, the Bharti Airtel building is unmistakably visible due to its multi-coloured facade which is visible from afar both during the day and night. It fulfils its purpose of creating a hi-tech image and being a loudly noticeable corporate office building for India's premier mobile telecommunications service provider. The futuristic headquarters of Bharti Airtel Limited portrays the company's modern-day ideology. The building is designed to meet the requisites of the corporate world and ensure a controlled work environment. Modern amenities such as a health club, day care and a cafeteria in the courtyard with a skylight are a welcome addition to the complex. The plan of this 8-storey building is simple and functional. A circular courtyard with its water fountain forms the epicentre of the surrounding hub. The office blocks encircle the courtyard, providing daylight and an external view for their occupants. The landscape, cut to geometric patterns, further highlights the profile of this distinct structure. Its external multi-coloured facade is made of high-performance glazing. The facade has integrated lighting provision which highlights the hi-tech digital Airtel logo in its trademark red and white colours.

District Centre ≫
Kuldip Singh (2009)
🚇 Malviya Nagar
Press Enclave Road

185 B

The District Centre is situated on a site of 21.8 hectares, with a total built-up area of 245,000 square metres. Access to the site is through an underpass system, with a view to segregating the local and through streams of traffic as well as providing an uninterrupted flow of pedestrians between the bus stands and major nodes of activity. The District Centre has a shopping-cum-residential complex of 123,297 square metres, an office complex of 95,693 square metres, a cultural complex of 10,750 square metres, a 5-star hotel of 14,757 square metres and other service facilities. The buildings have a maximum height of 36 metres. The District Centre was conceived as the heart of the community in South Delhi. It has been subdivided into essentially five distinct areas: a five-star hotel plot on one side; a huge chain of three-storeyed shopping malls all interconnected, interspersed with serviced apartment blocks at regular intervals; two complexes comprising offices, institutions and multiplexes, the latter connected to the malls at two levels; and a cultural centre at the front. The shopping area has been designed to form a partial ring around a large green area, integrated with the masterplan green belt across the main road. Below the green area, very generous parking space has been provided over 3 levels. A major service road connects the plots at the rear. This is intended to provide service facilities and access to long-stay car parks reserved for shop-keepers and employees. Visitors parking have been completely segregated into separate car parks in the vicinity of major shopping areas. Practically all car parking is multi-level and hidden with generous landscape provision. The entire development is subject to controls given in drawings, which specify facade dimensional controls, materials to be used (two specific types of granite cladding slabs used with dry cladding), basements, heights and building form. The location of service structures like cooling towers and lift machine rooms. has also been planned in such a way that no service structure is visible from outside. There have been some violations by the developers, but they have, by and large, adhered to these controls. Despite these carefully formulated controls, the developers have been given ample freedom to plan their spaces in a manner most suited to their requirements. This project has proved to be one of the best urban design projects of such a scale ever executed. Its vast popularity with residents living in south Delhi and other parts of the city testify to what a well planned District Centre can do to enhance their commercial, cultural, and social activities.

Polyclinic for the Destitute ≫
*Romi Khosla Design Studio
(2009–2010)*
🚇 Chandni Chowk
Lahori Gate, Old Delhi

186 A

In the heart of the old city of Delhi, on the edge of the railway line, sandwiched between a *masjid* and the remains of a burnt-out slum, is a modern Polyclinic. It was built to provide medical treatment and rehabilitation for the poor, drug addicts and HIV patients who live on the pavements of Lahori Gate. The Polyclinic also functions as a day care referral medical relief centre. This simple, elegant building is four floors high and is equipped with a hospital lift. A large area in the basement provides ample space for a modern pathological laboratory. The ground floor houses reception as well as the Out Patient Department cubicles for daytime doctors and consultants. Built in metal and glass, the new Polyclinic is a beautiful contemporary intervention in an otherwise historical part of Delhi. Each floor has a surface area of 200 square metres where laboratories, reception, consultation rooms,

daytime wards, doctors and nurse stations are situated. The fully glazed front facade provides a transparent view into the building, which invites the poor to enter within. A lift designed for carrying stretcher patients has also been installed for emergency treatment. The choice of primary colours that combine the yellow and blue louvered facade and brightly ventilated areas seem radical for this forgotten area of Delhi. The building is a rare example of a contemporary architectural addition in the old part of the city. While the facade on the entry side presents a colourful and welcoming front, the opposite facade with its white plastered surface surrounding windows on all floors resembles an 'urban window' itself. The contrast of the old and new is striking. The hallmark of the project is the infusion of vibrance and colour to an otherwise mundane programme.

Office for Agilent Technology 187 J

Sanjay Prakash,
SHiFt: Studio for Habitat Futures
(2009)
⊜ HUDA City Centre
Manesar, Gurgaon, Haryana

Agilent Technologies is one of the world's premier scientific measurement companies. Its facility located in the industrial suburb of IMT Manesar imparts a distinctive character to enhance productivity while maintaining the sanctity of a quiet work environment. Integrating various stand-alone features with energy efficiency, the project serves as an international model in ecologically appropriate office architecture in continental tropical climates. A large cantilevered office section with distinctive tensile structures marks the staff entrance and characterizes the eastern approach within the campus. This side lets the morning light filter in from certain portions. Elsewhere, the interplay of small square glass windows and local sandstone respond to the need to block the sun from the west. Despite this, the largely glazed (but protected) north and south facades instigate a feeling of the 'modern' glass office. The north-west formal entrance, under a triple-height space, integrates a water body and a concrete shear wall. This entrance leads to a grand atrium with a tree, which is the connecting element of all the spaces within the complex. Intermediate spaces have been provided for repose from the intense work environment in the form of a rooftop cafeteria, gardens, terraces and the atrium itself. Intermittent provision of internal and external courtyards also ensures enhanced indoor air quality. Meeting rooms project outwards, as distinct entities offering good views of the building and the landscape. Personalized work environments utilize a hybrid under-floor air conditioning system based on the principle of cooling the user (not the space). The extra height, as well as the limited floor plate depth, allows much of the office to operate in natural light. The building currently uses only about a quarter of the permissible floor area, allowing for future expansion to full coverage in the future. For now, this land (at the south) not only serves to create valuable outdoor spaces for recreation, but also enhances biodiversity by stepping the landscape, cutting dust and noise. The flexible circulation patterns, tall daylit spaces, exposed concrete wall finishes and unhindered hill views to the south impart the structure integrity in concept and planning.

National Coordination Office for SOS Children's Villages of India

188 B

Neeraj Manchanda Architects (2009)

🚇 Chattarpur

Plot No. 4, Block C-1,
Nelson Mandela Marg, Vasant Kunj

The National Coordination Office for the SOS Children's Villages of India is located on the busy Nelson Mandela Marg in South Delhi. A pivotal facility for one of the world's leading child-care organizations, it is designed as a workspace for the national office and a meeting place for co-workers from more than fifty initiatives around the country. Located in an institutional zone, the facility is accessed from the south, and looks into the residential green spaces of Vasant Kunj on the north. Its larger eastern and western sides face adjacent institutions. On account of the relatively small site dimensions, the building is planned to create the maximum workspace on each floor while isolating stairs and facilities on the west, creating an effective buffer from heating during office hours. The building uses red Agra stone as its cladding material, which, in conjunction with the playfully organized openings and coloured panels on the west, symbolically connects the building, to the focus of the organization: its children.

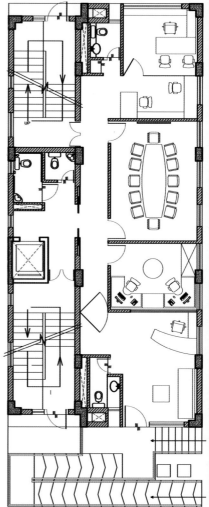

Ground floor

O. P. Jindal Global University   189

SPA Design (2009)
Sonipat-Narela Road,
Near Jagdishpur Village,
Sonipat, Haryana

The campus for the O. P. Jindal Global University is situated on entirely flat agricultural land, 10 kilometres away from the city of Sonepat. It sits on the remains of the Grand Trunk Road that crossed Northern India, from Afghanistan to Burma. As a Greenfield project with no built context, the design started on a very rigorous geometrical framework of squares and golden rectangles, reminiscent of both European as well as Indian architecture. The project is designed like a vast classical garden where nature has been tamed by the rule of geometry, as a metaphor for man pacified by the rule of law. At the centre is the academic square based on six courtyards, clubbing together lines of classrooms and faculty offices, while auditoria, reception, a library and a cafeteria occupy the centre of each courtyard. The main structures are large-span steel bridges, entirely flexible inside. All buildings are on pilotis to offer a continuous shaded park below the structures. Galleries and staircases are exposed on the facades to appreciate the constant movement of the students behind the coloured screenprinted glass panes, reminiscence of Indian *jaalis*. Beside the academic square are two students, complexes made of pavilions in exposed concrete, varying in heights and covered with terrace gardens. They create four courtyards of different proportions. The faculty housing is a line of villas forming the visual boundary of the campus. These exposed brick buildings compile experimental typologies, featuring of three-bedroom duplexes with a double-height loggia, two-bedroom duplexes and single-bedroom flats. Apartments benefit from generous gardens or terrace gardens. All the buildings come together around a network of gardens and parks, reintroducing the lost landscape of agricultural fields and vegetable gardens into the university.

New Wing of National Gallery of Modern Art (NGMA)

190 F

Team Snehanshu Mukherjee (2009)

🚇🚇 Central Secretariat
Jaipur House, India Gate

The design of the New Wing at the NGMA was the outcome of a collaboration between three young architects, A. R. Ramanathan, Anurag Gupta and Snehanshu Mukherjee, on a national architectural competition held for the project in 1984. The competition was organized to build an extension to Jaipur House, primarily to increase much-needed display space and add supporting ancillary facilities. On the 3.15-hectare site of Jaipur House the building programme envisaged adding a new wing, which was six times the size of the older palace building. The main challenge of the project was to design a distinctive New Wing for the NGMA that would share the site comfortably with the original 1930s Art-Deco palace of the Maharaja of Jaipur, designed by the British architect Arthur Bloomfield. The design of the extension is based on the original building's siting and strong architectural character. The three proposed blocks are placed orthogonally to the site edges to derive maximum possible use of the space available on site, and to keep as substantial a distance as

possible between the extension and the original building. To align the New Wing with the siting of the older building, a free standing colonnade has been built as a screen parallel to the rear facade of Jaipur House, forming a garden court between the old and the new building. The colonnaded screen and the garden create a grand entrance to the proposed extension, while restoring and reinforcing the original axis and clearly establishing the greater architectural hierarchy of the older Jaipur House. The trees present on site have been incorporated into the landscape design of the complex in a way that screens the newer buildings, presenting their facades as fragments against the relatively fuller appearance of the older building. The various courts and courtyards were designed to provide an appropriate setting to display outdoor art objects.The external walls of the New Wing are clad in sandstone of a colour similar to that of the existing building. The pattern of red and buff sandstone bands at the base of the older Jaipur House have been carried through to the new buildings, though here only red sandstone has been used — the banding effect has been achieved by recessing alternate bands. The facades are designed as layers or planes that overlap to generate the impression of generous verandahs and entrance porticos typical of the older institutional buildings that

stand on either side of Raj Path. The facades of the three blocks are designed asymmetrically and composed to deconstruct the solid mass of the New Wing, in effect allowing the new building to appear less imposing despite its larger volume and therefore creating a backdrop for the older building. The entrance lobby and reception is formed by the corner of the 'angled' square which sits within the triple-height atrium of the first gallery block. This atrium visually unites

and orients different floors within this block. Ramps placed at the corner of each of the new blocks, located on the external face, function as buffer spaces between the windows of the external screen walls and the gallery floors, allowing in diffused daylight to illuminate the gallery floors. The galleries are also lit from above by means of specially designed skylights that allow only indirect, diffused daylight to light the deeper central spaces of the gallery floors.

77 / 32

Morphogenesis (2009)

🚇 HUDA City Centre
Sector 32, Gurgaon

191 Ⓙ

Located in Gurgaon, the office hub in the suburbs of New Delhi, this building moves away from the typical office typology, providing an alternative with interweaving open social spaces and closed workspaces. The design brief specified 50,000 square feet of pre-fitted, rentable office spaces for a range of clients. The architect created two types of informal spaces — one at the public level and another at the individual office level. The ground floor is designed to be a recreational, informal meeting space, which defines the entrance. A passive cooling strategy is adopted to create a modified environment, which is non-air-conditioned. This is done through the creation of water bodies, and allowing for built mass only on two sides. The remaining two sides are left open to allow for wind movement. A café is designed as a part of the recreation zone. Each individual office has been provided with a terrace garden, which becomes its private,

informal breakout zone. To address the environmental issues that concern the contemporary office, orientation is optimized in the creation of built volumes. The east and west sun are blocked off with the help of solid stone walls that act as a thermal buffer. The two long sides, north and south, are provided with glazing and punctures respectively. Each floor plate is designed to be 15m wide to allow for daylight penetration. The use of post-tensioned beams allows for the creation of column-free spaces, which permits maximum flexibility within the office space. Rainwater harvesting is achieved across the site and all wastewater gets recycled and reused. Each floor has two separate office. A heat recovery wheel re-uses the exhausted air-conditioned air to pre-cool the fresh air supplied to the offices. The amalgamation of design principles and environmental imperatives creates a building that responds to its setting and programme in a visually aesthetic manner. The outward appearance lends character to the urban fabric through its massive stone walls and punctured facades, all done by using natural materials like wood and stone.

India Glycols Limited
Morphogenesis (2009)
🚇 Botanical Garden
Plot No. 2B, Sector 126,
NOIDA, UP

192 C

The design for the corporate office of India Glycols embodies issues concerning the workplace today, and explores the paradigm of office space as a social scene. Sited in a non-contextual suburban area of Delhi, the setting led to the development of an introverted scheme that would address environmental and socio-economic issues from first principles. The architects were asked to exemplify the identity and corporate ideology of equity and transparency in the workplace as an integral part of the architectural vocabulary. Conceived as a solid perimeter scheme with a more fluid interior, the morphology blurs the interface between the inside and outside. The site surroundings and context, along with an optimum enclosed square volume, enabled a built form with minimum exposed surface area. 8m-wide office bays optimize the natural day lighting and help to define the programmatic requirements of the office. A stacking system is used to generate a variety of open spaces such as courtyards, verandas, terraces and green roofs, which help to structure the office spaces. A central spine traversing the built volume serves as the common activity zone, with other departments branching out. The spatial organization creates overlaps between the exterior and the interior and between the various programmatic requirements, hence creating a vibrant and creative work environment. Energy consciousness dictates the internal spatial and programmatic composition through a series of open and semi-open spaces. Passive design techniques were employed throughout. Solar exclusion is achieved by means of a solid external perimeter, which only permits diffused daylight into the office environs. Reliance on artificial lighting is substantially reduced as courtyards are created to increase natural light levels on the floor plates. The courtyards also help to keep the solar heat gain in the interiors to a minimum. External spaces are tempered using courtyards and terrace gardens that facilitate thermal insulation. A shaded outer facade with air cavity construction, very small slit windows on the outside, and courtyards with microclimate controls (shading and mist gardens, water bodies and plantations) all help to reduce heat gain. Green roofs and terrace gardens also provide a high level of thermal insulation. Water bodies aid evaporative cooling, thereby reducing dependence on artificial means of cooling. They also create an environment rich with the potential for social transactions. Rhythmic articulation of volumes and spaces generates a scheme that is a radical departure from the structured differentiated spaces of the traditional office and the monotony of the open-plan halls that have dominated office planning.

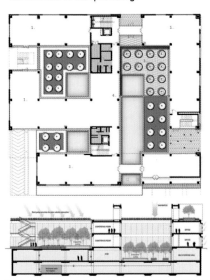

Development Alternatives Headquarters

193 B

Ashok B Lall Associates (2010)
🚇 Hauz Khas
Qutab Institutional Area

Development Alternatives (DA), a Non-Governmental Organization, was established in 1983. In 1985 the young organization acquired a 3,316 square metre plot of land in Qutab Institutional Area on the fringe of a beautiful forest. Neeraj Manchanda, a graduate of New Delhi's School of Planning and Architecture and George Varughese, a young civil engineer, worked on DA's first building with limited resources. They used mud as the main building material. Combining an ancient construction method with modern engineering, thick walls and domes made of compressed-earth blocks took shape and the building was completed in 1988. By 2006, DA needed space for 150 to 200 occupants and was forced to consider its options. It finally decided to demolish and replace the building. The client and architects decided that the new building should carry on the spirit and evoke the memory of the original one, which it does in several ways. Forms and elements of the new building recall those of the old — a domed lobby, vaulted ceilings and central courtyard. The old seminar room, circular, sunken and covered with a prominent dome, is reborn in the same form and location. The new building is also very different from the old one. With 4,500 square metres of usable area instead of 1,000 square metres and six storeys instead of one and a half, it is four and a half times larger. It fully utilizes the maximum permissible floor area of the site and includes underground parking. The building is efficient in utilization of space, materials, and energy. It is built with a degree of technical sophistication appropriate for contemporary cities. The building establishes a visual termination of the street. This happens almost by default because the building is aligned with the street, which ends in a cul-de-sac at the site. From this vantage point, the building presents itself obliquely. Entering the building, after passing through the entrance lobby, one discovers a shaded courtyard with sky above, pools of water below and the sound of trickling water echoing all around. A variety of spaces are arranged around the courtyard: meeting rooms, offices, corridors, stairs and terraces. The spaces are visually connected, vertically and horizontally, to other spaces across the courtyard, blurring the barrier between inside and out. The ground floor is open to the public who visit the shop and use DA's resource centre. One can ascend from the amphitheatre and from the cafeteria garden and cross the bridge from the middle wing to the curved wing. Ascend further to the terrace above the conference room and eventually one reaches the yoga terrace outside the gym. The building volume is modulated in response to the climate, shading against the sun in summer while welcoming it in winter, and capturing the monsoon breezes. The design of each facade is different, especially the fenestration, in response to solar orientation and view. The windows in the west facade are blinkered with prism-shaped protrusions that block the afternoon summer sun while permitting views of the forest. Vines climb the pergolas and the east and west walls. Inset clay pots offer nesting places, inviting bees, parrots, and squirrels from the forest. The shading grills with planters and daylight reflectors on the north and south sides moderate the summer sun and intense light.

The unified palette of materials is woven into a variety of textures, colours, and patterns. The building includes moulded terracotta tiles that form a *jaali* feature common to traditional buildings in northern India. The tiles are filled with insulating vermiculite plaster and recycled mirror fragments that glint sunlight and enhance the dimensional effect. Ninety per cent of the interior and exterior walls are made of cement-stabilized compressed-earth blocks or cement-stabilized fly ash lime gypsum blocks. The earth removed from the site after demolition of the original building was recycled into compressed-earth blocks using simple machinery. The fly-ash blocks used in the building were made using fly-ash from a local power plant. Nearly all masonry and architectural concrete is fair faced. Floors are unpolished granite and sandstone. The project tests innovative specially designed elements and components such as hybrid air-handling that integrates evaporative cooling and refrigerant-based cooling to reduce energy consumption for air-conditioning by 30% and to reduce water consumption. The hybrid cooling has been used throughout the building except in the conference hall. All workspaces are illuminated by daylight, which is modulated for glare-free distribution. The conference room has roof lights that can be closed with shutters when the room needs to be darkened. Rainwater is used to recharge the groundwater. Waste water is recycled, treated on site and used for irrigation and flushing toilets. Economical local materials, simple technology and local labour were employed to keep construction costs low. The project illustrates traditional, environmentally-efficient construction materials and systems that can be economically developed for low-energy mass production and adopted by the mainstream building industry, especially in developing countries. The work of architecture is a symphony in masonry with nearly a dozen types of brick block and stone used in a variety of patterns to create walls, columns, arches, domes, floors, and stairs — orchestrated to create a harmonious whole that delights the senses.

Jawaharlal Nehru Stadium

gmp Architekten and
schlaich bergermann und partner
(2010)

194 A

⊜ JLN Stadium
Bhishma Pitamah Marg, Lodi Road

From 3rd to 14th October 2010, the Jawaharlal Nehru Stadium in New Delhi hosted not only the athletics and rugby events of the Commonwealth Games but also the opening and closing ceremonies. This was the largest sporting event ever staged in New Delhi. The city had previously hosted the Asian Games in 1951 and 1982. An international competition was held in 2007 for the design of the stadium; gmp's scheme in collaboration with schlaich bergermann und partner of Stuttgart emerged victorious. The point of revitalizing the stadium built for the last Asian Games was to create a totally different look without changing the existing terraces. The aim was both to offer the world a new architectural image of the Commonwealth Games and to preserve the stadium's firm place in

public awareness thanks to its long history. These apparently irreconcilable requirements determined the design, making the various 'layers' of the building scheme clear. All 57,000 spectators are under cover, thanks to a membrane roof springing from the triangles and lozenges of the vertical support structure. Visible from afar with its white-coated steel profiles, the structure is arranged round the existing terraces, giving the stadium a wholly distinctive appearance. New access ramps are located between the two spatially separate levels of the lozenge-shaped fields of the supports, distributed around the entire geometry of the stadium in a cascade. The ramps and expressive structure form the 'new' layer around the existing terraces, creating interplay between old and new. These ramps, which are deliberately distinctive in colouration from the rest of the support structure and the existing terraces, replace the original access features, which took up too much space and looked a jumble as well as being incompatible with modern safety requirements. With

their removal, spacious areas are created in front that can be used as open space and entrance zones for different groups of visitors and are no longer obstructed by the ramp structures. The existing floodlight masts were dismantled and replaced by a floodlighting system integrated into the edge of the roof. The roof structure is based on the spoked wheel principle, with two external compression rings. Running right round, two steel compression rings made of welded rectangular box sections carried by V and X-shaped supports with the same profiles form the main load-bearing structure. The radial cables are attached alternately to the upper and lower compression ring, creating a folded substructure. Fully enclosed high-strength cables are used for the load-bearing cables along the spokes, offering the optimal solution for this kind of application in respect of assembly, load bearing capacity and durability. The roof membrane consists of a self-cleaning, PTFE-coated glass fibre membrane with very high material strength and low maintenance

requirements. The rainwater drainage and cleansing effect it has are further reinforced by the steep inclination of the membrane surfaces. These large, smooth membrane zones can be used for temporary projections and lighting effects of all kinds. Access to the roof is via four radial catwalks leading to the ring-shaped catwalk suspended from the inner edge of the roof, where all technical installations such as loudspeakers and floodlighting are installed.

DLF Cyber City

Hafeez Contractor (2010)
🚇 Sikandarpur
DLF Cyber City, Phase II,
Gurgaon

195 J

DLF Cyber City is part of development phase II and III of the DLF City masterplan. Around ten major commercial buildings so far have been designed by architect Hafeez Contractor in this approximately 100-acre development. The DLF metro rail line also passes through Cyber City and the firm has been actively involved in its route planning, placement and elevation features within this commercial park. Most buildings are road facing, so employees will have easy, walkable access from the metro stations. Major IT players like Ericsson, Google, IBM, along with financial institutions like RBS, Standard Chartered and SBI have bought or leased offices in this city, which partly falls under the Special Economic Zone. All buildings in Cyber City have steel, glass, metal and ACP facades. All blocks are of varied, irregular shapes, making each and every one a statement piece and giving the area a very futuristic feel. Each building offers an intelligent workplace to new-age professionals within the IT/ITES Special Economic Zone. The office blocks are designed to ensure a dynamic interplay of open and enclosed spaces. The overall development has a campus feel, with buildings and landscape visually integrated into one complete environment. The program of most buildings called for added features like a gym, swimming pool, health club, and cafeteria as well as business centres. Most buildings also have a covered pedestrian plaza protecting its occupants from the harsh summer sun and providing its young employees with places for rejuvenation.

Building 8

Building 8 is spread across an area of approximately 1.4 million square feet and is divided in to three blocks with a range of six to 15 floors. The building was designed and constructed in three stages. The design of this complex is contemporary with a mixture of glass, ACP and granite used for its facade. The front elevation has an interesting geometric pattern with vertical, horizontal and diagonal lines dividing the facade into sections. The three wings of the complex are connected by two atriums which act as buffer space in this otherwise dense uninterrupted office space.

Castro Café

Romi Khosla Design Studio (2010)

🚇 Jasola-Apollo

Jamia Milia Islamia University,
Jamia Nagar

196 C

The Cafeteria in the Jamia Milia Islamia university is located near the auditorium, cultural centre and the mass communication block, and was expected to become a hub of all social activities on Campus. Most student canteens in India are not air-conditioned, and are often poorly ventilated, making them very hot and oppressive in the summer and very cold in the winters. Due to the extreme climatic conditions of New Delhi, where the summer sees temperatures of above 45 degrees centigrade, and the winters often see temperatures below 5 degree centigrade, this canteen was proposed as a 'Semi-open-air Café'. This allowed it to have an ambient temperature for most of the year along with good ventilation, and a variety of degrees of shade from the climate. The building has a kitchen block to the east, which is a fully enclosed space for cooking and serving food. As one walks along the length of the building westwards, initially the eating enclosure is defined by two walls and a roof. Further down, the sense of interior is defined by one wall and the roof from where the space progresses to be articulated by only one wall. Finally there is only the floor, which ends to demarcate the edge of the canteen space. Throughout this changing sense of interior and exterior, the eating surface and the seating surfaces continue, almost acting like stitches that tie the entire space together. The idea was to try to blur the boundaries between inside and outside, where these undefined boundaries act as a negotiator between the user and the climate of Delhi. All the elements of the building are defined distinctly and independently from each other. The walls don't touch the floor and the roof does not touch the walls. This was the first steel building built at the university campus.

Vatika City
Studio U+A (2010)
⊜ HUDA City Centre
Golf Road Extension, Gurgaon,
Haryana

197 **J**

Studio U+A were the Design Consultants for this project. Vatika City is conceived as a totally designed environment encompassing urbanism, landscape, architecture and interior design. The 53-acre urban district in Gurgaon is envisioned as a family-oriented, pedestrian-friendly community of neighbourhoods. The site is organized as a legible network of traditional streets and open spaces. Approaching from the Sohna Road, the public face of Vatika City is represented by an L-shaped two-storey podium housing retail shops, professional offices and a banqueting facility backed by community facilities. The residential blocks that rise above this base are accessible only from the triangular park. Upon entry, one travels along the Crescent Park

Road. This gently curving thoroughfare feeds a series of radiating tree-lined streets leading to and from a distinct set of neighbourhoods, each characterized by a specific building typology and open space treatment. On the right lies the Crescent Park, a landscaped buffer which serves as the setting for the wedge-shaped Club Ambrosia. Rising on the left, the nine-storey Emilia blocks conform to the crescent and feature landscaped courtyards. The five-storey Iris row houses each have two through units per floor flanking a central hall. Inspired by the cross-section of the London townhouse, the first two floors comprise a duplex apartment which has its lower floor a half-level below and upper floor a half-level above grade. The zone between the public walkway and the building face contains a sunken garden accessible to the lower duplex level. The rear of the row houses look onto a landscaped Common, directly accessible from the upper duplex level and available to

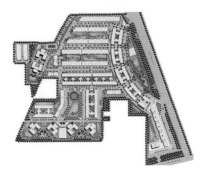

bars bridged by connecting passages and vertical circulation elements. The landscaped courtyard gardens are continuously connected at the ground level. These mid-rise blocks define three sides of the Crimson Park. With its amphitheatre, lawn and playground, Crimson Park is conceived as a public square. Crimson Park is joined along its western edge by the four diagonally-set Sovereign Towers. Comprising two pairs of eighteen-storey point blocks, the pairs flank a central Health Club and Pool. Each of the three wings of a given tower comprises a single 'house in the sky' having no fewer than three exterior exposures. All of Vatika City's buildings share a vocabulary inspired by traditional Indian design precedents, realized in a contemporary architectural language. The narrow building cross-section enabling natural ventilation, the use of screen walls and deep overhangs for shade and privacy, and the courtyard as a place of cool shadow and common use offer a sensitive response to climate and culture.

all residents through a series of apertures which penetrate the blocks. The eight-storey Primrose apartments, along with the Aster blocks north and south of Crimson Park, are composed of a series of abutting buildings forming two parallel

The Westin «
Studio U+A (2010)
MG Road
No. 1, MG Road, Sector 29,
IFFCO Chowk Gurgaon, Haryana

198 J

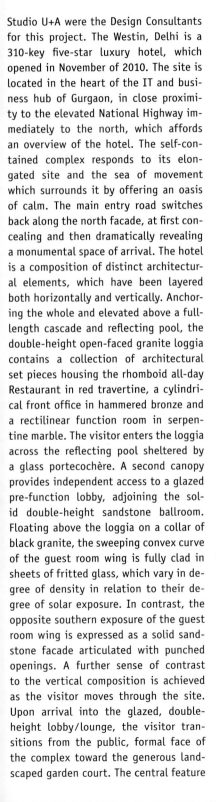

Studio U+A were the Design Consultants for this project. The Westin, Delhi is a 310-key five-star luxury hotel, which opened in November of 2010. The site is located in the heart of the IT and business hub of Gurgaon, in close proximity to the elevated National Highway immediately to the north, which affords an overview of the hotel. The self-contained complex responds to its elongated site and the sea of movement which surrounds it by offering an oasis of calm. The main entry road switches back along the north facade, at first concealing and then dramatically revealing a monumental space of arrival. The hotel is a composition of distinct architectural elements, which have been layered both horizontally and vertically. Anchoring the whole and elevated above a full-length cascade and reflecting pool, the double-height open-faced granite loggia contains a collection of architectural set pieces housing the rhomboid all-day Restaurant in red travertine, a cylindrical front office in hammered bronze and a rectilinear function room in serpentine marble. The visitor enters the loggia across the reflecting pool sheltered by a glass portecochère. A second canopy provides independent access to a glazed pre-function lobby, adjoining the solid double-height sandstone ballroom. Floating above the loggia on a collar of black granite, the sweeping convex curve of the guest room wing is fully clad in sheets of fritted glass, which vary in degree of density in relation to their degree of solar exposure. In contrast, the opposite southern exposure of the guest room wing is expressed as a solid sandstone facade articulated with punched openings. A further sense of contrast to the vertical composition is achieved as the visitor moves through the site. Upon arrival into the glazed, double-height lobby/lounge, the visitor transitions from the public, formal face of the complex toward the generous landscaped garden court. The central feature of the garden court is the plateau of an infinity-edged fountain set atop convex battered spillway walls and embedded with a gridded grove. Housing a gymnasium and support areas, this form encloses the pool deck further to the south as the zone of greatest privacy in contrast to the active areas of the garden court. A full-length vegetated screen wall softens and defines the southern boundary of the site. Rising beyond the battered, textured wall of the water table, the outward canting walls of the kidney-shaped Signature restaurant/nightclub are shingled in sheets of smooth bronze.

Vatika City Point ⌄
Studio U+A (Design Consultants) (2010)
MG Road
MG Road, Gurgaon, Haryana

199 J

Vatika City Point is a composition of built elements comprising a slender stone-clad side-core office tower with an appended curved metal-clad shield above a skylit two-storey retail base. All are linked at the base by a fully glazed facade, which stretches from end to end along the public face of the site. The Tower's south-facing facade is shaded by a series of continuous horizontal louvers. At night, the louvers feature integral up-lighting culminating in the glazed lantern, which completes the building's crown.

Residence at Defence Colony 200 B

Vir Mueller Architects (2010)

🜔 Moolchand

C-386, Defence Colony

In the city of New Delhi, the valuation of land is now so intense that property owners seek to build on the maximum permissible extent of the property. Hence, the city is slowly being overrun by masonry boxes, devoid of kinetic energy. For the Defence Colony residence, Vir Mueller Architects designed the dwelling as a combination of two duplex units. The family would live in one and obtain rental income from the other. The project derives its material and tectonic vocabulary from the load-bearing brick-masonry walls, designed to withstand the loads of a Zone 4 seismic location. The machine-moulded brick has been sourced from a brick factory near Chandigarh. The mass of the bricks is expressed in the thickness of the walls, keeping the house thermally temperate, and endowing it with a rich earthen hue. Simultaneously however, the brick transforms into an effervescent and lacy veil in the screens that shade the west facade of the building. All doors and windows, made from teak timber sections, were fabricated by the carpenters on the site. Mirror-polished stone floors reflect the light within, offering a luminous counterpoint to the masonry walls. This is a simple, hand-crafted, modern/medieval house, seeking to restore the relationship of inhabitants to their material context.

Educomp Academic Block

201

Morphogenesis (2010)
🌐 Botanical Garden
Raffles Millennium Institution,

Plots No. 5, 6, 7 & 8 (adjoining Wipro),
Knowledge Park 4, Greater NOIDA, UP

The design brief was to create a new urban development on the outskirts of the city—an urban spread that allows for flexibility, yet defines the academic settlement, and is derived from its local climatic conditions. The campus consists of three main zones—a public zone (academic), a semi-public and a private zone (residential). The masterplan aimed to create a mini urban settlement that could generate a socio-cultural built environment similar to that of a city. The architects aimed to achieve an optimum sense of balance between the built and open spaces on campus. They also wished to create a sustainable eco-friendly campus, with spaces that respond to local climatic conditions. Vehicular movement is restricted along the peripheral network, while the internal primary, secondary and tertiary streets are for pedestrian movement. The shaded walkways and narrow streets are articulated by exploring the nature of traditional streets to create a pedestrian-friendly environment. The building is an elevated structure with a scooped-out underbelly that is thermally banked to create a recreational space, which remains cool throughout the summer. The underbelly is an enclosed space, cooled by water bodies, and is approached through stepwells leading down from the corners of the building that are open for entry and exit, finished with landscape greens. The intent was to define each corner of the building as a different design element so that no two corners looked the same. One of the unique features of the building is a centrepiece staircase on the south-east inner courtyard of the building, with interweaving stairs spilling out into small break-out spaces at the edges. The ground floor area includes the reception, offices and other administrative rooms. The first and second floors are equipped with the library next to the staircase for easy access, while the third floor is dedicated to classrooms and seminar rooms. The facade was carefully designed with *jaali* screens that help protect sun-exposed areas in the summer months. The *jaali* pattern is in the shape of louvers that closely follow the summer path of the sun across the facade and provide the most shade during the summer, while allowing in the most light during the winter. The courtyards and corridors are cooled through evaporative cooling and allow natural cross-ventilation of the buildings. Vegetation further enhances evaporative cooling in the courtyard and helps insulate the roof from the direct rays of the sun. The campus is being built in three phases, with the first phase being the construction of the Academic Block. The remaining phases involve the development of a sports centre, student centre and public facilities like a convention centre, auditorium and the remainder of the residential block.

Indira Gandhi National Centre for the Arts
Ralph Lerner (2010)
🚇 Central Secretariat
Mansingh Road

202 F

A competition to design the Indira Gandhi National Centre for the Arts (IGNCA) was held in 1986. The 10.2-hectare site for the Centre was located on the northern side of the Rajpath, where it intersects Janpath, and opposite the National Archives building designed by Luytens. The competition brieflisted a vast array of facilities for the study and display of India's fine and performing arts heritage. Above all was the goal of gaining an internationally recognised symbol of modern India in the way that Chandigarh had done earlier. The competition drew almost two hundred entries from forty-six different countries. Ralph Lerner, an architect and educator from Princeton University with a practice in that city, won the competition. Gautam Bhatia's scheme was placed second. Significant Indian entries also came from such well-known architects as Raj Rewal, Romi Khosla, Chandra Prakash Kukreja and Anil Laul. Lerner's winning scheme, unanimously chosen by the jurors, recognised the importance of the existing context and sought monumentality in design. It was a neo-classical, courtyard composition that integrated its parts into the whole. Visually, the elements of the scheme reflected certain Indian building types, such as the temple *shikhara* and parts of Fathepur Sikri. The full project had envisaged a large, enclosed square, reminiscent of the Naqsh-e-Jahan in Isfahan, Iran. But it appears as if the IGNCA shaped the architectural vocabulary of current official building — specifically, the reluctant verticality, *ziggurat*-like heaviness, plate-glass windows deeply inset, rectangular play of volumes rather than surface adornment, and of course the use of Agra and Dholpur stone on the facade. The original scheme with a vast array of activities was to be a mammoth eight-building complex on prime land on the Central Vista. It was to be completed in 1993. It has been almost 30 years since IGNCA was set up in November 1985, but only about 20 per cent of the work on its building has been completed.

Jaypee Greens

203

ARCOP (2011)
Sector 128, Greator NOIDA, UP

ARCOP has been a pioneer in creating Jaypee Greens, a premium 450-acre golf-centric real estate development integrating homes with a golf course, landscaped spaces, resort living and commercial developments. Jaypee Greens offers a complete lifestyle real-estate destination offering individual homes and apartments amidst an 18-hole golf course designed by Greg Norman, an exclusive clubhouse, conference and banquet facilities, eateries, spa and health club, a golf academy and a host of entertainment and recreation options. It is a place where nature connects to a recreation destination, social activities and gracious living. It is a mixed-use development with different residential options and recreational facilities like golf, landscaping, play areas and parks. The townships are less dense with large green landscapes all around, to give the residents an experience of elegant living. The project is a unique place to live, with very well refined pieces of Indian residential architecture. Jaypee Greens has a repertoire of various forms of residential typologies. Low-density high rise housing features towers with luxurious open spaces in between them. Thus the opportunity was exploited by making the urban design a composition of well refined forms that addressed the planning requirements of the client's brief for the various towers. Owing to the large scale of the project and the ever-changing requirements of the clients, the masterplan and architectural design of the complex was based on flexibility of planning and design as the most important criterion.

Triburg Headquarters
SPA Design (2010)
◉ MG Road
Udyog Vihar, Haryana, Gurgaon

204 **B**

Triburg is one of the leading apparel sourcing companies in India. Prior to its relocation to new premises, it was operating out of multiple buildings located in the Sultanpur area of South Delhi. As the company was itself well versed with contemporary design trends, it wanted the head office building to express the contemporary as well as well crafted spaces, which could promote interaction amongst its teams. The site for the project was located in the industrial sector of Gurgaon. In spite of being surrounded by nondescript buildings all around, the immense size of the site had the potential to create an oasis-like environment within itself. Thus the project aimed to recreate the transparent character of the Adalaj stepwell and the terraces of the mythical hanging gardens of Babylon in a contemporary manner. A snake-like shape characterizes the construction, creating four large courtyards giving diffused light to the offices, adapted to the harsh climate of Delhi. The new structure consists of two to five storeys, increasing gradually towards the back of the building. The back portion is structurally designed to accommodate three more floors. A large basement runs beneath the entire building, housing parking and services. The structure is Reinforced Cement Concrete using large spanned beams and shallow slabs with clay brick arches underneath, offering open-space offices with 11-foot-high vaulted ceilings. Arched facades overlook an enclosed garden and courtyards with different types of landscapes, from water bodies to desert and jungle, keeping the vistas protected from neighbouring developments. Extensive use of natural clay bricks for outside paving, walls and vaulted ceilings gives the precinct a warm and tactile character. Hanging gardens cover the green terraces at all levels to protect the structure from direct heat. The top floors have skylights to take full advantage of natural light. Facades to the south-east, south-west and west are equipped with clay louvers to modulate light in the offices and lobby. The design of the Triburg Headquarters relies on a simple geometry to give it architectural clarity and strength. Although the forms are forceful, the architecture is not monumental. Instead, the building assumes a human scale in spite of its large size.

Delhi Metro
2001–2011

After India's independence and partition in 1947, Delhi saw a huge inflow of migrants, which led to a rapid growth of its population from 700,000 to 1,700,000 in just five years. Over the past 60 years, the city has continued to grow exponentially with rapid development and urbanization transforming it into a major cultural, political, and commercial centre of India. The result has been an increase of the population to over 16 million in Delhi alone. The National Capital Region (which includes the suburban towns of NOIDA, Gurgaon, Faridabad and Ghaziabad) has a population of over 22 million, making it the eighth-largest metropolis in the world. The need for an efficient and affordable public transport system was made all the more urgent in the early nineties. As a result of liberalization, a large number of multinationals started setting up offices in the upcoming suburbs of Gurgaon and NOIDA, creating jobs for an ever-increasing number of immigrants from across the country. The only way to transport all these people safely and efficiently was to develop a Mass Rapid Transit System. Planning for the metro started in 1984,

when the Delhi Development Authority and the Urban Arts Commission came up with a proposal for developing a multi-modal transport system for the city. The Government of India and the Government of Delhi jointly set up the Delhi Metro Rail Corporation (DMRC) in 1995. Construction started in 1998, and the first section, 8.5 kilometres between Shahdara and Tis Hazari, opened in 2002. Since then the network has grown to six lines with a total length of 189.63 kilometres (117.83 mi) connecting not only the vast region of the capital but also the suburbs of NOIDA, Gurgaon, Faridabad and Ghaziabad. With the completion of Phase II, the system has 142 stations of which 35 are underground, and has a combination of elevated, at-grade and underground lines which use both broad gauge and standard gauge rolling stock. The Delhi Metro has been the largest public works project undertaken by any city in India. The Calcutta Metro, which predates Delhi's by over a decade, was overrun with delays and covered a much shorter area over a longer construction period. To avoid similar delays and to make the construction process more efficient, the DMRC was established as an autonomous body with full control over financing, operations, hiring and contracting.

Airport Express, New Delhi Railway Station

The urban landscape of Delhi has undergone some radical changes because of the Metro. Most of the network operates above ground on heavy concrete pilasters running along the arterial routes of the city. Elevated stations are designed as monolithic structures with a concourse on the lower level and the platforms on top. Underground stations reverse the layout with the platforms at the lowest level. The major interchange stations are larger and have a stronger architectural impact on their contexts. Rajiv Chowk, one of the busiest interchange stations on the network, transformed the urban landscape of Connaught Place with the addition of Central Park, a large landscaped public park in the rotunda, creating much-needed breathing space. Kashmiri Gate, another major interchange station with both above- and below-grade lines, has completely transformed the busy Kashmiri Gate area.

Despite the similarity in layouts, the exteriors of many metro stations have been designed to reflect the local visual fabric. Alternatively, many use glass and aluminum facing that fits in well with the more 'modern' aesthetic that DMRC wants to project. The metro stations at Central Secretariat on the Yellow and Violet lines use Dholpur stone louvers in a contemporary minimalist *jaali* formation. These reflect the finish of Most government buildings on Raisina Hill. In stark contrast, the station at Nehru Place, one of Delhi's busiest commercial complexes, is a two-storey glass and aluminium-clad structure reflecting a more 'modern' aesthetic. As part of the plan to recover the costs of constructing the Metro, the DMRC has developed land acquired around metro stations as commercial properties like malls and office complexes. The DMRC also opened South Asia's first Metro Museum

Karol Bagh Metro Station

Dwarka Sector 21 Metro Station

in 2011 at the Patel Chowk Metro Station. This Museum showcases the genesis, history and journey of the DMRC. A vast collection of display panels, historical photographs and exhibits traces the development of the Delhi Metro over the 32 years it took to start operations in 2002 from the drawing boards.

The Delhi Metro has also won recognition from various organisations for its environmentally-friendly practices. Most of the Metro stations conduct rainwater harvesting as an environmental protection measure. It is also the first railway project in the world to earn carbon credits after being registered with the United Nations under the Clean Development Mechanism, and has so far earned 400,000 carbon credits by saving energy through the use of regenerative braking systems on its trains.

Phase III of the metro, already under construction in some parts of central Delhi, will add another 65 kilometres to the Metro network in Delhi and the National Capital Region. The next phase, expected to be operational by 2015, will see the Metro take an entire circle around the city, much like the surface Ring Road in Delhi. It will be a mixture of elevated and underground stretches.

The Metro is accelerating growth and transforming the city all along its corridors. Property values have increased exponentially and the government has proposed to increase the Floor Area Ratio along Metro routes to accommodate a growing and mobile population. A sharp increase in users of public transport has spurred the government into rethinking its urban transit policies. This will involve redesigning roads to be more pedestrian-friendly and encourage cycling. These policies are years away from becoming reality, but are a positive step towards developing a sustainable, livable city.

Lajpat Nagar Metro Station

Elevated Metro Stop

Post-Liberalisation

Chandigarh

City Centre, Sector 17, Le Corbusier

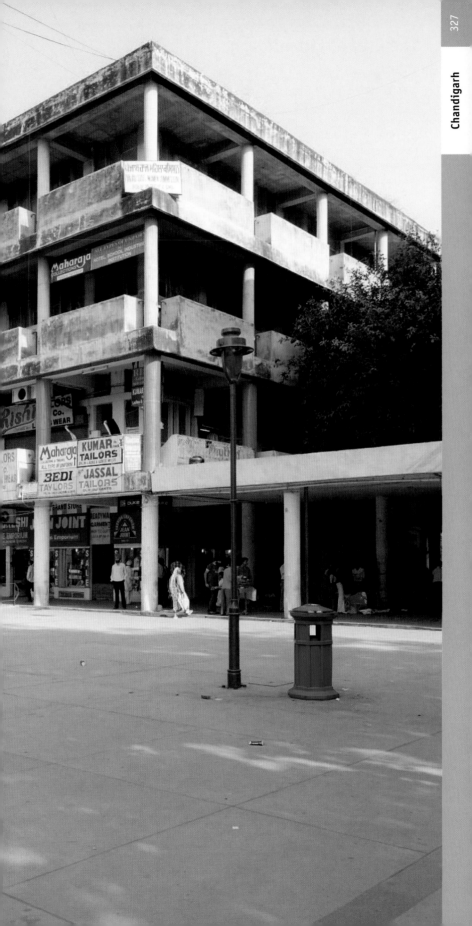

The City of Chandigarh

Ashish Nangia

The city of Chandigarh is situated at the base of the Shiwalik Range of the Himalayas, at 333m above sea level, approximately 260 kilometres northwest of India's capital, New Delhi. In 1947, at the command of the British viceroy and with the consent of the future leaders of India and Pakistan, Sir Radcliffe drew a line dividing the British empire in the Indian subcontinent into two new entities: the nations of India and Pakistan.

The state of Punjab, through which the line was to be drawn, was an incredibly homogenous mix of three communities—Hindu, Muslim and Sikh—living together in close proximity and sharing the same physical space in villages, towns and cities, and bound together by social and economic ties fostered by generations of cohabitation. It was inevitable, thus, that entire villages and communities found themselves on the wrong side of the line, Muslims finding themselves in the heart of Hindustan and Hindus and Sikhs being stranded in Pakistan.

The aftermath of the partition of India led to the greatest known exchange of population in history. It is estimated that 15 million people crossed the Radcliffe line both ways, leaving behind in a now foreign land the major part of their immovable property, as well as most of their wealth. For north India, most of the 1950s were occupied by a mammoth effort to undo the damage of partition. To resettle people, attract capital, build up infrastructure, and to provide housing and employment to its citizens.

The state of Punjab was the most grievously affected. Not only did it have the maximum number of refugees from across the border, it had suffered greatly both economically and socially. Its administrative and historic capital, Lahore, the pride of the Punjabi population, was now across the border in Pakistan. Reconstruction efforts in this state thus assumed a symbolic value—not only was this effort a Punjabi initiative, but it was also deemed to be a microcosm of India's post-independence effort, and its success or failure would be India's measure of its post-independence capability.

For Punjab, and thus India, the building of a new capital city was to quickly assume the importance of a project of national priority. This city was to be a showcase of the new India, a confident new nation, though based on its ancient traditions. It was also as much a social as a political experiment, designed to have space for all, from the poorest sections of the population to the richest. In this sense, the new capital was also an expression of the Republic of India, based on the principles of liberty and equality. The socialist leanings of Nehru translated into his personal backing for this project.

Having taken the decision to treat Chandigarh as a material expression of the optimism and the dynamism of a newly independent nation began the struggle for locating the city within the complex matrix of Indian architecture, the history of which, in pre-independence India, stretches from the 5000 year old Indus Valley Civilization to the British Imperial Capital of New Delhi.

Located in between these extremes are examples such as the cities of Jaipur or—closer home to Chandigarh, Patiala, which like all medieval cities in India, were structured around a centrally positioned royal palace, fitted with gardens for the king and his privileged few. But, for the majority of the Indian populace, living conditions in the average

Nehru and Le Corbusier

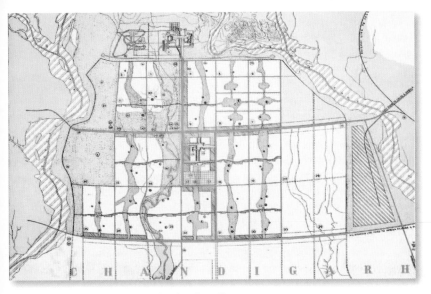

Chandigarh's City Map, Le Corbusier (1952)

Indian city of 1947—whether of colonial or indigenous origin—were no better than confinement to extremely cramped and obsolete structures. Since none of the existing could have served the purpose of an appropriate symbol or an architectural and social model for a newly independent, democratic nation, it became important to have a conscious departure and create, in the words of Nehru, 'a new town, unfettered by the traditions of the past...'

Utopian Dreams

The brief presented to the architects was essentially a reflection of such individual and collective perceptions of what a utopian, modern capital of independent India should be. Chandigarh would be an aesthetic and social utopia and was described as '... a capital which would be a cultural, commercial and industrial centre ... from it would flow life and activity throughout the Province.' Above all, Chandigarh would be the first Indian city where opportunities for healthy living—interpreted as access to 'water, drainage and electricity' and 'sun, space and verdure'—would be available to even the poorest of the poor. The vision was of a capital that would serve as a model in city planning for the nation.

The near vacuum of indigenous expertise needed to realize this dream prompted the search for Western skill. Conscious

of the specificities of their situation, the search was narrowed to '...a good modern architect who was not severely bound by an established style and who would be capable of developing a new conception originating from the exigencies of the project itself and suited to the Indian climate, available materials and the functions of the new capital.' The Chandigarh Project was, at first, assigned to the American planner Albert Mayer, with his associate Matthew Nowicki working out architectural details. Le Corbusier's connection to the city—as also that of his three associates, Pierre Jeanneret, E. Maxwell Fry and Jane Drew—was purely fortuitous, a result of Nowicki's sudden death in August 1951. The agreement with the second team had included acceptance of the Mayer Plan. Beginning with the practical necessity of re-locating the Capitol, this first scheme, with its concept of a fan-shaped city with a curved network of roads and varying shapes of superblocks, was soon set aside. Le Corbusier's plan for Chandigarh conformed to the modern city planning principles of Congrès International d'Architecture Moderne (CIAM), in terms of division of urban functions, an anthropomorphic plan form, and a hierarchy of road and pedestrian networks. The urban form of Chandigarh derives from the well-ordered matrix of the generic 'neighbourhood unit' and the hierarchical circulation pattern resulting from

Le Corbusier's theory of the 7Vs, with a regular grid of the fast traffic V3 roads defining each 'Sector'. The sector itself was a self-sufficient introverted unit, making contact with the surrounding fast traffic roads at four specified points.

A *sector*, a neighbourhood unit of size 800 metres × 1,200 metres with population of each sector varies between 3,000 and 20,000 depending upon the sizes of plots and the topography of the area. Connections with adjoining neighbourhoods were made through its V4, the shopping street, as well as the bands of open space that cut across in the contrary direction. Day-to-day facilities for shopping, healthcare, recreation and the like were arrayed along the V4 — all on the shady side. The vertical green belts, with the pedestrian V7, contained sites for schools and sports activities.

The natural edges formed by the hills and the two rivers, the gently sloping plain with groves of mango trees, a stream bed meandering across its length and the existing road and rail lines — all were to play their role in influencing the distribution of functions and establishing the hierarchy of the roads, giving the city its ultimate civic form. Connecting the various accents of the city — such as the Capitol, the City Centre, the University, The Industrial Area, etc. and scaling its matrix were the city's V2s, of which the Jan Marg (People's Avenue), was designed as the ceremonial approach to the Capitol with the Leisure Valley, reinforcing its directionality. The second V2, Madhya Marg (Middle Avenue), cutting across the city, connects the railway station and the Industrial Area to the University. The third V2, Dakshin Marg (South Avenue) demarcates the Phase I of Chandigarh.

Architectural Components

Le Corbusier's masterplan regulated the built mass of the new city by including an extensive range of architectural controls covering volumes, facades and textures — especially for the major commercial and civic hubs such as the V2s. Recognizing the crucial role of trees as elements of urban design, he also devised a comprehensive plantation scheme, specifying the shape of trees for each category of avenues, keeping in view their potential for cutting off the harsh summer sun.

Besides deciding the city's layout, Le Corbusier had assumed the responsibility of establishing the architectural controls of the City Centre and designing the Capitol group of buildings. The Capitol was to contain the three major functions of democracy — the Legislative Assembly, the High Court and the Secretariat. Besides the fourth major building, the Governor's Palace (later changed to Museum of Knowledge) the complex also had a number of other 'Monuments' such as the Tower of Shadows, the Martyrs' Memorial and the Open Hand. In time he would also be assigned the responsibility for designing the Government Museum and Art Gallery, the College of Art as well as some other smaller works such as the Boat Club and parts of the Sukhna Lake.

To the other three architects was assigned the role of designing 'places for people', containers for ordinary, everyday functions such as government housing, schools, hostels, buildings for work and entertainment and of grappling with the complex exigencies of the situation. Occupying vast tracts of land all over the First Phase of Chandigarh, these lesser-known constructions were to define the constructed volume and architectural vocabulary of the city and, in general, direct the course of Modernism in India. (www.boloji.com)

Capitol Complex

Le Corbusier conceived the masterplan of Chandigarh as analogous to the human body, with the Capitol Complex as a clearly defined head. The complex comprises of the 'Secretariat', the 'High Court' and the 'Legislative Assembly', separated by large piazzas. A fourth building, originally proposed to be the Raj Bhavan (Governor's Palace), and later demarcated as a Museum of Knowledge, were never realized. Le Corbusier established a harmonious relationship between various buildings of the complex through the consistent use of exposed reinforced concrete. The most significant

Open Hand, Le Corbusier (1957)

aspect of the layout is the facilitation of uninterrupted pedestrian linkages throughout the complex. A vast concrete esplanade between the High Court and the Assembly thus became the central design feature, along which were arrayed the six 'Monuments' and various pools of water. All vehicular circulation was arranged, and dug out where necessary, at 5m below the esplanade. The large quantities of earth thus obtained were used to create 'artificial hills', enabling partial enclosure of the Complex and emphasizing its careful orientation towards the magnificent view of the hills beyond.

Main facade of the High Court in Chandigarh, Le Corbusier (1955)

High Court
Le Corbusier (1955)
Sector 1, Capitol Complex,
Chandigarh

205

The first of the buildings to be built in the Capitol Complex was the High Court, which was constructed from 1951 to 1957. The High Court houses nine courts of law and the required administrative and support units. Besides the architecture, Le Corbusier also designed some furniture and light fittings, and tapestries for each of the nine courts. The structure has a double roof projecting over the office block, which looks like an inverted umbrella. Three vertical piers rising 60 feet from the floor and painted in bright colours form the entrance to the building. A distinctively Corbusian brise-soleil shields the glazed facade from the harsh Indian sun, an attempt to negotiate the climate with passive mechanisms to avoid a reliance on mechanical systems. The most striking aspect of the monument is the magnificent sweep of its upper roof, symbolic of the assurance of protection and justice to people.

Secretariat Building

Le Corbusier (1966)
Sector 1, Capitol Complex,
Chandigarh

206

The Secretariat was constructed from 1953 to 1959 and is the largest and tallest of the three structures that form the Capitol Complex. The long horizontal concrete slab form, 240 metres long, 24 metres deep and 50 metres high, marks the edge of the Capitol Complex on the left side. The structure was seen as a solution to 'problems of modern offices' such as adequate lighting, ventilation, economy and efficiency. The plan incorporated two ramps for vertical pedestrian movement. The exposed concrete ramps perforated with small square windows, along with its distinctive brise-soleil-louvered screen of deeply sculptured two-storey porticos in the centre, gives the building a sculptural appearance. The Secretariat building, designed to house the offices of various ministries, helps in defining the space of the Capitol Complex by emphasizing a sense of hierarchy of facades, and by its sheer cliff like size and volume. Multi-level interior spaces and the terrace garden are also key design features of the building.

**Legislative Assembly
(Vidhan Bhavan)**
Le Corbusier (1957)
Sector 1, Capitol Complex,
Chandigarh

207

The Legislative Assembly at the north-eastern end of the Capitol Complex is the most sculptural structure of the group.

The building was conceived as a horizontal rectilinear structure, square in plan, with a monumental portico facing the main plaza. The design of its top-lit Forum, the sickle-shaped Portico, and the thin hyperboloid shell of the immense, column-free, circular Assembly Hall, displays the immense plastic and structural potential of concrete. Sun

protection louvers 'brise-soleil' on lateral walls protect the interiors against the harsh Chandigarh sun. The two legislative chambers are surrounded by a space 'forum' which serves for circulation as well as informal meetings. The Assembly Chamber, 128 feet in diameter at the base and rising to 124 feet at its highest point, is crowned by a massive hyperbolic tower which extends well above the roof line and looks very dramatic against the backdrop of distant hills. The Legislative Assembly completes the complex. Located in the centre is the Open Hand Monument. This metallic sculpture, designed by Le Corbusier, is the official emblem of Chandigarh and represents the ideology of 'open to give and open to receive'.

Rock Garden by Nek Chand ≈   208

Nek Chand (1975)
Sector 1, Chandigarh

Nek Chand was an avid collector of rocks and stones from the foothills of the Himalayas, which he said had a soul of their own. The region's odd, sometimes anthropomorphically shaped stones struck him as ancient and alive beings. As the collection grew, Nek Chand started to store them in an abandoned gorge near Sukhna Lake, a property designated as a land conservancy, a forest buffer established in 1902 that nothing could be built on. Chand continued to build his sculptures surreptitiously for eighteen years, before being discovered by the authorities in 1975. By this time, the gorge had turned into a 12-acre (49,000 square metres) complex of inter-linked courtyards, each filled with hundreds of pottery-covered concrete sculptures of dancers, musicians, and animals. His work was in serious danger of being demolished, but with public opinion on his side, the park was inaugurated as a public garden in 1976. Nek Chand was then officially asked to continue making his sculptures in the garden with a workforce of 50 labourers. An unpretentious entrance leads to a magnificent, almost surrealist arrangement of rock fossils, broken chinaware, discarded fluorescent tubes, broken and cast away glass bangles, building waste, coal and clay—all juxtaposed to create a dream

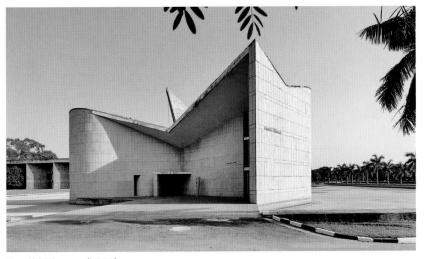

Gandhi Bhavan (1962)

folk world of palaces, soldiers, monkeys, village life, women and temples. These are open air sculptures, one display separated from the other by a clever use of tunnels, twists, turns and concealed gateways such that this magical world unfolds in phases.

and consequential, cannot be fully grasped — much less perpetuated — if the principles regulating the concept are not properly understood through the study of various components of the city in use.' He intended for this study to be carried out at the CCA.

Chandigarh College of Architecture (CCA) ≽
Le Corbusier (1975)
Sector 12, Chandigarh

209

CCA was established in 1961 after Le Corbusier succeeded in establishing it as an integral part of Chandigarh. His conviction was that '... the creation of the built environment, however brilliant

Punjab University ≽
Pierre Jeanneret and
B. P. Mathur
Sector 14, Chandigarh

210

The Punjab University with its various departments and adjoining technical and non-technical government colleges, spread in an area of over 500 acres in sectors 14 and 25, form

the educational zone of the city. The masterplan was done by J. K. Chowdhury and later revised by Pierre Jeanneret and B. P. Mathur. The layout is a loose gridiron plan, in which the buildings are placed like objects within the space, each object having the same geometry and set parallel to each other. The three-winged structure of Jeanneret's Gandhi Bhavan is one of the most sculptural on campus, and sits poised atop a large reflecting pool. The three pinnacles symbolise the ascension into the three worlds of Indian philosophy. The Student Centre, a major landmark of the city of Chandigarh, was inaugurated in 1975. The unique cylindrical structure with a ramp spiralling up to the cafeteria on the top floor houses the office of the university students' council, recreational spaces and a cafeteria with a panoramic view of the city.

**Government Museum
and Art Gallery ☆**
Le Corbusier (1975)
Sector 10-C, Chandigarh

211

Situated in the heart of the city planned
by Le Corbusier, and very close to the city
centre in beautiful view of the Shivalik
range of mountains, the Museum has a
sprawling campus at one side of which is
located the Government College of Art.

Ahmedabad

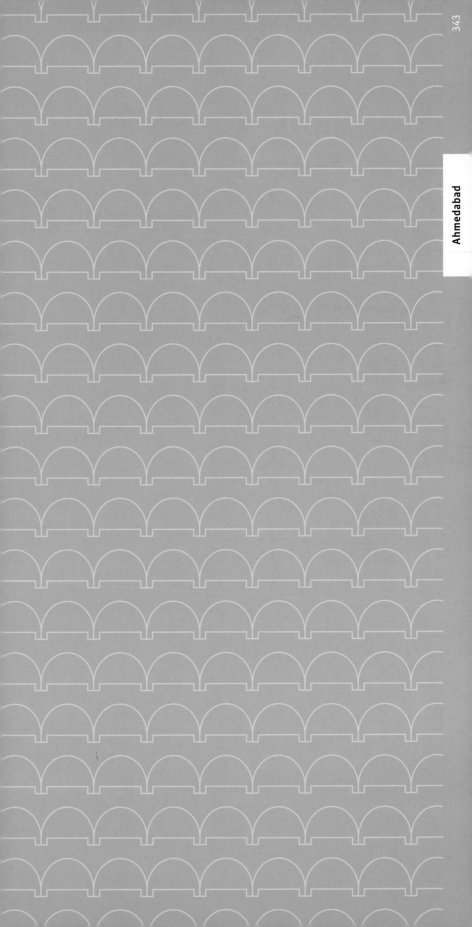

Millowner's Association, Le Corbusier (1954)

Architecture of Ahmedabad

Shahana Dastidar

Ahmedabad is the largest city in India's western state of Gujarat and has a population of about six million people. It was founded on February 26th, 1411 by Sultan Ahmed Shah as the capital of the Gujarat Sultanate and has been an important centre of trade and industry for several centuries now. The city is split in two by the River Sabarmati and connected by a series of bridges.

The old City of Ahmed Shah (simply called the 'City' in common parlance, even in the Gujarati language) lies on the Eastern bank of the river. It was built as a walled city punctuated by gates, some parts of the walls and the gates still existing. The settlement enclosed by the walls is characterized by neighbourhood units called 'Pol' and timber courtyard houses called 'Haveli'. While the old city with its dense urban fabric, narrow winding lanes, colourful markets and numerous monuments is worth exploring by itself—most architects and designers visit Ahmedabad because it is, today, one of the hubs of contemporary design and architecture in India.

One of the reasons for this is the geology of the state where it is located. Much of Gujarat is covered with Black 'Cotton' Soil, perfect for the raising of cotton. Due to the extensive farming of cotton as a cash crop, Ahmedabad saw the rise of the textile industry in the late 19th century with numerous mills located in and around the city. Mahatma Gandhi, himself a Gujarati, lived in Ahmedabad for a while. The local textile industry benefited from the civil disobedience movement during the fight for Independence where Gandhi promoted the use of 'Swadeshi' or Indian-made goods and the boycott of fabrics being imported from England. The mill-owners, thus involved in the Independence movement, were also involved in the development of science, technology and education in post-Independence India. So, in the 1960s, Ahmedabad saw the rapid founding of the Indian Space Research Organisation, Physical Research Laboratories, National Institute of Design, Indian Institute of Management Ahmedabad and the School of Architecture at the Centre for Environmental Technology and Planning. One of the more prominent mill-owning families was the Sarabhai family, owner of Calico Mills and involved in many of the institutions mentioned above and much of the architecture discussed below.

Post-colonial architecture in India was influenced by many factors, some indigenous and some foreign, and consequently followed many different paths. External influences comprised mainly of the Bauhaus in the 1920s and 1930s and later, Le Corbusier who was invited by Jawaharlal Nehru, first Prime Minister of Independent India, to design Chandigarh in 1950.

Some of the Bauhaus influence can be seen in the early work of the Indian architect, **Achyut Kanvinde**, in Ahmedabad. His design for the **Ahmedabad Textile Industry's Research Association** (ATIRA, 1950–1952) and **Physical Research Laboratory** (1953–1954) in Ambavadi appear to reflect the philosophy of Walter Gropius and the Bauhaus with clear forms, an organisation of spaces based on function and the use of new building technologies. The facades of ATIRA reflect its geographical orientation, the windows on the north side being flush with the face of the building while the southern elevation has continuous sunshades running the length of the building. At both ATIRA & PRL, Kanvinde made pioneering use of the column-beam grid

Textile Industry's Research Association, Achyut Kanvinde (1950–1952)

Villa Shodhan, Le Corbusier (1954)

that quickly became popular, and later standard in building construction all over India. He was also one of the first architects to work with a concrete waffle slab in his Bank of India building in the Bhadra area of Ahmedabad. ATIRA/PRL being research institutions have highly restricted access while the Bank of India, being a public institution, has some limited areas of the building open to all.

The other strong external influence was the work of the Swiss architect, **Le Corbusier**. As Le Corbusier's direct association with India began with the design of Chandigarh, he was invited by the mill-owning families of Ahmedabad to design a number of buildings in the city. The first of these was the **Villa Shodhan** (1954) near the Nagri Hospital. The villa is defined by its strong cubical form in exposed concrete punctuated by large glass windows and tiny slits. Many of Le Corbusier's signature elements are present here including the flat 'parasol'

roof, the brise-soleil facade and a ramp leading straight to the mezzanine. Some scholars have noted in the Villa Shodhan influences from Le Corbusier's earlier studies in house design especially, the Maison Citrohan. Today, it is a private residence (as it was designed to be) and not accessible to the public.

The exposed concrete, approach ramp and brise-soleil is also evident in his other residence in Ahmedabad—the **Sarabhai House** near the Calico Museum in Shahibag (1955). However, in form, the Sarabhai House is completely different—being a strongly horizontal building in contrast to the cubical Villa Shodhan. Spatially, the building is very different as well, composed as it is of ten 'Catalonian' parallel brick vaults of equal width. The vaults are supported by large concrete beams. All the walls are underneath these beams, hence parallel to each other and intermittently punctuated by openings. This building is still home to a member of the Sarabhai family and, as such, is not open to the public. However, visits are sometimes possible by appointment and it may be a good idea to combine it with a visit to the Calico Museum nearby (also owned by the Sarabhai family and also accessible only by appointment). Interestingly, as a side-note, Frank Lloyd Wright's only design for India was the unbuilt Calico Mills Administrative Office, also for the Sarabhai family.

Floor plan of the Villa Shodhan

Sarabhai House, Le Corbusier (1955)

The third residence that Le Corbusier designed in Ahmedabad, the Chinubhai House, was never built. Fortunately, his two other works are public buildings and accessible to all. Perhaps his most famous building from Ahmedabad is the **Ahmedabad Textile Millowners' Association (ATMA)** opposite City Gold Cinema on Ashram Road, known by local architects as 'atma'.

The distinctive entrance facade of ATMA (1954–1956) is composed of an imposing brise-soleil (this being the west-facing elevation), a dramatic approach ramp leading straight to the first floor and a sculpturesque free-standing staircase. The building is cubical in form and made of exposed concrete. Internally, it is almost completely open—with concrete columns, a few free-standing concrete walls and very few enclosed spaces. Upon entering visitors can feel the breeze that flows unimpeded through the building and see straight through to the river on the other side. The lack of enclosed spaces also means that the building has always been of little practical use, perhaps exemplifying architecture as a work of art. Until recently, the same could be said of Le Corbusier's other public building here—**the Sanskar Kendra** (1957), opposite NID in Paldi. Designed as a museum of culture, the building is located at the western end of the Sardar Patel Bridge in Paldi. The entire structure is raised on exposed concrete 'pilotis' columns. The walls on the upper floors

Sanskar Kendra, Le Corbusier (1957)

Millowner's Association, Le Corbusier (1954)

Indian Institute of Management, Louis I. Kahn (1962)

are made of an exposed concrete framework with exposed brick infill walls on the facade. The scale of the building feels somewhat monumental, possibly because of the large expanses of exposed brick. The entrance is from an open court on the ground floor with a pool and a ramp that leads to the first floor. Though designed as a museum, it did not house one until only very recently. Today it hosts a limited exhibition focusing on the city of Ahmedabad, a kite museum and some offices of the Ahmedabad Municipal Corporation. Much of the building remains empty.

The Indian Institute of Management (IIM) comprises of a group of public educational institutions in the country that impart a variety of post-graduate qualifications. Entry to these institutions is through an open exam and there is stiff competition. The second IIM to be started in India was in the Vastrapur area of Ahmedabad. Today, IIM-Ahmedabad or IIM-A (as it is commonly known) has two campuses—the Heritage Campus and the New Campus connected by an underground passage. The 'Heritage Campus' (1962–1964) was designed by Louis I. Kahn, and is located near the Blind Men's Association in Ambavadi. This series of buildings in exposed load-bearing brick walls is arranged around a series of courtyards. The walls are articulated with a series of exposed concrete arches, some of which are full circular and some segmental—though not all the arches are load bearing. The arrangement and varying sizes of courtyards provide scale to the open and built spaces of

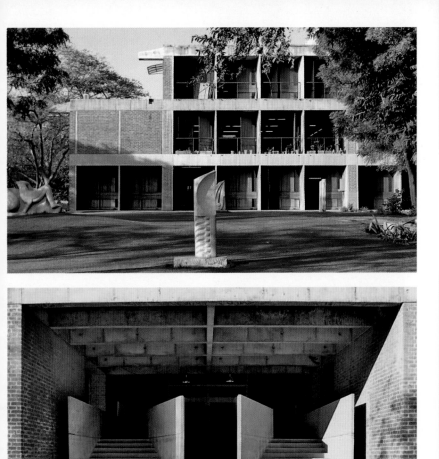

**Centre For Environmental Planning and Technology (CEPT),
Balkrishna V. Doshi (1972–1981)**

the Institute, as well as framing a series of vistas that change as one move in and out of the courts — one of which is named the Kahn Plaza. Kahn died in 1974 while the large complex was still under construction. The design responsibility was taken over by the Indian architect Anant Raje, who had previously worked with him in Philadelphia. Anant Raje had worked with Kahn from 1964 to 1969 though not on IIM. He completed the project with the dining hall (1979), the Management Development Centre (1982) and the Ravi Mathai auditorium. Raje used the same palette of materials as Kahn, thereby maintaining visual continuity while spatially expressing his own design ideas.

Another Indian architect who had worked with Kahn on the IIM project, and

earlier as site architect for Le Corbusier in Chandigarh, is **Balkrishna V. Doshi**. He was one of the key founding members of the School of Architecture at the **Centre for Environmental Planning and Technology (CEPT)**, near Dada Saheb in the university area of Navrangpura, Ahmedabad. In addition to developing the institution, he also designed the buildings for it (1967–1968). The structures are in parallel load-bearing brick walls with exposed concrete slabs, beams and staircase. The buildings lie on a longitudinal axis in an East-West direction with all openings on the North-South facades.

Sunken courts on one side of the building result in open double-height spaces on the south side. On the north side, lawns cover a mound over what used to

Husain Doshi Gufa, Balkrishna V. Doshi (1992–1995)

Husain Doshi Gufa, Balkrishna V. Doshi (1992–1995)

be brick kilns, sloping down towards the building and leveling out at basement level. The upper floors consist of studios for the students, each of which consist of two distinct volumes — on one side a large double height space lit by north light trusses, on the other a lowered roof slab creating a single height space opening onto balconies facing the south. As the institution has grown and developed, Doshi has been involved in the design of other structures in and around CEPT. A few years previously, Doshi designed the **L. D. Institute of Indology** (1952–1962), opposite the LD Engineering College on University Road. This building in exposed concrete shows the clear influence of Le Corbusier. A few decades later, towards the south of the campus and in complete contrast to both the Institute of Indology and CEPT, he designed an art gallery with the artist M.F. Husain. The gallery was previously known as the **Husain-Doshi Gufa** (Husain-Doshi Cave, 1992–1995) after

its founding members. Due to a somewhat violent controversy surrounding Husain's art, the gallery was threatened and, consequently, later re-named Amdavad ni Gufa (Cave of Ahmedabad). The gallery consists of a series of sunken underground caves with tree-like columns holding up a thin ferro-cement shell roof. The shell is covered in a mosaic of broken ceramic tiles and punctuated with protruding skylights that provide a dim light to the sunken cave-spaces beneath. The gallery is located near the Vikram Sarabhai Community Science Centre on University Road.

Similar ceramic tile mosaic also covers the vaults of Doshi's own office, **Sangath** (1979–1980), opposite Doordarshan Tower on the Drive-In road in Memnagar, Ahmedabad. These vaults are made of two skins of thin ferro-cement shells with cylindrical tiles filling the space in between. One long barrel vault houses the main studio, with smaller barrel vaults over other offices and guest rooms.

Sangath, Balkrishna V. Doshi (1979)

He used similar vaults in the **Gandhi Labour Institute** (1984) opposite the Lotus Temple on Gurukul Road in Navrangpura. Though the institute is much larger than his studio, with three blocks (academic, housing, dining) around a courtyard, the attempt appears to be to modulate scale so as to make it more approachable and less institutional. Near the Sanskar Kendra in Paldi, and on the banks of the Sabarmati River, is the **Tagore Memorial Hall** (1971) also designed by Doshi. Though also in exposed concrete, this building is distinctly different from both Doshi and Le Corbusier's other exposed concrete buildings and was designed in collaboration with the structural engineer, Mahendra Raj. Here, the structure and resolution of forces is expressed architecturally with 15-centimetre-thick folded plates in reinforced concrete, 17-metre high and spanning

Tagore Memorial Hall (1971)

about 33.5 metres. The Memorial Hall is located opposite the NID in Paldi. Close to the Sanskar Kendra and Tagore Memorial Hall in Paldi, on can find the **National Institute of Design** (NID, 1961) designed by Gautam and Gira Sarabhai. The initial idea for the Institute came from a 1958 report by Charles and Ray Eames that discussed the educational curriculum for an Institute of Design — thereby influencing the actual physical design of the Institute itself. The Sarabhais had worked with Frank Lloyd Wright at Taliesin and some have seen his influence in the design of NID.

However, it can be argued that the concrete frame structure with brick infill and the use of courts to create a distinct solid-void relationship was already present in the architectural vocabulary developing in Ahmedabad at the time, and in particular — at Sanskar Kendra

Gandhi Labour Institute, Balkrishna V. Doshi (1984)

Gandhi Smarak Sangrahalaya, Charles Correa (1958–1963)

and contemporaneously at CEPT. In any case, the pre-cast floor at NID and its brick-shell roofs are definite innovations. The NID campus is worth a visit not just because of its architecture, but also to see the students' work in their studios and in their internal exhibitions. NID also periodically hosts other exhibitions of art, photography and design. Roughly when the NID was being set up, a memorial museum designed by the Indian architect Charles Correa was being constructed across the city on the banks of the Sabarmati.

The **Gandhi Smarak Sangrahalaya** (1958–1963) is located at Sabarmati Ashram where Mahatma Gandhi lived from 1917–1930 and commemorates his life and work. The materials used in the construction are similar to the existing buildings in the ashram — consisting of tiled roofs, brick walls, stone floors and wooden doors. Light and ventilation is provided by wooden louvers and glass is not used anywhere in the building.

Correa's innovation was in the use of a geometric modular grid to order the spaces, opening up some of the spaces to form courtyards, covering others to form exhibition spaces. The grid permitted the future expansion of the complex by adding modules. The grid is expressed structurally through the use of reinforced concrete channels laid as beams along the grid. Each module consists of a four-way pyramid roof with tiles, resting on the RCC channels on all four sides. The channels act as both structural beams to take the load of the roof as well as rainwater channels for the sloping roofs. The modules, each with its own tiled roof, are arranged in a pattern such that the visitor is gradually led towards the central water court.

The architect describes a design typology analogous to the villages that were central to Gandhi's philosophy — in fact, the entire design marries Modernist ideals with Gandhian philosophy. The play of light/shade/shadow, the

National Institute of Design (1961)

Ramkrishna House, Charles Correa (1962)

open spaces and their human scale reflect the tranquility of the Ashram and the central role that meditation, modesty and quiet thought played in Gandhi's life. Charles Correa also designed the **Ramkrishna House** in the Shahibaug area of Ahmedabad (1962) for a mill-owner. He had previously worked on the concept of a long, narrow 'Tube' house as a response to Ahmedabad's extreme climate. The Ramkrishna house reflects his studies of the Tube house. As the architect describes, this residence consists of parallel massive brick load-bearing walls punctuated by interior courts and a 'cannon' shaped skylight in the roof section.

The linear plan terminates in the living room that opens out into the garden on the south, creating a point of interest and arrival in the sequence of spaces. Correa also used his Tube house studies for the design of the Parekh House (1967–1968) in Ahmedabad. This building had a cubical form and the spaces were arranged as per the ambient temperature. The house itself was split into three bays — the Winter Section (for early mornings/night), the Summer Section (for day) and a Service Bay for circulation, kitchen and toilets. The Winter and Summer bays consisted of two different stepped pyramidal sections that

Parekh House, Charles Correa

Torrent Research Centre,
Parul Zhaveri and Nimish Patel (1997)

were inverted with respect to the sea-son—the Winter section opens up the terraces to the sky while the Summer section protects the interior from the heat. The building uses Le Corbusier's 'Parasol' roof, but as a pergola, shading the walls during daytime.

The **Parekh house** was demolished for unknown reasons, while the fate of the Ramkrishna House is unknown. It is worth making an effort to try and vis-it Ramkrishna House (by appointment/personal request), if it still exists. If nothing else, it may interest visitors to see how the building works climatically after more than 40 years.

Another building that has been de-signed to respond to climate, is the **Torrent Research Centre** (1997) by **Parul Zhaveri and Nimish Patel**. This building is outside Ahmedabad, near Kanoria hos-pital in the village Bhat. While the lab-oratories are centrally air-conditioned, the building was designed together with Brian Ford Associates, London, so that all the other spaces were cooled by ven-tilation shaft towers that enabled a down-draft evaporation system. These cooling towers are a distinctive element in the building's appearance. Additional-ly, other passive features such as cavity walls and reduced openings on the East and West facade keep the indoor temper-ature much lower than the ambient tem-perature outside in the summer months. Another factory/office building built in the 1990s that has attempted to re-spond to climate is the **Inductotherm** building in Bopal, on the outskirts of Ahmedabad. Designed by **Kiran Pandya,** this factory complex comprised of pro-duction building, administration build-ing and a building housing the confer-ence and dining centre. The buildings are connected internally and arranged around a landscaped courtyard, used as a passive element to affect a micro-climate within the complex. Both Tor-rent and Inductotherm are not open to the general public, as they are industri-al/research institutions.

The building complex of the **Centre for Environmental Education** (1988–1990) was designed by **Neelkanth Chhaya and Kallol Joshi** off SG Road, opposite the Gurudwara. The centre is open to the public and visitors are welcome to see how the building has been designed as a response to its local topography, and how the landscape and planting is used to enhance the flagship branch of an insti-tution that focuses on the environment.

Entrepreneurship Development Institute, Bimal Patel (1985–1987)

Additionally, the design has focused on making the complex feel less institutional and more intimate — the scale of the buildings and sequence of spaces and views modulated accordingly.

Coming back to the discussion on Gropius and Le Corbusier, some have noted their continued influence on Indian architecture particularly on relatively recent buildings like the Ahmedabad Management Association (AMA, 1997) in the ATIRA Campus on IIM Road, Ambavadi.

Extension of IIM, Hasmukh Patel (2008)

Designed by the architectural firm HCPDPM (composed by Hasmukh Patel and his son, Bimal Patel), the AMA is a non-profit organization of over 400 industries housing classrooms and a bookshop on the ground floor and a 250-seat auditorium, a library and an exhibition space on the upper floor. The building in reinforced concrete demonstrates a careful detailing, with the exterior treated with anti-fungal repellant against weathering and window frames in mild steel. The AMA building won the World Architecture Award in 2001 and an ar+d High Commendation the same year.

Another award-winning building by Bimal Patel is the **Entrepreneurship Development Institute** (EDI, 1985–1987) on the outskirts of Ahmedabad, near Indira Bridge at the village Bhat. This is a non-profit educational institution whose design was awarded on the basis of a national competition that called for an innovative concept to evoke a combined sense of modernity and

tradition. The campus covers 23 acres with 6,000 square metres of built-up area and the buildings are erected in exposed brick, concrete and steel. The brick buildings are arranged around a courtyard and other outdoor spaces, a structure reminiscent of Kahn's IIM complex. Windows are recessed, walls made thick and plenty of verandahs provided to deal with the hot and harsh climate of Ahmedabad. Yet, while paying homage to the Modernist tradition, the building does deviate from it in the detailing of its brickwork and its placement on an elevated plinth. Like in the CEE, the design makes an effort to de-institutionalize the building and the campus was awarded the Aga Khan Award for Architecture in 1992.

Bimal Patel and his firm, HCPDPM, are also responsible the **Extension to the IIM-A in Vastrapur** (2008) the 'New Campus'. The design was awarded on the basis of a national competition. As previously mentioned, this new campus is

Alliance Francaise, Christopher Charles Benninger (2008)

connected to the Louis Kahn designed 'Heritage' campus by means of an underpass, which houses an exhibition on Louis Kahn's work. The new campus' buildings have been designed in exposed concrete and brick, with fenestrations in a combination of mild steel and wood. While adhering to a palette of materials and forms similar to that used in the existing campus, the architect has designed a complex of buildings that are dramatically different in spatial quality, scale and articulation.

About ten years after the School of Architecture started at CEPT, an American architect, **Christopher Charles Benninger**, became the first Head of the School of Planning at CEPT in 1972. During that time he designed the **Alliance Francaise** (1973) on the Ellis Bridge Road of Ahmedabad. The design reflected Benninger's sculptural intensions as well as his concern for context. The materials adopted reflected the architect's preference for natural materials, and were in keeping with those used in the

Prathma Blood Centre, Gurjit Singh Matharoo (1998–2008)

Theological College of Gujarat where the building is situated.

The language was one of exposed concrete molded into columns, water spouts, window boxes, lintels and skylights, all framed in a load bearing wall system of naturally expressed materials. The structural grid of the beams, carried up into the skylights, reflects the system of proportion built on multiples of a 2'-6" rhythm, with 2'-6" square windows; 7'-6" square doors and 15' square floor modules. The combinations within this simple system created a variety of spaces. The architect describes the building as a classic Modernist statement, fused into the structure of an existing 19th-century symmetrical campus plan through an informal courtyard.

Architects in Ahmedabad have been able to move beyond the association of exposed concrete with 'Modern' architecture. Their continued experiments have ensured that the material has remained within the domain of contemporary architecture. One such building is the

Prathma Blood Centre, Gurjit Singh Matharoo (1998–2008)

House with Balls, Gurjit Singh Matharoo (2004)

Prathama Blood Centre (1998–2000) designed by **Gurjit Singh Matharoo** and located near the Shreyash School in Jivraj Park. Awarded in a design competition, the non-profit foundation hoped to revolutionize the system of voluntary blood collection and blood component disbursement. Therefore the building had to be a new 'type' where the service intensive medical entity had to become what the architect describes as a 'playful, intuitive receptacle, by removing the repulsion associated with medical facilities and transforming it into an inviting public domain'. The nondescriptive site was given by the Ahmedabad Municipal Corporation and offered no specific context. The building was designed in such a fashion that exterior 'skin' disintegrates into sub-spaces as soon the entrance leads the visitor into a four-storey high 'void'.

Elements like the blast freezer, conference room and balcony protrude from a glass wall. Additionally, the architect also designed the auditorium chairs, fully automatic donor chairs, hot and cold-water dispensers, blood storage and identification systems, moving ladders and even two specially conceived blood donation mobile vans. Large fixed furniture is all set in situ concrete while the staircases are composed of precast concrete.

Architects like Gurjit Singh Matharoo are re-examining Modernism and re-interpreting not just program briefs but also, basic building types. This is evident in Matharoo's explorations in residential design in Ahmedabad — **the House with Balls** (2004) that serves as a weekend retreat/fish breeding centre and the **Net House** (2010), a 12 metres × 12 metres column free space wrapped in layers of

Net House, Gurjit Singh Matharoo
(2010)

Dada Miya Mosque, Hiren Patel (2010)

mosquito nets, bamboo chiks and glass. Other architects are re-examining architectural traditions in the context of modernity or, conversely, Modernism in a traditional context.

This can be seen in Kulbhushan Jain's school on Khamasa Road in the Chhipawad neighbourhood of the old city of Ahmedabad; and the **Dada Miya Mosque** designed by **Hiren Patel** in Dariyapur, again located in the dense fabric of the old city.

The examples mentioned in this chapter hope to provide a sampling of architecture in Ahmedabad from post-Independence to contemporary times for the interested visitor. Of course, by necessity, it is a limited sample. Yet if one had to identify a characteristic common to all the architecture from Ahmedabad discussed above, that may be how in all of these examples '... *the primary principle of architectural autonomy resides in the tectonic rather than the scenographic ...,*' summarized by the architectural historian, Stanford Anderson when he wrote: '*Tektonik referred not just to the activity of making the materially requisite construction ... but rather to the activity that raises this construction to an art form ...*' (*Towards a Critical Regionalism*, Kenneth Frampton, 1983)

Appendix

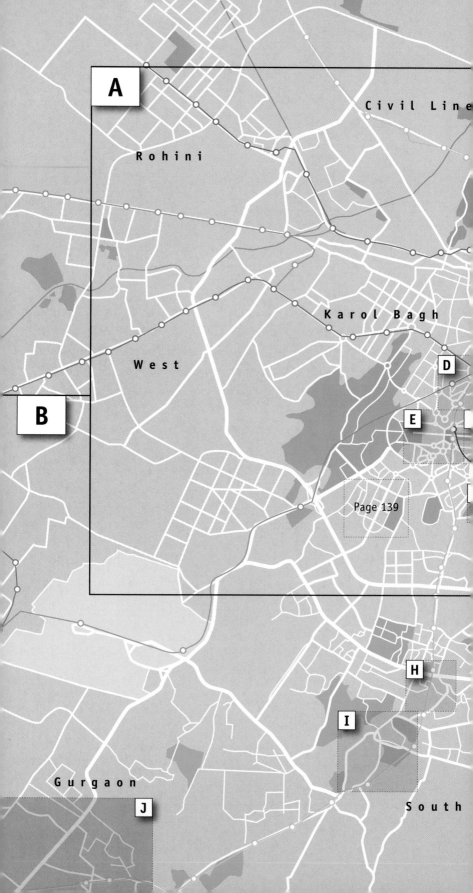

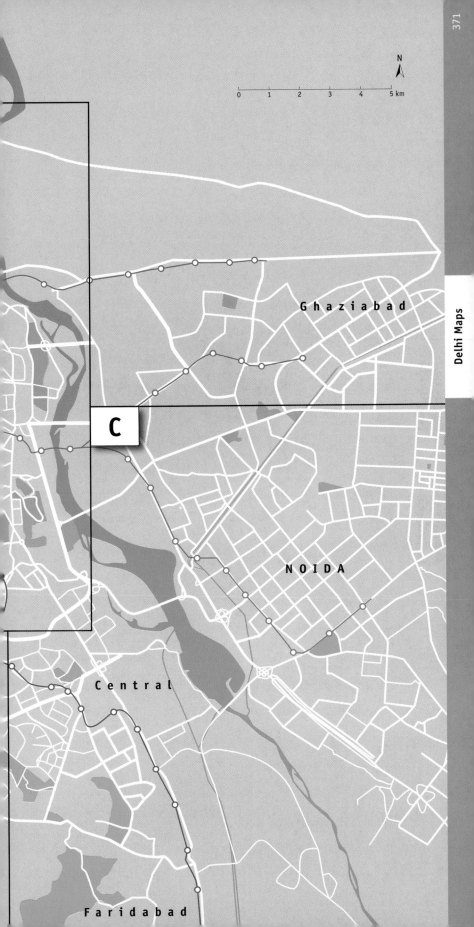

N

0 1 2 3 4 5 km

Ghaziabad

C

NOIDA

Central

Faridabad

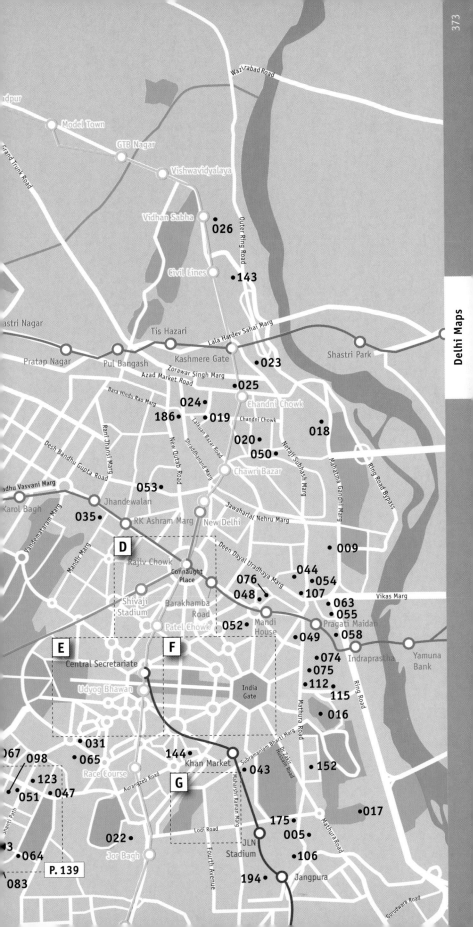

B

A

Pankha Road

Dwara Sector 9

Dwara Sector 8

Indira Gandhi International Airport

IGI Airport

Rao Tu

Gurgaon Road

• 090

Delhi Aero City

← 159

Mehrauli Road

Old Jaipur Road

135

002 •   188 •

Old Gurgaon Road

128 •   • 204

J

Ghitomi

• 118

147

Sikandarpur   Guru Dronacharya

Arjangarh

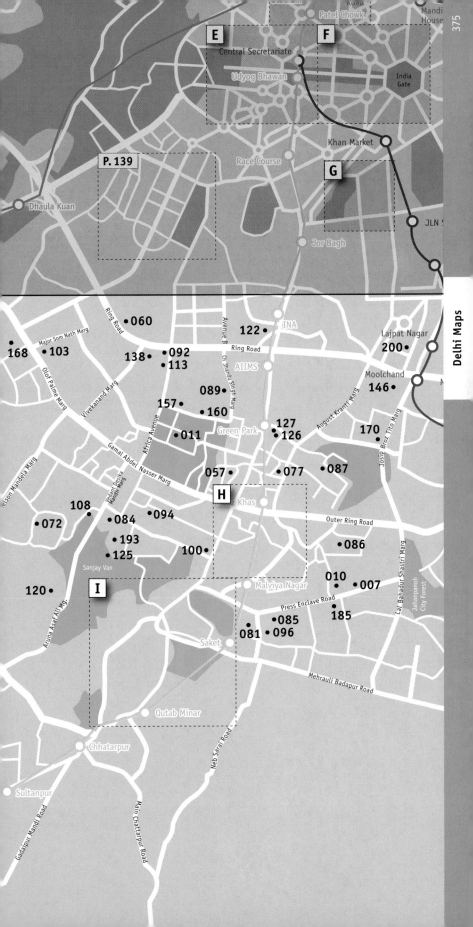

Hapur Bypass

161 •
155 •

Institutional Area

Sec. 63

Sec. 63

• 172

Sector 62

Sector 62

Logix Cyber Park

Sec. 64

Sec. 65

Sec. 69

Sector 67

Sec. 55

Sec. 58

Sec. 59

Sec. 56

Sec. 57

Sec. 66

Sector 70

Sector 121

Sector 11

Sector 54

Sector 60

Narbada Marg

Sec. 61

Sec. 71

Sector 72

Sector 122

.8

Sec. 12

Sec. 22

Ashok Marg

Sec. 53

Sector 120

Sahana Lal Bajaj Marg

Sec. 21A

Sec. 24

Sec. 33

Kanal Marg

Sec. 52

Sector 73

.9

Har Singh Marg

Vidhyachal Marg

Tulsi Marg

Sec. 34

Capt Shashi Kant Sharma Marg

Sector 51

Sec. 20

Sec. 25

Sec. 32

Shivalik Marg

Sec. 35

Sector 75

Sector 74

Sec. 26

Maharaja Agrasen Marg

Sec. 31

• 104

Noida City Center

Sector 77

Sector 116

Sec. 27

Sec. 30

Sec. 36

Major Anurag Naudiyal Marg

Sec. 76

oida Sector 18

Sec. 28

Shaheed Smarak Marg

Sector 50

Sector 78

Sector 79

Sec. 29

Sec. 37

Golf Course

Jalin Road

Sector 43

Sector 113

Sec. 40

Sec. 41

A Garden

Botanical Garden

Dadri Road

Sector 43

Sec. 42

Sector 48

Sec. 103

Sector 80

114 •

38 A

• 176

Sector 44

Sector 46

Sector 47

Sec. 101

Sec. 102

149 →

4

124

Sector 45

Sec. 107

Sec. 106

Sector 81

or 125

Sector 96

Sector 99

Sec. 100

Sector 104

• 192

Greater NOIDA Espressway

Sector 97

Sector 98

Sec. 110

Sector 126

Sector 105

Sector 127

Sector 108

Sec. 82

Sec. 84

Sector 93

Sec. 83

Sector 128

Sec. 92

Sec. 85

Sector 131

Sec. 93A

Sector 132

Sector 93B

Sector 133

Sector 134

Sector 136

Sector 129

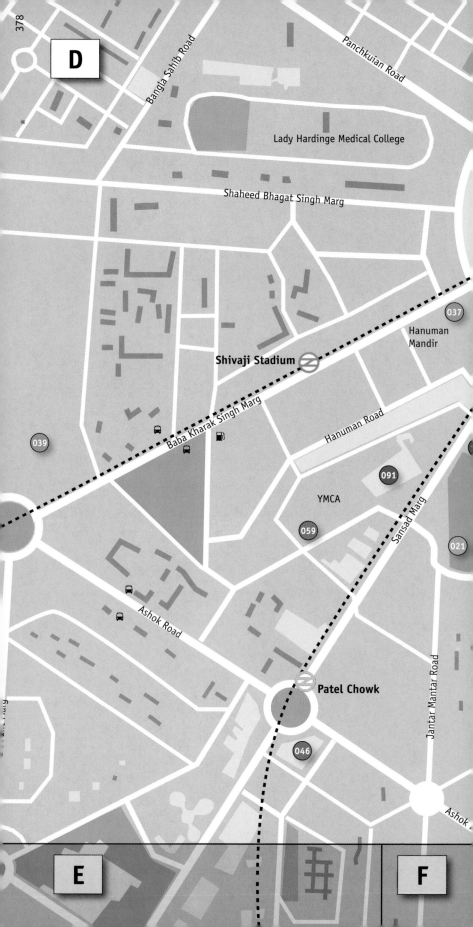

D

Bangla Sahib Road

Panchkuian Road

Lady Hardinge Medical College

Shaheed Bhagat Singh Marg

Shivaji Stadium

037

Hanuman
Mandir

039

Baba Kharak Singh Marg

Hanuman Road

091

YMCA

059

Sansad Marg

021

Ashok Road

Patel Chowk

046

Jantar Mantar Road

Ashok

E

F

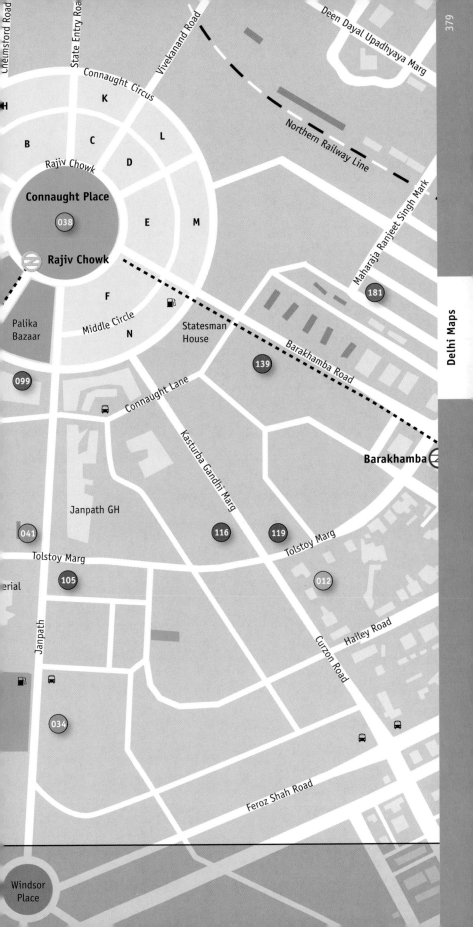

Chelmsford Road

State Entry Road

Connaught Circus

Vivekanand Road

Deen Dayal Upadhyaya Marg

K

H

B

C

L

D

Rajiv Chowk

Connaught Place

038

E

M

Rajiv Chowk

Northern Railway Line

Maharaja Ranjeet Singh Marg

181

F

Palika Bazaar

Middle Circle

N

Statesman House

139

Barakhamba Road

099

Connaught Lane

Barakhamba

Kasturba Gandhi Marg

Janpath GH

116

119

041

Tolstoy Marg

Tolstoy Marg

012

105

erial

Hailey Road

Janpath

Curzon Road

034

Feroz Shah Road

Windsor Place

E

North Avenue

040

Church Road

Brassey Avenue

Mughal Garden

033

Dalhouse Road

South Avenue

Thyagaraj Marg

Willingdon Crescent

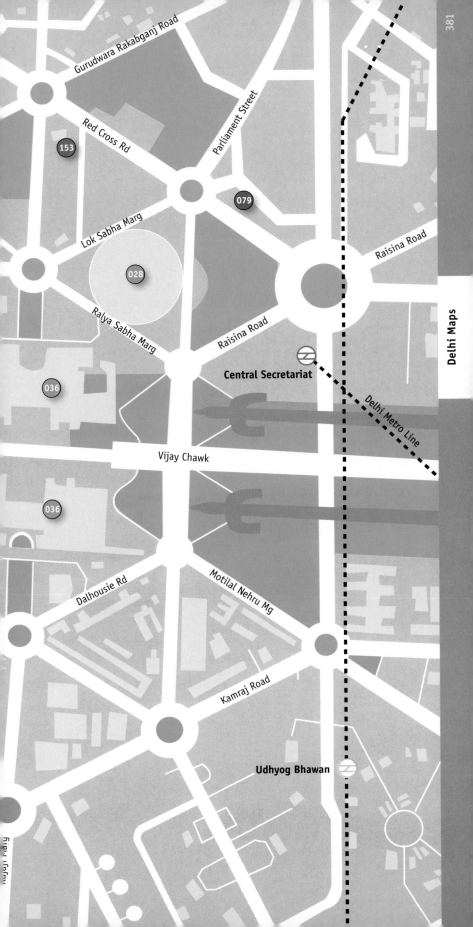

Gurudwara Rakabganj Road

Red Cross Rd

Parliament Street

153

079

Raisina Road

Lok Sabha Marg

028

Raisina Road

Ralya Sabha Marg

036

Central Secretariat

Delhi Metro Line

Vijay Chawk

036

Dalhousie Rd

Motilal Nehru Mg

Kamraj Road

Udhyog Bhawan

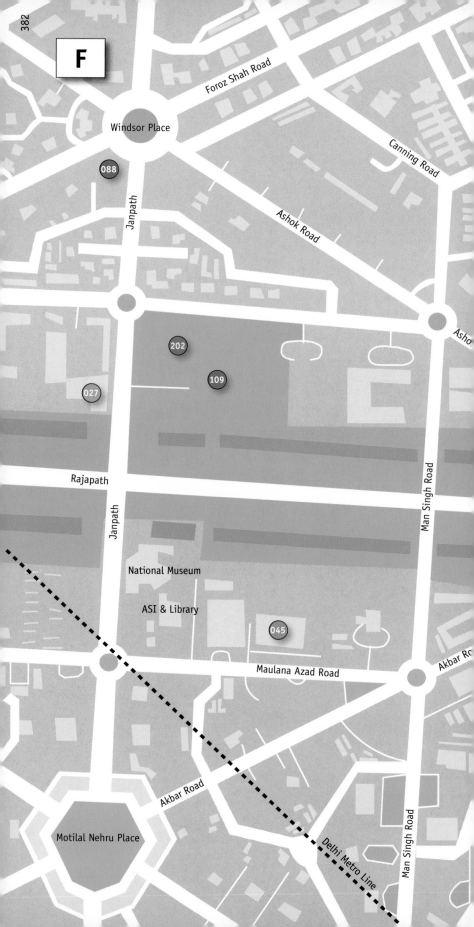

166

Canning Road

Kasturba Gandhi Marg

029

Baroda House

Copernicus Marg

Tilak Marg

032

042

190

Dr Zakir Hussain Marg

Shahjahan Road

Pandara Road

G

Lodi Garden

014

056

066

Joseph Stein Lane

062

KK Birla Marg

124

132

158

Max Mueller Marg

Lodi Road

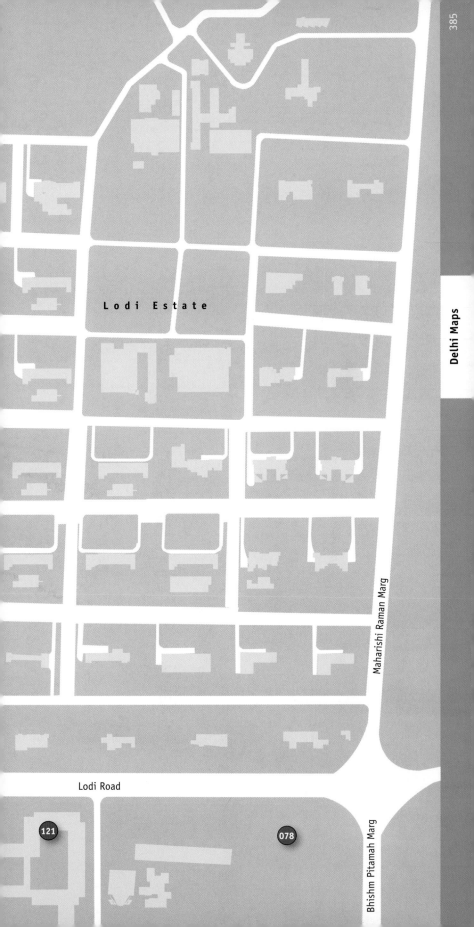

Lodi Estate

Maharishi Raman Marg

Lodi Road

Bhishm Pitamah Marg

121

078

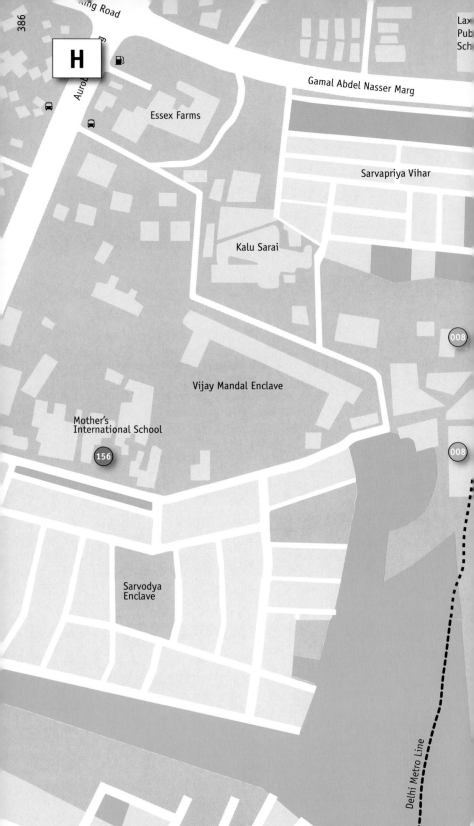

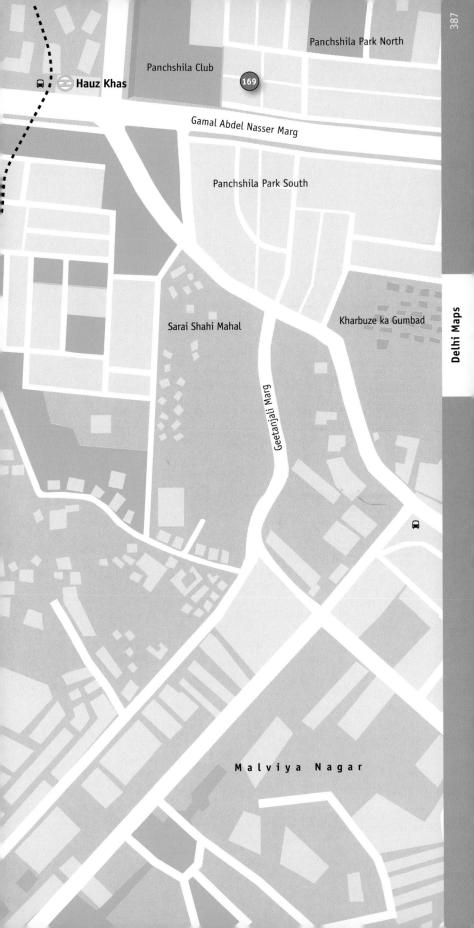

Panchshila Park North

Panchshila Club

169

Hauz Khas

Gamal Abdel Nasser Marg

Panchshila Park South

Sarai Shahi Mahal

Kharbuze ka Gumbad

Geetanjali Marg

Malviya Nagar

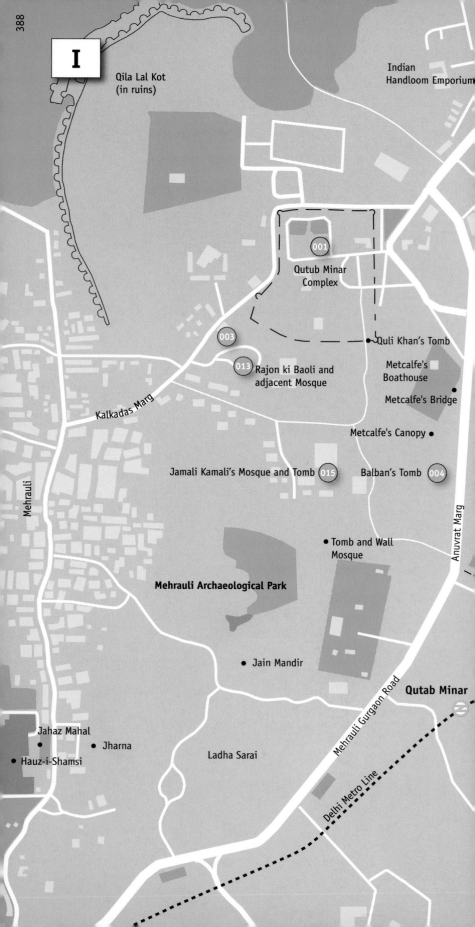

I

Qila Lal Kot
(in ruins)

Indian
Handloom Emporium

001

Qutub Minar
Complex

003

Quli Khan's Tomb

013 Rajon ki Baoli and
adjacent Mosque

Metcalfe's
Boathouse

Metcalfe's Bridge

Kalkadas Marg

Metcalfe's Canopy •

Mehrauli

Jamali Kamali's Mosque and Tomb 015   Balban's Tomb 004

• Tomb and Wall
Mosque

Anuvrat Marg

Mehrauli Archaeological Park

• Jain Mandir

Qutab Minar

Jahaz Mahal

• Jharna

Ladha Sarai

Mehrauli Gurgaon Road

• Hauz-i-Shamsi

Delhi Metro Line

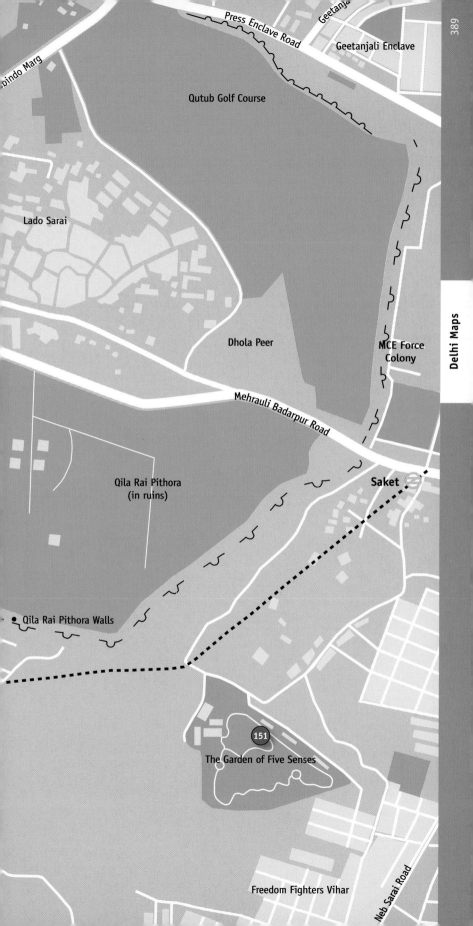

Press Enclave Road

Geetanj

Geetanjali Enclave

bindo Marg

Qutub Golf Course

Lado Sarai

Dhola Peer

MCE Force
Colony

Mehrauli Badarpur Road

Qila Rai Pithora
(in ruins)

Saket

Qila Rai Pithora Walls

151

The Garden of Five Senses

Freedom Fighters Vihar

Neb Sarai Road

J

Daultabad Main Road

Ajghera Road

Gurgaon RS

Sec.2

Sector 23

Wooded Area

Sec.3A

Railway Road

Sec.5

Lt Atul Katariya Marg

Sector 4

Sec.6

Sector 13

Secto

Delhi Road

Sector 7

Sector 12

Sec

Sector 9A

Basai RS

Sector 9

Sadar Bazar Road

Sector 15-II

Basai Road

Sec.8

Sector 15-I

Sec.32

Sector 10

191

Se

Sec.32

Pataudi Road

Sector 10A

Khandsa Marg

137

167

174

140

Sector 37

Sector 33

Sector 38

•182

NH8

Sector 34

Sector 33

Sector 47

Sector 36

Sector 35

Sohna Road

Sector 74

Sector 74A

Sector 48

Sector 71

Sector 73

Sector

187

Sector 76A

Sector 72

197•

150

178

Sector 75

Sector 70

Sector 69

Sector 70A

Sector 68

Sector 22

Vihar Road

Old Jaipur Road

Sector 18

Sec. 19

Expressway

Maruti Udyog

• 130

• 195

DLF City
Phase III

• 184

DLF City
Phase II

• 111

Akashneem Marg

Guru Dronacharya

199

MG Road

Sikandarpur

• 148

or 17

198 •

• 162

141

Expressway

c. 17

DLF City
Phase I

IFFCO Chowk

Sec. 29

Sector 28

136

th City

Sector 27

c. 30

Sector 42

177

Sec. 41

Huda City Centre

• 163

Sec. 44

Sector 43

DLF Golf
Course

• 173

Maj Gopinath Marg

St. Thomas Marg

Sector 44

Sec. 43

Sector 45

Sector 54

Vikas Marg

tor 46

Sec. 52

• 180

Sector 53

Sector 51

Sector 56

Sector 55

Sector 57

Sector 57A

Sector 58

Golf Course Extn Road

ector 50

Sector 61

Sector 62

Sector 65

Baharampur Road

Sector 59

Sector 62

Sector 64

145
↓

Kadarpur Road

Architects and Projects

Digits indicate the project numbers.

Directory (Delhi Metro)

Digits indicate the project numbers.

⊖ Yellow Line

Civil Lines
026, 143

Kashmere Gate
023

Chandni Chowk
018, 019, 020, 024, 025, 050, 186

New Delhi
053

Rajiv Chowk
021, 037, 038, 041, 088, 091, 099, 105, 110, 119, 181

Patel Chowk
034, 039, 046, 109

Central Secretariat
027, 028, 032, 033, 036, 040, 042, 079, 109, 153, 190, 202

Udyog Bhawan
045

Race Course
031, 047, 051, 065, 067, 093, 098, 123, 144, 165

Jor Bagh
014, 022, 056, 062, 066, 121, 124, 132, 158

INA
064, 122, 123

AIIMS
060, 092, 113, 138

Green Park
011, 057, 087, 089, 126, 127, 146, 157, 160

Hauz Khas
008, 072, 077, 084, 094, 100, 103, 108, 156, 168, 169, 193

Malviya Nagar 007, 010, 081, 085, 086, 096, 125, 185

Saket
151

Qutab Minar
001, 003, 004, 013, 015

Chattarpur
002, 120, 135, 188

Arjangarh
118, 147

Guru Dronacharya
111, 128, 130, 148, 184

Sikandarpur
180, 195

MG Road
162, 198, 199, 204

IFFCO Chowk
136, 141

HUDA City Centre
137, 140, 150, 163, 167, 173, 174, 177, 178, 182, 187, 191, 197

⊜ Violet Line

Central Secretariat
*027, 028, 032, 033, 036, 040, 042, 079,
109, 153, 190, 202*

Khan Market
*014, 043, 056, 062, 066, 121, 124, 132,
144, 152, 158*

JLN Stadium
005, 017, 078, 175, 194

Jangpura
106

Moolchand
142, 146, 170, 200

Kailash Colony
134

Kalkaji Mandir
097

Govind Puri
080, 082

Jasola-Apollo
061, 073, 131, 179, 183, 196

Tughlaqabad
006

Badarpur
068, 069, 070

⊜ Red Line

Rithala
133

Netaji Subhash Place
164

Kashmere Gate
023

⊜ Orange Line

New Delhi
053

Shivaji Stadium
059

Dhaula Kuan
168

IGI Airport
090

⊜ Blue Line

Dwarka Mor
159

Janakpuri West
101

Ramakrishna Ashram Marg
035

Rajiv Chowk
*021, 037, 038, 041, 088, 091, 099, 105,
110, 119, 181*

Barakhamba Road
012, 116, 139

Mandi House
029, 048, 052, 076, 166

Pragati Maidan
*016, 044, 049, 054, 055, 074, 075, 107,
112*

Indraprastha
009, 055, 058, 063, 115

NOIDA Sector 15
149, 154

NOIDA Sector 16
102, 149

NOIDA Sector 18
129

Botanical Garden
176, 192, 201

Golf Course
104

NOIDA City Centre
114, 155, 161, 172

Vaishali
155, 161, 172

⊜ Green Line

Paschim Vihar West
095

Bibliography

Books:

Byron, Robert. *New Delhi*, AES Reprint of *Architecture Review*, London. Vol. LXIX NO. 410, January 1931, Asian Educational Services, New Delhi, Chennai. 2007

Correa, Charles and Frampton, Kenneth. *Charles Correa*, Perennial Press, London. 1996

Corporate Offices in India, White Flag Media & Communications Ltd, Mumbai. 2011

Davies, Philip. *Splendours of the Raj*, John Murray, London. 1985

Delhi: A Living Heritage, IGNCA & INTACH, New Delhi. 2010

Desai, Madhavi, Desai, Miki and Lang, Jon. *Architecture and Independence: The Search for Identity — India 1880 to 1980*, Oxford University Press, New Delhi. 2000

Grover, Satish. *Building Beyond Borders — Story of Contemporary Indian Architecture*, National Book Trust of India, New Delhi. 1995

Irving, Robert Grant. *Indian Summer; Lutyens Baker and Imperial Delhi*. Yale University Press, New Haven & London. 1981

Khanna, Rahul and Parhawk, Manav. *The Modern Architecture of New Delhi 1928–2007*, Random House, India. 2008

Lang, Jon. *A Concise History of Modern Architecture in India*, Permanent Black, New Delhi. 2002

Mehrotra, Rahul. *Architecture in India Since 1990*, Pictor Publishing Pvt. Ltd., Mumbai. 2011

Peck, Lucy. *Delhi — A Thousand Years of Building*, Roli Books, New Delhi. 2005

Rewal, Raj, Sharma, Ram and Veret, Jean-Louis. *Architecture in India*, Electa Moniteur, Paris. 1985

Singh, Malvika, Mukherjee, Rudrangshu and Kapoor, Pramod. *New Delhi: Making of a Capital*, Lustre Press, Roli Books, New Delhi. 2009

Taylor, Brian Brace. *Raj Rewal*, Mimar Publications, London. 1992

White, Stephen. *Building in the Garden: The Architecture of Joseph Allen Stein in India and California*, Oxford University Press, New Delhi. 1993

Articles:

Narayani Gupta. 'Military Security and Urban Development: A Case Study of Delhi 1857–1912'. *Modern Asian Studies*, 5, I, 1971

Acknowledgements

This book is dedicated to the people of Delhi; we hope that they will take time from the everyday madness of living in this city to stop and take note of the environments that surround them, and continue to demand that architecture fulfill the Vitruvian edicts of firmness, commodity and delight.

This guide would have been impossible but for Philipp Meuser initiating the idea and showing us the importance of this endeavour. A chance meeting with Malini in the Metro made it a reality when she agreed to co-author with me. After almost exactly a year of starting on this project, we find that a recent facebook moniker describes us perfectly as 'nillionaires', immeasurably richer for all that we have learnt, with 'nillions' in our bank accounts.

We have had the good fortune of meeting some of the most amazing people while researching this book. Tightening security over the years has resulted in a majority of public buildings in the capital being out of bounds for photographers — regardless of intent or interest. Our search for alternative means of photographs, especially of the vast majority of Modernist buildings built in the years after independence, lead us first to Ram Rahman. We are eternally grateful to Ram for being an invaluable resource in our research for Habib Rahman's projects and for directing us to Madan Mahatta, who was generous enough to allow us access to his extraordinary collection of photographs of Delhi and its architecture. His photographs became the largest resource and contribution by a single individual for this book, making Mr. Mahatta indispensable to its making. We are also grateful to Ram for introducing us to Ethan and David Stein, who have been extremely generous and allowed us to access Joseph Allen Stein's vast archives of drawings and photographs. Thanks also to Varun Shiv Kapur, for graciously granting us access to his vast collection of contemporary photographs of Delhi.

A special thanks goes to the authors who contributed chapters to the guide — Shahana Dastidar for her comprehensive and insightful text on Ahmedabad Architecture, Ashish Nangia, for his indispensable background of Chandigarh, Abha Narain Lambah and Meena Bhargava for their insight into historical Delhi. We are also grateful to Mr. A. G. K. Menon for his guidance and for facilitating access to the maps and articles commissioned by INTACH.

Numerous other individuals who have been extremely helpful in providing us with supplementary and equally significant information and assistance are Nitin Lalwani, who provided us the necessary books, Rahul Khanna, who offered insights into the available architectural resources of Delhi, Mr. Suneet Paul, editor A+D, who gave us important articles and officials at the Finish Embassy who granted us the permission to photograph the embassy premises.

Special thanks also to Nidhi Sharma, Gurnoor Kaur and Manish Verma for being in the line of fire while doing all the compilation, layout and production work in the office. Finally, we would like to say a special thanks to all the architects who put up with our constant nagging and contributed drawings and photographs for the guide, their enthusiasm and encouragement for the project kept us going in spite of all the odds.

Anupam Bansal

Authors

Anupam Bansal

is a Delhi based architect. He founded ABRD Architects with Rajesh Dongre in 1996. ABRD Architects have designed several prestigious projects all over India. He has taught design, history and theory of Architecture at School of Planning & Architecture, TVB School of Habitat Studies at Delhi and Sushant School of Art and Architecture in Gurgaon, Haryana. He has an avid interest in the modern architecture of Delhi. (anupam@abrdarchitects.com)

Abha Narain Lambah

is a conservation architect and recipient of Eisenhower, Charles Wallace, Attingham Fellowships, Sanskriti Award and seven UNESCO Asia Pacific Awards for conservation. Her architectural practice covers a range of projects such as a 15th-century Maitreya Temple, Ladhakh, Chandramauleshwar Temple in Hampi, Jai Vilas Palace, Gwalior and the Viceregal Lodge, Shimla. She has prepared management plans for ancient sites of Ajant Caves and Sisupalgarh and UNESCO nomination dossiers for Santiniketan and Hyderabad. She is based in Mumbai and her work in Mumbai covers a range of Victorian buildings including the Convocation Hall, Old Secretariat, Tata Palace, Mani Bhavan Gandhi Sangrahalaya and the Municipal Head Offices. Abha has edited *Architecture of the Indian Sultanates* for MARG and authored *Through the Looking Glass: The Grade I Heritage of Mumbai* among other publications.

Malini Kochupillai

is an architect and photographer based in Delhi. She has taught design at Sushant School of Art & Architecture, Gurgaon and University School of Architecture and Planning, Delhi. She is currently involved in various art and urbanism related projects in Delhi.

Ashish Nangia

is an architect by training, and specializes in the history of modern and Indian architecture. He has a PhD in architecture and the built environment, a reflection of his interest in rewriting architectural history and making the topic relevant to a wider audience. Ashish has lived, studied and worked in India, France and the United States.

Meena Bhargava

is Associate Professor, Department of History, Indraprastha College, University of Delhi. She has published several articles in journals and collected works. She is the author of *Stae, Society and Ecology: Gorakhpur in Transition, 1750-1830* (Manohar, New Delhi, 1999); co-authored *Women, Education and Politics: The Women's Movement and Delhi's Indraprastha College* (Oxford University Press, New Delhi, 2005) and edited *Exploring Medieval India: Politics, Economy, Religion, vol. I* and *Exploring Medieval India: Culture, Gender, Regional Patterns, vol. II* (Orient Black Swan, New Delhi, 2010)

A.G. Krishna Menon

is an architect, urban planner and conservation consultant who has been practising and teaching in Delhi since 1972. In 1990 he co-founded the TVB School of Habitat Studies and was its director from 1994-2007. As the Convener INTACH-Delhi Chapter he has undertaken many pioneering urban conservation projects in India and authored several documents setting guidelines for conservation practice in India, including *The Charter for the Conservation of Unprotected Architectural heritage and Sites in India*, 2004. While maintaining an active professional practice he remains a passionate interlocutor in mediating the development of Delhi as a Heritage City.

Shahana Dastidar

is an architect from Delhi. She completed her Bachelors in Architecture from CEPT Ahmedabad and later read for a Masters degree at UCL London. She has lived and worked as an architect in Oman, India, the UK and Mauritius. Shahana has previously taught as full-time and visiting faculty in architecture schools in Delhi. She has a keen interest in academic research on the built environment and pedagogical methods used in the teaching of architecture. She hopes someday to do her doctoral thesis on the socio-economic challenges involved in conserving historic settlements in India.

Jörn Düwel

Professor Jörn Düwel was born in 1965. After studying art history and German studies at the Ernst Moritz Arndt University in Greifswald from 1986 to 1991, he obtained his PhD in 1994 with a study on the architecture and urban planning of the Soviet occupation zone and of the early German Democratic Republic. After a period of freelance work in Berlin, he became research associate at the architecture faculty of the University of Stuttgart. He was academic counsellor at the architecture faculty of the Technical University Darmstadt from 1998 to 2002. Since 2002 he has been professor for the history and theory of architecture at HafenCity University, Hamburg. He has published on the architecture and urban planning of the 19th and 20th centuries in Europe and has been involved with several exhibitions, including at the Academy of Arts, Berlin, and the Dutch Architecture Institute (NAi), Rotterdam. His other major professional focus is built heritage studies and surveys. Currently, he is involved with the conservation effort for the overall refurbishment of the building complex of the German Embassy, New Delhi.

Bibliographic information:
Die Deutsche Nationalbibliothek lists this publication in the *Deutsche National-bibliografie;* detailed bibliographic data are available at http://www.dnb.de

ISBN 978-3-86922-167-0

DOM publishers

Final proofreading
Mariangela Palazzi-Williams

Design
Masako Tomokiyo

Maps
Anupam Bansal (G, Page 139)
INTACH (D, E, F, H, I)
Masako Tomokiyo (A, B, C, J)

QR-Codes
Christoph Gößmann

Printing
Tiger Printing (Hongkong) Co., Ltd.
www.tigerprinting.hk

Also available:
Architectural Map Delhi
ISBN 978-3-86922-367-4